T0328535

WHEN ALL ROADS LEAD TO THE STANDOFF

WHEN ALL ROADS LEAD TO THE STANDOFF

HOW CORPORATE GOVERNANCE

FUELS WHITE SUPREMACY

JEANNE M. HASKIN

Algora Publishing
New York

Library of Congress Cataloging-in-Publication Data —

Names: Haskin, Jeanne M., 1964- author.
Title: When all roads lead to the standoff: how corporate governance fuels
    white supremacy / Jeanne M. Haskin.
Description: New York: Algora Publishing, [2016] | Includes bibliographical
    references and index.
Identifiers: LCCN 2016001372 (print) | LCCN 2016004101 (ebook) | ISBN
    9781628941869 (soft cover: alk. paper) | ISBN 9781628941876 (hard cover:
    alk. paper) | ISBN 9781628941883 (pdf)
Subjects: LCSH: White supremacy movements—Political aspects—United States.
    | Corporate governance—United States. | Business and politics—United
    States. | Government, Resistance to—Economic aspects—United States. |
    Social conflict—United States. | United States—Race relations. | United
    States—Economic policy. | United States—Social policy. | United
    States—Politics and government.
Classification: LCC E184.A1 H355 2016 (print) | LCC E184.A1 (ebook) | DDC
    305.800973—dc23
LC record available at http://lccn.loc.gov/2016001372

Printed in the United States

To my mother, who inspires me
And for Marquita, who brought us love

Acknowledgments

As ever, I would like to thank Algora Publishing for their invaluable input and willingness to publish this manuscript. Their ideals and many years of support matter more than I can say. I also owe a special debt of gratitude to author Leonard Zeskind, whose book *Blood and Politics* may be the definitive work on militant white supremacists.

Too, I would like to thank Elizabeth Hull, my dear friend and fellow author (who writes under the byline of C.N. Lesley), my husband, and my mother for providing honest feedback at every stage of this project.

Table of Contents

INTRODUCTION: A SYMPTOM WITHOUT A CURE

This book recasts the Ruby Ridge standoff and the Branch Davidian siege as symptoms of a larger battle between two different forces, using a psycho-social theory of political economics.

On one side, the wealthy and politically powerful manipulate the market to atomize world polities and reorganize their societies in service to transnational conglomerates that seek the services and assets controlled by the nation state. Defined as Corporate Governance (or upside-down dictatorship, when corporations rather than the state make and enforce national policies), the rule of transnational conglomerates can never be benevolent if they control everything. Because their focus is on outcomes, abstract calculations for maximum impact through minimal expenditure hold neither malice nor promise. Often touted as the champions of world peace and a higher standard of living, transnational conglomerates diminish expectations (by driving down wages, cutting out other employment benefits, and prolonging economic recessions), induce social instability, and render increasing numbers of people not just jobless but rootless and rightless.

On the other side, the post-desegregation growth of racist, bigoted and anti-Semitic groups into a cohesive and self-aware movement of "Leaderless Resistance"[1] produced a collective that seeks white purity above and beyond all else. This was not from socioeconomic marginalization (although recruiters

---

[1] This became the preferred method of organization for militant white supremacists after their cell formations underwent thorough infiltration in the mid- to late 1980s. Instead of cells, Louis Beam proposed a web formation that ultimately led to the idea of Leaderless Resistance. As the most secure form of organization, Leaderless Resistance relies on web pages and Internet bulletins to disseminate information.

for white supremacy certainly exploit fears of a non-recoverable economy, illegal immigration, and America's diminishing greatness—a case in which transnational conglomerates push concerned and fearful people toward militant white movements), but rather from a belief that nonwhites must suffer for "polluting" the white Christian "race." Having sanitized their hate-filled criminal past, white supremacists seek to seize the state and would use it to carry out ethnic cleansing as well as the grand-scale elimination of "traitorous liberal elites and policymakers," or those who hold liberal views. Because their leaders would sacrifice anyone (whites included) to achieve a "whites-only" world, so-called "real" Americans must fight the "corrupt liberal elite establishment" by any means necessary, even if it requires temporary alliances with the movement's contemptible enemies (to be disposed of afterward).

In the meantime, it is easy for whites-only leaders to invoke proxy wars, pitting citizens against the government as a matter of random violence, privately planned and implemented. This places the onus on just one man or a small group of men, thereby protecting the overall movement from exposure and prosecution. "Leaderless resistors" magnify their violence by burning black churches and gunning down women and children or blowing them up in buildings. The greater the shock value and the more they attack what is sacred, the more they inspire others to follow in their footsteps and to do so with more frequency. The campus shootings in Oregon, for example, inspired a week of violence. The point is to build up momentum while evading a solution. Thus, the powerful NRA refuses to block sales of weapons to terror suspects on the FBI's watch-list, knowing that some of them will be militant white supremacists. Supported by Republican presidential contenders and high profile Republican media figures, who urge us to pray and buy guns in response to the killings, the movement as a whole deliberately promotes the perception that the government can't defend us and thereby gains more converts for militant white supremacy.

This is the meaning of the modern-day standoff.

The government faces off with the "symptoms" because there is no "cure" when people with racist, bigoted, and other deeply-held hostile views oppose corrective national policies that might curtail their violence. Much like the IRA (the Provisional Irish Republican Army), which was associated with Sinn Fein (the nationalist political party that articulated and pressed the IRA's demands), "Leaderless resistors" strike fear into those who oppose them while Republican presidential contenders Donald Trump, Dr. Ben Carson, Ted Cruz, Marco Rubio and others align themselves with the Tea Party and the Republican Freedom Caucus as they vie to impose their demands.

If, as a result, the government assimilates white supremacy in an effort to stop the killings, then tolerance, rights, and equality will vanish in short order, as will millions of "undesirables," from Latinos to Muslims to liberals, whether they are forcibly expelled from the country, collectively detained, or forced to flee persecution.

If the government represses white supremacy, violence can only grow exponentially, and the conflict we sought to avoid will erupt anyway. In other words, either path could destroy the United States and much of the world as we know it.

The only thing more disastrous would be a marriage of convenience between Corporate Governance and white supremacists. Via corporo-fascism, they would end life and hope for many millions of people, leaving those who survive to fight for the miserable scraps discarded along their paths.

Chapter 1. Held Hostage to the Human "Story"

Since this book portrays the standoff as a symptom of asymmetric conflict between militant white movements and transnational conglomerates (where the conglomerates have the advantage via influence over legislation, research, lobbying, fundraising, diplomacy, militarization and strategy, as well as armaments and allies), we'll first look at the standoff as a standardized concept, using Robin Wagner-Pacifici's *Theorizing the Standoff: Contingency in Action*. Then, because Wagner-Pacifici's work flows naturally into seeking the "human story" behind the phenomenon of the standoff, we'll look at what brought about the control of transnational conglomerates, the resurgence of white supremacy, and their asymmetric relations. From there, I will diverge from, and contrast, the work of Robin Wagner-Pacifici with a psycho-social interpretation of militant white movements to be applied to the Ruby Ridge standoff in chapters 7 and 8 and the siege at Waco, Texas, in chapters 9 and 10.

THE WORK OF WAGNER-PACIFICI

In *Theorizing the Standoff: Contingency in Action*, author Robin Wagner-Pacifici proposes a nexus between Pragmatism (a theory of situations) and Structuralism (a typology of situations) that meet at the point of contingency—what happens when things could literally go one way or the other.

In her words:

> By proposing the standoff as a privileged archetypal situation, the project has read contingency through the standoff and the standoff through its own contingency. Of course I am concerned with moments of danger and imminent violence for the damage they can do to lives and

social systems. But I am also, and equally, concerned with ferreting out the "standoffish" aspects of everyday interactions and charting the various thresholds we all work hard to elude, thresholds that will take a conversation into the realm of the confrontation.[1]

If the definition of contingency, as provided by Wagner-Pacifici, is "what happens when things could literally go one way or another," then what she proposes in her study is that there is a path leading up to the standoff where uncertainty prevails and a path leading through the standoff where the same is equally true. In other words, ignorance abounds regardless of where we begin, but there is a caveat—that we can gauge some probabilities, if not certainties, based on observable patterns, and we can approach the situation based on that understanding. In other words, crisis responders may be helped by crossing theories with typologies and examining their byproduct—although this simply means that there are preconceived notions about behavioral dynamics and often, if not always, the categorization of a crisis tells responders which type of dynamics to expect and vice versa.

Most responders do operate on the basis of standardized categories. (That being said, I prefer to cast "identities" as the basis of group formation, rather than typologies—not as a matter of semantics but from a need to eliminate the status of non-persons to which all typologies relegate their subjects. To me, "typology" leaves no room for different states of mind, different degrees of resolve, and the various attachments between and among individual immersed in white militant movements.)

As Wagner-Pacifici says:

> One of the striking aspects of researching responses to real-life standoffs is the discovery of the habitual connections made between situations and standardized categories. The book attempts to locate and theoretically press the idea of standard operating procedures as agents of the law and adversaries alike summon up their warrants, ultimatums, deadlines...and so forth when an "emergency" has been declared. One category of standard agent, the "Hostage Rescue Team," has particular theoretical resonance. As a specific group within the Federal Bureau of Investigation, this team is obviously trained to rescue hostages in situations of danger and potential violence. As will be explored, sometimes this team is sent into situations where there is no clear hostage (this was particularly true in the case of the Ruby Ridge, Idaho standoff of the Randall Weaver family). At such a moment, a kind of aporia opens up, a conceptual and strategic gap between the reality of the situation and the means determined to deal with it. Much of the book's investigation will peer into that gap to

---

[1] Wagner-Pacifici, Robin, *Theorizing the Standoff: Contingency in Action* (Cambridge: Cambridge University Press, 2000), p. xi.

try and understand it. *But in a larger sense, if the claim here is that all social situations are working overtime to avoid becoming standoffs, then perhaps we do need a kind of metaphorical Hostage Rescue Team to periodically rescue us hostages of social life from ourselves and each other.*[1] [Emphasis added.]

"THEY JUST NEED SOMEONE TO TALK TO"

Interestingly, Wagner-Pacifici's concern with basic civil discourse is fully half the justification for producing her subject work. To me, it echoes the earnest (if not always substantive) view that "people just need someone to talk to" when their world is falling apart and nothing promised has emerged.

For example, policy-makers who focused on diminishing American economic expectations presumed that "talking Americans through it" would allow further marginalization without social upheaval—a theory that was disproved by Tea Party rallies (where one sign read: MY CHILD IS NOT YOUR ATM!) and the Occupy Wall Street movement.

OCCUPY WALL STREET

During the Wall Street occupation, Fox News commentators (seemingly baffled by the movement) disingenuously asked, "Isn't this class warfare?" and "What do they actually want?"

In fact, they had thirteen demands.

The amusement of the *Washington Times* in that regard is obvious: "Read the Demands of 'Occupy Wall Street'...and Try Not to Laugh."[2]

FIRST DEMAND: Restoration of the living wage. This demand can only be met by ending "Free trade" by re-imposing trade tariffs on all imported goods entering the American market to level the playing field for domestic family farming and domestic manufacturing as most nations that are dumping cheap products onto the American market have radical wage and environmental regulation advantages. Another policy that must be instituted is to raise the minimum wage to twenty dollars an hour.

Let's deal with the wage gap first. According to Ravi Batra, the preconditions for economic "bubbles" that over-inflate expectations to the benefit of the rich are a significant lag between earnings and production, plus a great deal of public debt (regardless of whether the debtor is the government, big business, Wall Street, or consumers). Because a "bubble"

---

[1] Ibid., pp. xi-xii.
[2] Pickett, Kerry, "Read the Demands of 'Occupy Wall Street"...and Try Not to Laugh," *Washington Times*, http://nation.foxnews.com/occupy-wall-street/2011/10/04/read-demands-occupy-wall-street-and-try-not-laugh

economy is one that banks, investors and traders know how to wring every dime from (by engaging in privileged betting on both the upside and the downside), we will see this over and over, with something new in the form of a "product" to be blamed for fraud each time. Although it might be argued that a real living wage would approach parity with production, it must be recalled that we are largely a de-industrialized nation. Since there is little or no production in an economy devoted to services, the resulting inflation of prices on the things we do produce will manifest as a hidden consumption tax, negating the hoped-for gain.

This is a two-part demand, however, including, secondarily, the abolishment of free trade. For anyone who has studied Western history and particularly The Great Depression, this form of recidivism on free trade and protective tariffs is common to all periods of severe economic contraction. As measures that are typically instituted by conservatives responding to nativist sentiments, they antagonize other countries with no appreciable gain. Seen in the present day as the threat of a "currency war," where nations either devalue their currency to increase export potential at the expense of other nations or create a closed-loop alternative to replace the world's predominant currency with one specific to a new-formed trading bloc, one actor's loss is always the other's gain. But when it comes to market "voters" attempting to reshape a nation's policies, the manipulation of currency values is tolerated and even encouraged. The IMF is always eager to offer a bail-out plan, contingent on draining a country's foreign reserves at an unsustainable rate. In this, the IMF rewards currency speculation by protecting the withdrawal of foreign investment and only allows devaluation when impoverishment is assured. In a way, the only real difference between a currency war and a run on a nation's currency is that the latter is "market driven." They are both wars, regardless of who starts it.

Parallel to this, a new trade agreement (The Trans-Pacific Partnership— TPP), is a deal written *by corporations for corporations* under which they can sue participating countries for "lost opportunities" (or barriers to trade) and include in their demand for damages a projection of future profits even though the plaintiff corporations have never invested a dime. Worse, the TPP comes equipped with a supra court that represents only corporations, and is staffed by corporate lawyers, who act as both judge and jury. This will end the sovereignty of nations because countries will have no reciprocal right to civil litigation.

Opposing the TPP is part of the Democratic Platform for the 2016 election, but it also outrages U.S. Constitutionalists, who object to the secret negotiations behind the TPP and the mandatory five-year nondisclosure provision embedded in the Treaty.

In large part, however, goods that are "dumped" on the U.S. market have helped to mask the pinch on wages. An abundant supply of cheap produce comes from poor countries exporting identical products (in accordance with "advice" from the IMF) for little or no profit. Otherwise, the problem is home-grown in terms of cheap foodstuffs produced by Big Agriculture under horrific conditions.

SECOND DEMAND: Institute a universal single payer healthcare system. To do this all private insurers must be banned from the healthcare market as their only effect on the health of patients is to take money away from doctors, nurses and hospitals preventing them from doing their jobs and hand that money to Wall Street investors.

Before Obamacare, those who were young and able often eschewed health insurance, which provided a strong incentive for government intervention to secure a new source of revenue which would also dilute the risk pool. Because this was the market sector that healthcare insurers desperately wanted to capture, Obamacare was suffered as the means to make health insurance a legal obligation, upon which the abandonment of support for Obamacare really began in earnest. That said, Obamacare was not about reforming the health care system to standardize costs and equalize treatments, but rather a deal with insurers[1] for a disease management system.

Senator Bernie Sanders hopes to enact a single-payer system through the expansion of Medicare. Conservatives have responded by claiming it will cost the American people an outrageous $18 trillion. But the Congressional Budget Office (a nonpartisan government agency responsible for fact-gathering and analysis) projects that it will save hundreds of billions of dollars.

THIRD DEMAND: Guaranteed living wage income regardless of employment. [See answer to Demand One.]

FOURTH DEMAND: Free college education.

This is also a plank in the Democratic Platform for the 2016 election.

FIFTH DEMAND: Begin a fast track process to bring the fossil fuel economy to an end while at the same time bringing the alternative energy economy up to energy demand.

---

[1] Suskind, Ron, *Confidence Men: Wall Street, Washington, and the Education of a President* (New York: Harper, 2011), pp. 269-272.

Although this is not specifically a plank in the Democratic Platform, high hopes for a windfall from Arctic drilling proved to be unfounded once permission to drill was granted. Too, the fracking industry, which extracts oil from shale, may be the latest bursting bubble. Leaders and investors in the industry have had to write down their assets to the tune of heavy losses.

Moreover, the oil industry is in the process of being de-funded as a strictly private endeavor, spearheaded by actor Leonardo DiCaprio. DiCaprio, 400 institutions, and 2,000 other people committed to pulling out $2.6 trillion in investments in a drive toward demanding clean energy.[1]

SIXTH DEMAND: One trillion dollars in infrastructure (Water, Sewer, Rail, Roads and Bridges and Electrical Grid) spending now.

This, too, is a plank in the Democratic Platform for the 2016 election, best represented by Senator Bernie Sanders.

SEVENTH DEMAND: One trillion dollars in ecological restoration planting forests, reestablishing wetlands and the natural flow of river systems and decommissioning of all of America's nuclear power plants.

This has not been addressed in depth by Democrats or Republicans. However, it certainly runs contrary to the bid of the Koch Brothers to buy America's park lands and protected reserves for commercial exploitation.

EIGHTH DEMAND: Racial and gender equal rights amendment.

As with the end of slavery, legislating rights does not mean the end of discrimination. For some, it only creates "specially recognized" groups that are hated twice as much. Moreover, the Reconstruction Amendments (from the Thirteenth to the Fifteenth) are already rejected by the far-right and the Tea Party. Likewise, the Marriage Equality Act has lately led to rebellion by a Kentucky civil servant, who not only refused to issue marriage licenses to gay couples but also tampered with licenses already issued. After being temporarily jailed, Ms. Davis became a rallying figure for the far right and the Christian Coalition. These groups have been rightly ridiculed for equating Ms. Davis with the legendary civil rights activist Rosa Parks (who fought discrimination instead of imposing it on others).

NINTH DEMAND: Open borders migration. Anyone can travel anywhere to work and live.

---

[1] "Leonardo DiCaprio calling to bring down Big Oil Corporations," ewao. com, September 13, 2015, http://www.ewao.com/a/1-defund-oil-with-leonardo-decaprio

President Obama has issued a call for illegal immigrants who reside in the United States to become naturalized citizens, and has streamlined the process to make it easier and more affordable.

As for whether border-hopping will become a global phenomenon, this is certainly the hope of transnational conglomerates. They measure the success of Corporate Governance by how willing (or desperate) people are to uproot themselves from their communities, and even become transients, in pursuit of scarce employment.

TENTH DEMAND: Bring American elections up to international standards of a paper ballot precinct counted and recounted in front of an independent and party observers system.

The deployment of such systems, particularly in deeply divided countries, has not always guaranteed respect for unpopular electoral outcomes. However, the U.S. must invest in maintaining the same quality of equipment in all voting precincts. Most notably, the voting machines in poor regions are decrepit and prone to errors (such as registering a vote for a candidate who is not the voter's choice).

Too, the upcoming presidential election has forced racism out in the open like no recent election before now. The state of Alabama has imposed stringent requirements for voter registration while closing down the DMV (Department of Motor Vehicles) offices in predominantly poor, black districts.

ELEVENTH DEMAND: Immediate across the board debt forgiveness for all. Debt forgiveness of sovereign debt, commercial loans, home mortgages, home equity loans, credit card debt, student loans and personal loans now! All debt must be stricken from the "Books." World Bank loans to all Nations, Bank to Bank Debt and all Bonds and Margin Call Debt in the stock market including all Derivatives or Credit Default Swaps, all 65 trillion dollars of them must also be stricken from the "Books." And I don't mean debt that is in default, I mean all debt on the entire planet, period.

Not that this would ever happen, but it would end the banking system and the means to control countries as well as people, wiping out along with it the savings and assets of small holders. In effect, there would be a run on all currencies, leading to a disaster worse than The Great Depression.

TWELFTH DEMAND: Outlaw all credit reporting agencies.

Since lenders must have some criteria to predict payment performance, this would return us to the days when credit was apportioned on condition of social status rather than individual effort. But in the spirit of this demand, Senator Elizabeth Warren has proposed legislation to prohibit employers from accessing applicants' credit histories to prevent poor credit from justifying non-hiring.[1]

THIRTEENTH DEMAND: Allow all workers to sign a ballot at any time during a union organizing campaign or at any time that represents their yeah or nay to having a union represent them in collective bargaining or to form a union.

Although this targets "right to work" states, the tendency of unions to amass political power and collectively support candidates without input from union members (let alone consent) has made them part of the party machines, both as a condition of their continued survival and to ensure their relative weakness in representing the working class. As yet, what remains of organized labor has not endorsed either party.

THE DEREGULATION DILEMMA

While I understand the disgust of the Occupy Wall Street organizers with the subprime mortgage meltdown and subsequent bank bailout, the persistence of too-big-to fail and the network of global debt are the preferred tools of the wealthy in managing the world. They have learned from experience that the supremacy of a few wealthy families requires spreading the wealth, not to the desperate bottom 90 percent mired in poverty or distress, but to other top tier businesses and families who would otherwise contest their rule to wrest away wealth for themselves.

The two most recent and boldest examples of this inside the U.S. were the Savings & Loan scandal and the toxic asset rescue built into the subprime mortgage meltdown. The Savings & Loan scandal required regulations to be relaxed or rewritten to allow self-dealing, not just to executives, but also to friends, relatives and an unlimited number of subsidiary endeavors, resulting in highly leveraged and zero-collateral loans with no prospect for repayment. In short, it represented fraud on a smaller scale than what became clear by 2008-2009 but set the stage for the same pitfalls with

---

[1] Levine, Sam, "Elizabeth Warren Points Out How Unfair This Hiring Practice Can Be," Huffington Post, September 15, 2015, http://www.huffingtonpost.com/entry/elizabeth-warren-credit-checks_55f82335e4b09ecde1d9a3eb?ncid=fcbkln kushpmg00000013&section=politics

"exotic innovation" upon further deregulation. In the case of the S&L scandal, the Federal Reserve later admitted to "calming fears too long," as well as to outright incredulity that the public "bought the ruse," allowing the problem to become much larger as well as the cost of resolution.

Government intervention under the Obama administration likewise aimed to instill confidence in the stability of the market until all toxic assets had been purchased for their original value (even though they had lost that value) from the megabanks whose overwhelming exposure to "creative innovations" (like collateralized debt obligations and credit default swaps) would otherwise have destroyed them. Although the introduction of new regulations requires the megabanks to submit orderly plans for dissolution in the event of another meltdown to the Federal Reserve, Senator Elizabeth Warren failed to get a definitive answer from Fed Chairman Janet Yellen as to whether such plans (submitted in 2012, 2013 and 2014) fulfilled the requirements of the law.

Presumably, the plans submitted to the Federal Reserve are what Senator Bernie Sanders would utilize to dismantle the megabanks should he become president-elect. Whether he'll actually get credible plans is doubtful at best.

THE BACKLASH AGAINST THE TEA PARTY

Because of its strident rhetoric, which caused several Republicans to step down from office well before the lead-up to the 2016 presidential election,[1] the Tea Party originally lost support within the Republican Party. According to a two-year-old poll conducted by the *Wall Street Journal* and NBC News:

> 41% of non-Tea Party Republicans believe [that] the Tea Party has too much influence. Of self-described Tea Partiers, 56% say they have too little influence. [A]bout the same portion of Republicans—43%— identify with the Tea Party as [those who] say they do not.[2]

As it pertains to harassment, the Tea Party was targeted by the IRS because, according to a Fox insider story, mainstream Republicans *wanted* this:

> "When you have 71 percent who want an investigation, 64 percent who believe it is a sign of corruption...the reason is the establishment Republicans want the IRS to go after the Tea Party. Got It?"[3]

[1] Edwards, David, "Fearing Tea Party violence four Arizona Republicans resign," The Raw Story January 12, 2011, http://www.rawstory.com/rs/2011/01/12/fearing-tea-party-violence-arizona-republicans-resign/

[2] Epstein, Reid J., "Tea Party Wing Irks Some Republicans—WSJ/NBC Poll," Washington Wire, http://blogs.wsj.com/washwire/2014/06/18/tea-party-wing-irks-some-republicans-wsjnbc-poll/

[3] Massie, Mychal, "Republican Leadership Wants IRS to Intimidate Tea Party," The Daily Rant, February 19, 2014, http://mychal-massie.com/premium/

As noted by Lois G. Lerner, then head of the IRS division that oversaw tax-exempt organizations, the words "Tea Party," "patriot," "9/12 Project," "We the People" and "Take Back the Country" were singled out as keywords to flag tax-exempt applications for the most intensive investigation. Maine Republican Sen. Susan Collins told CNN's "State of the Union."

> "This is truly outrageous and it contributes to the profound distrust that the American people have in government.... It is absolutely chilling that the IRS was singling out conservative groups for extra review. And I think that it's very disappointing that the president hasn't personally condemned this."[1]

Not much else was said by Republicans until it became clear that a new IRS rule (planned for the last five years) would prevent 501(c)(4) tax-exempt groups (which spent "more than $310 million over the two-year 2012 election cycle") from "running television ads, organizing get-out-the-vote efforts and voter registration drives," and distributing political literature.[2]

Reacting to the proposal in a joint letter to IRS Commissioner John Koskinen, House Speaker John Boehner and Senate Minority Leader Mitch McConnell wrote:

> It is our view that finalizing this proposed rule would make intimidation and harassment of the administration's political opponents the official policy of the IRS and would allow the Obama Administration to use your agency as a partisan tool.[3]

Since this constitutes an effort to de-legitimize the Tea Party, we should look at what the Tea Party wants before asking why the Department of Homeland Security initially placed some of the party's organizers on the watch list for potential domestic terror.

THE TEA PARTY MANIFESTO

1) Protect the Constitution

Require each bill to identify the specific provision of the Constitution that gives Congress the power to do what the bill does.

---

republican-leadership-wants-irs-to-take-us-down/
[1] FoxNews.com, "Republicans slam IRS targeting of Tea Party as 'chilling,' a form of intimidation," May 12, 2013, http://www.foxnews.com/politics/2013/05/12/rogers-irs-targeting-tea-party-and-other-political-groups-intimidation/
[2] Batley, Melanie, "McConnell, Boehner to IRS: 'End Intimidation and Harassment of Tea Party Groups," Newsmax, July 19, 2014, http://www.newsmax.com/Newsfront/mcconnell-boehner-irs-tea/2014/02/06/id/551290/
[3] Ibid.

If, as they have said, the Tea Party rejects the Thirteenth, Fourteenth, and Fifteenth Amendments, their alleged racism is not unfounded. It would therefore mean the end of any public program aimed at redressing discrimination, economic or otherwise.

2) Reject Cap & Trade

> Stop costly new regulations that would increase unemployment, raise consumer prices, and weaken the nation's global competitiveness with virtually no impact on global temperatures.

As deniers of global warming (which has been both over- and understated), the Tea Party will obviously press for exploitation of protected federal lands, just as the Koch brothers are currently doing. Too, the supposed concern of the Tea Party for rising consumer prices misinterprets the actions of the Federal Reserve from Fed chairman Alan Greenspan forward, since the whole point of monetary inflation and/or "quantitative easing" is to buttress commodity prices with cost-push inflation during economic downturns. By adding liquidity to the system to encourage lending and credit, the Fed creates purchasing power, confidence in the market, and ensures continued buying. The seeds for this policy were sown in the Great Depression, when, from the perspective of the wealthy, there was a glut of overproduction because people had money but were deemed afraid to spend it.

3) Demand a Balanced Budget

> Begin the Constitutional amendment process to require a balanced budget with a two-thirds majority needed for any tax hike.

For this author, the words "begin the amendment process" are ominous. If an amendment to balance the budget is only the first measure, then anything else can follow without involving the public.

Conversely, 57 percent of Republicans wish to dissolve the Constitution and declare Christianity the national religion.[1]

4) Enact Fundamental Tax Reform

> Adopt a simple and fair single-rate tax system by scrapping the internal revenue code and replacing it with one that is no longer than 4,543 words—the length of the original Constitution.

A single-rate tax system would be a distinctly regressive program because the true financial burden depends on the proportion of the tax rate to one's

---

[1] Brekhus, Keith, "57% of Republicans Say Dismantle Constitution and Make Christianity National Religion," PoliticusUSA, February 25, 2015, http://www.politicususa.com/2015/02/25/57-republicans-dismantle-constitution-christianity-national-religion.html

level of earnings. In other words, a worker with $18,000 in annual earnings would have less left over than someone earning $50,000. In practice, a flat tax of 10% would leave the first with $16,200 after taxes, whereas the second would have $45,000. Notably, $16,200 is not even a living wage but rather a measure of poverty.

5) Restore Fiscal Responsibility & Constitutionally Limited Government in Washington

> Create a Blue Ribbon taskforce that engages in a complete audit of federal agencies and programs, assessing their Constitutionality, and identifying duplication, waste, ineffectiveness, and agencies and programs better left for the states or local authorities, or ripe for wholesale reform or elimination due to our efforts to restore limited government consistent with the US Constitution's meaning.

Who precisely gets to determine the Constitution's meaning? For one thing, federal oversight of primary and secondary education could be viewed as "unconstitutional," thereby deleting the Board of Education and leaving it to the states to oversee their curricula. For better or for worse, this would open the door for introducing religion into the system as well as the controversial use of vouchers. This is one way to move liberals out of states that enact such provisions, achieving in the process "voluntary" ethnic cleansing.

6) End Runaway Government Spending

Impose a statutory cap limiting the annual growth in total federal spending to the sum of the inflation rate plus the percentage of population growth.

Since anti-inflationary measures are a mainstay of conservative politics as the means to tamp down wages, the Federal Reserve tolerated no more than 3 percent inflation under the chairmanship of Paul Volcker. At the same time, it cannot be ignored that a tight money policy, or one that pushes up rates of interest, has a devastating effect on debtors, particularly poor countries that received IMF bail-outs as the means to finance the liberalization of their economies and their integration with the global marketplace. Even as liberalization left these countries impoverished, the redoubling of their debt ensured that they became easier to control while prior debt relief was effectively erased.

Inflation above 3 percent is tolerated during recessions to buttress commodity prices. Only when the stock market signals that the boom is about to go bust does the Federal Reserve reverse policy to raise interest rates, which, in turn, signals investors to bet on market failures and thereby rake in additional wealth.

Lastly, the issue of population growth is contentious. Pro-life forces seem to think that the marginalization of America's white male Christians is due to the availability of birth control and abortions as choices for white women, which means they are losing their pride of place due to a war of attrition in which they have no say. On the other hand, the U.S. population is, of course, expanding, but as Jeb! Bush, contender for the Republican presidential nomination, stated: We shouldn't help refugees [or support non-integrated communities] because "we should not have a multicultural society."[1]

Whereas the Obama administration is working to legalize immigrants and aid refugees, Republican legislators are solidly against him.

7) Defund, Repeal, & Replace Government-run Health Care

Defund, repeal and replace the recently passed government-run health care with a system that actually makes health care and insurance more affordable by enabling a competitive, open, and transparent free-market health care and health insurance system that isn't restricted by state boundaries.

By gutting and reforming what Americans were legally forced to buy into, those who looked to the state for assistance will suffer the punitive damage of being redirected to the private sector-in-waiting with the outcome of higher costs, lost protections and so on.

8) Pass an All-of-the-Above Energy Policy

> Authorize the exploration of proven energy reserves to reduce our dependence on foreign energy sources from unstable countries and reduce regulatory barriers to all other forms of energy creation, lowering prices and creating competition and jobs.

As noted, events have already overtaken this demand to show that the long hoped-for windfall regarding Arctic drilling turned out to be groundless. Likewise, the fracking industry is in the process of going under. At this point, Republican focus is on allowing U.S. oil exportation now that climate-conscious investors are ditching their oil investments.

9) Stop the Pork

> Place a moratorium on all earmarks until the budget is balanced, and then require a 2/3 majority to pass any earmark.

Like President Clinton before him, President Obama has balanced the budget with a plan that extends through the year 2017. But wars against foreign countries, the most explosive cause of debt, will remain a

---

[1] Parker, Elisabeth, "BUSTED: Jeb Bush Tells Voter 'We Should Not Have a Multicultural Society.'" Reverb Press, October 4, 2015, http://reverbpress.com/politics/battlegrounds/jeb-bush-multicultural-society/

Congressional power. This means, on the one hand, that the president-elect will have his or her financial hands tied for their first year in office unless they can pass enabling legislation regarding the planks of their platform. On the other, Republicans who are determined to scuttle President Obama's peace deal with Iran will have overwhelming support from the trillion-dollar disaster industry launched by President George W. Bush.

10) Stop the Tax Hikes

> Permanently repeal all tax hikes, including those to the income, capital gains, and death taxes, currently scheduled to begin in 2011.[1]

Since events have already overtaken this demand to the benefit of the wealthy, let it suffice to say that Jeb! Bush champions the next biggest tax cut as a Republican contender for the presidential nomination. But now that society's top earners are measured as the wealthiest *tenth of one percent*, prominent figures, such as Cartier chief Johann Rupert, publicly admitted that he loses sleep at night from fearing where our inequality will lead us:

> We are destroying the middle classes at this stage and it will affect us.... How is society going to cope with structural unemployment and the envy, hatred and the social warfare?[2]

That said, Bernie Sanders, who has declared war on the rich and is currently leading the polls as a Democratic contender for the presidential nomination, counted over one million online campaign donors by the close of September, 2015. He raised more money in this stage of the campaign process than did President Obama. Most notably, none of this came from corporate donors.

THE RANT HEARD 'ROUND THE WORLD

To understand the Tea Party's emphasis on constitutional interpretation and a return to the limited government preceding World War I, we need to look past the provisions that conservatives have wanted for decades to the Tea Party's rallying rhetoric.

According to John R. Coyne, Jr.:

> The Tea Party movement was christened officially on February 19, 2009, when Rick Santelli, reporting from the Chicago Mercantile

---

[1] Hoffman, Ben, "Tea Party Manifesto," *The Hoffman Post*, http://drudgeretort. wordpress.com/2010/04/27/tea-party-manifesto/
[2] Pulver, Matthew, "'We are destroying the middle classes': Why one of the world's richest men is starting to sound awfully like Bernie Sanders," *Salon*, June 16, 2015, http://www.salon.com/2015/06/16/we_are_destroying_the_middle_ classes_why_one_of_the_worlds_richest_men_is_starting_to_sound_awfully_ like_bernie_sanders/

Exchange for CNBC, after listening to a commentary on housing bailouts, broke into what Dick Armey, former House Republican majority leader and chairman of FreedomWorks, and Matt Kibbe, FreedomWorks' president and chief executive, call "the rant heard 'round the world." "The government is promoting bad behavior!" Mr. Santelli shouted. "This is America! How many people want to pay for your neighbors' mortgages that have an extra bathroom and can't pay their bills? Raise your hands! President Obama, are you listening?...It's time for another Tea Party."[1]

Then:

The political establishment reacted with predictable fury. Homeland Security reportedly put some of those associated with the movement on a watch list of potential "domestic terrorists."[2]

But in the words of Armey and Kibbe:

Unlike past political uprisings against a political establishment gone amuck [sic], this is a revolt from the bottom up. It is built on a coherent, unifying set of values—values that go back to the revolutionary traditions of our founding as a nation...it is built around traditions of respect and humility and hard work...Tea Party members, "beholden to no corporation, no union, no patronizing politician...are the future of American grassroots activism. To turn the Tea Party "ethos into public policy...we need to take over the Republican Party. By seizing control of the party, we can spend our time focused on ideas and use the party infrastructure that has been built over the past 156 years."[3]

Of all that is said by Armey and Kibbe, this last is most important. Although the Tea Party most recently engaged in a losing ploy to threaten a government shutdown over the de-funding of Planned Parenthood, it may, with the resignation of John Boehner, have achieved its more urgent need to redress its asymmetric relation to the mainstream political parties. The Tea Party is now in position to seize the Republican Party in its quest for recognition, both at home and abroad, even though their views are not mainstream:

The 13th, 14th, and 15th amendments to the United States Constitution—are targeted in many of the Tea Party and far-right Republican campaigns against the rights of immigrants and women,

---

[1]   Coyne, John R. Jr., "Book Review: Give Us Liberty: A Tea Party Manifesto" *The Washington Times*, August 30, 2010, http://www.washingtontimes.com/news/2010/aug/30/give-us-liberty-a-tea-party-manifesto/
[2]   Ibid.
[3]   Ibid.

marriage equality and LGBT rights, and voting rights for African Americans and other minority ethnic groups. The racist tinge of many of these attacks, whether openly stated or implied, is obvious.[1]

And:

> Consistent with the intense nativism and significant degree of racism that is prevalent among Tea Partiers, Pew found...pronounced... support among Tea Party Republicans for the draconian and racist Arizona immigration law, for increased enforcement of immigration laws and border security, and for changing the Constitution to abolish birthright citizenship for the children of illegal immigrants.[2]

This distinguishes the Tea Party from the "traitorous liberal elites and policy-makers" so hated by the right-wing fringe, thereby allowing the Tea Party to co-opt white militant movements on behalf of hyper-aggressive white nationalism.

To judge by their militant rallying, this symbiosis is understood.

WISHFUL THINKING

How the nature of the Tea Party could be initially misconstrued is a mystery to me. However, it was apparently believed that the Tea Party could be assimilated into the political left.

In the words of Paul Street:

> Much of the early left commentary on "The Tea Party"...was quite naïve. A number of prominent liberal and left thinkers and activists in the spring of 2010 advised progressives to reach out to "the Tea Party folks" and connect with its members as potential allies...At the outer margins of wishful thinking, the Washington-based antiwar activist Kevin Zeese called...for progressives to recruit "traditional conservative" Tea Party activists—described as "confused" by Zeese—to join a "left-right antiwar coalition" to demand "the end" of "the American empire" and form "a broad-based anti-war movement not limited to the left."[3]

> The first error [Street contends] was to think that many if not most of the Tea Party supporters came largely from the working class progressive base that had been abandoned by corporatist Democrats

---

[1] Miah, Malik, "Rolling Back Reconstruction," Solidarity, http://www.solidarity-us.org/site/node/3637
[2] Street, Paul, "Tea Party Republicans are Petit-Bourgeois Militarists," Z Commentaries, December 27, 2011, http://zcomm.org/zcommentary/tea-party-republicans-are-petit-bourgeois-militarists-by-paul-street/
[3] Ibid.

and whose legitimate populist anger against the financial and corporate elite (what became known this year as the 1%) had been hijacked and misdirected by Glenn Beck and his ilk. Many, perhaps most of the "Tea Partiers," this mistaken (and some might say desperate) line ran, were working class people "we" [the left] should be organizing."[1]

Crucially, Street says:

It is absolutely true that the corporatist and imperial Democrats in the Age of Obama have continued their long neoliberal betrayal and demobilization of the working (and lower) class voters they claim to represent. But the demographics of the Tea Party's support base have not been remotely working class. [Instead] that base is distinctly petit-bourgeois, relatively comfortable, [and] comparatively educated. It includes a particularly large number and outsized percentage of solidly middle class professionals and small business owners along with an outsized component of reasonably well off retired folks. But what most set it apart from the rest of the population was its older (predominantly middle aged and senior) composition, its disproportionately rural, exurban, and suburban residence, its extreme whiteness, and its extremely "conservative" (right wing) and partisan Republicanism.[2]

Political scientists David E. Campbell and Robert D. Putnam, who published the results of their research into the political attitudes and backgrounds of Tea Party supporters, found them to be:

"...overwhelmingly partisan Republicans" who were politically active prior to the Tea Party. [They] found Tea Party supporters "no more likely than anyone else" to have suffered hardship during the 2007-2010 recession. Additionally, the respondents were more concerned about "putting God in government" than with trying to shrink the government.[3]

Surprisingly, Street asserts that:

"The current liberty/Tea Party movement—which started off, if not as a third-party libertarian endeavor, but as an alternative to the prevailing political status quo—is being co-opted by Republicans and right wing conservatives..."[4]

In fact, it is the Tea Party that seeks to co-opt Republicans or vote them out of office. The threat that it could walk away from Republicans if they don't fall in line is the result of watching the polls (where support

---

[1] Ibid.
[2] Ibid.
[3] "Tea Party Movement," http://en.wikipedia.org/wiki/Tea_Party_movement
[4] Street, Paul.

for Republicans has declined to 28%) and realizing that the Tea Party has created a captive audience.

As noted by Molly Ball, Glenn Beck recently urged his listeners to defund the GOP. Seemingly, Republicans fail to understand that the Tea Party isn't a wing of the GOP.

> "It's an autonomous force," said Jenny Beth Martin, national coordinator of the Tea Party Patriots... In the Tea Partiers' view, the clueless establishment hasn't yet internalized the seriousness of the threat to its supremacy. The grassroots has taken control, and it will have its way or secede. [1]

For its part, much of the GOP:

> [Has] long seen the Tea Party as a destructive force. [T]he talk of a schism merely confirms what they've always suspected—that these activists are a radical, destabilizing force, nihilists devoid of loyalty. Some, like the renegade moderate David Frum, urge the Tea Party to go ahead and leave: "Right now, tea party extremism contaminates the whole Republican brand," Frum wrote on CNN.com, wondering "whether a tea party bolt from the GOP might not just liberate the party to slide back to the political center." Representative Charles Boustany of Louisiana lashed out at his intransigent colleagues Wednesday, telling *National Journal*, "I'm not sure they're Republicans and I'm not sure they're conservative." [2]

With the resignation of House Speaker John Boehner, another Republican stated that this opened the way for "the crazies."

For example, before withdrawing from consideration to be the next Speaker of the House, Kevin McCarthy promised Sean Hannity that he would force a government shut-down four times more before the elections.

As interpreted by David Corn:

> [The Tea Party] doesn't want a speaker who is going to try to govern in a time of divided government; [they] don't want a speaker who will endeavor to forge a compromise on behalf of the GOP conference and make the system work; and, as a government shutdown looms and a possible debt ceiling crisis approaches, [they] want a speaker who will step to the side and let the chaos reign. This is the congressional equivalent of "burn, baby, burn." [3]

---

[1] Ball, Molly, "The Conservative War on the GOP," The Atlantic, October 17, 2013, http://www.theatlantic.com/politics/archive/2013/10/the-conservative-war-on-the-gop/280637/

[2] Ibid.

[3] Corn, David, "House Tea Partiers to the World: Burn, Baby, Burn," Mother Jones, October 8, 2015.

The point that the Tea Party has not been "talked down" from its intransigence means that discourse, or the way we choose to talk,[1] is not necessarily the key to resolving a conflict, regardless of the locus, *when confrontation is desired as a challenge and end in itself.*

IN SEARCH OF MODERATION

Theorizing the Standoff is a deeply thoughtful work that demonstrates concern for society as a whole. In agreement, a good many Americans bemoan the lack of civil debate in contemporary politics. Repulsed by corruption, attack ads, gridlock, and aggressive government shut-downs, many feel dispossessed from the governmental process.

According to one study:

> Sixty percent of people said that corruption has increased over the last two years, while only ten percent said it has decreased by any amount.[2]

On the opposite side of the fence:

> Slightly more than 7 percent of Americans admitted to paying a bribe to any of eight major public services in the last 12 months. Of these people, 15 percent said they paid a bribe to someone who works in the judiciary. 14 percent paid one to registry and permit services and 11 percent paid off someone in education services.[3]

In a Gallup poll conducted from June 1–4 in 2013, Americans were asked to explain in their own words why they either approved or disapproved of Congress. In the top tier, 28% disapproved of Congress due to partisan gridlock. 21% cited the failure of Congress to take action and make decisions (of which 19% cited specific issues, such as healthcare, taxes, immigration, and gun control).[4] As it pertains to government shutdowns, a Pew Research Center survey found that 46% of Americans blame Republicans, whereas 37% blame the Obama administration. However, the same question, asked by an NBC/*Wall Street Journal* poll, yielded a wider, 22-point margin, showing that 53% blame Republicans.[5]

---

[1] Thus, trading tangible gains, or the need for more than "talk," is implicit in Game Theory.
[2] U.S. News and World Report, http://www.usnews.com/news/newsgram/articles/2013/07/10/majority-of-americans-say-corruption-has-increased
[3] Ibid.
[4] Saad, Lydia, "Gridlock is Top Reason Americans Are Critical of Congress," Gallup Politics, June 12, 2013, http://www.gallup.com/poll/163031/gridlock-top-reason-americans-critical-congress.aspx
[5] Blumenthal, Mark and Swanson, Emily, "Americans Mad at Everyone Over Federal Government Shutdown, but Most Blame Republicans," Huff Post

CONFRONTATION AS AN END IN ITSELF

Tea Partiers, or those who believe in "tough talk," are also determined to prove that they "walk the walk." This has raised fears that the violence of the 1960s will reemerge with a vengeance.

Two years before this writing, Susan J. Demas opined:

> Somebody is going to get shot. If I am wrong—and I hope desperately that I am—we will be extremely lucky. Because there is a suffocating, sweltering mood brewing in our country, like that of the anxious early 1960s. Consider the all-too-ubiquitous racist Tea Party signs and the rash of death threats against congressmen who voted for health care reform. There's the stomach-churning image of teabaggers calling civil rights hero U.S. Rep. John Lewis a "nigger" and U.S. Rep. Barney Frank a "faggot." Another tea partier caught on camera chucked a dollar at a health care supporter with Parkinson's disease, sneering, "Start a pot; I'll pay for you. I'll decide when to give you money"... And in a move only George Orwell could love, *Second Amendment patriots will be holding rallies on April 19 to commemorate the 15th anniversary of when far-right militiamen incinerated 168 people in Oklahoma City.* [Emphasis added.][1]

> There is a festering ugliness [Demas says] that's gained safe haven on the right and in the Republican Party. It makes no sense to deny it. Rush Limbaugh, Glenn Beck, Sean Hannity and [others] stoke the rage of the fearful, the unemployed and the generally unbalanced for fun and profit. GOP leaders, desperate to regain power, know that the only energy in their party is from the farthest of the far right. So Republican National Committee Chair Michael Steele declares that he's the Original Teabagger (O.T.) and...John Boehner whips up a frenzy warning that national Romneycare will beget Armageddon.[2]

This tragic and fearful prophecy has certainly been fulfilled with the murder of children at Sandy Hook and within the Amish community. And it happened again—three times in under ten days—with the Oregon shootings on college campuses.

Perversely, killing kids has become the new "normal" as the price we pay for "freedom." This, at least, is the bottom line in the words of:

Bill O'Reilly: "People around the world must wonder what's going on in the land of the free. And it is our freedom that allows insane

---

Politics, October 15, 2013, http://www.huffingtonpost.com/2013/10/15/federal-government_n_4102263.html
[1] Demas, Susan J., "Take it down a notch, GOP," Huff Post Politics, July 20, 2014, http://www.huffingtonpost.com/susan-j-demas/take-it-down-a-notch-gop_b_524201.html
[2] Ibid.

individuals to kill so many people. Guns are legal in America under the Second Amendment...The mass murder [in Oregon] could not have been prevented by any legislation in my opinion."[1]

Jeb Bush: "We're in a difficult time in our country and I don't think more government is necessarily the answer to this. I think we need to reconnect ourselves with everybody else. It's very sad to see. But I resist the notion, and I had this challenge as governor—look, stuff happens. There's always a crisis. The impulse is always to do something and it's not necessarily the right thing to do."[2]

Ben Carson: [I] grew up in the slums of Detroit. I saw plenty of gun violence as a child. Both of my cousins were killed on the streets. As a Doctor, I spent many a night pulling bullets out of bodies. There is no doubt that this senseless violence is breathtaking—but I never saw a body with bullet holes that was more devastating than taking the right to arm ourselves away.[3]

As the simplest, most eloquent defense, Jay Branscomb said, "You fear we'll take your guns. We fear you'll take our children."

President Obama spoke with visible anger about the need to find a solution, and when he appeared in Roseburg, Oregon to talk to the victims' families, he was met by a gathering of protestors carrying Confederate flags and others with "Don't Tread on Me." One sign even read: "Go back to Kenya!"[4]

The all-too-hysterical hatred of President Obama by the far-right and far-right fringe also inspired a page on Facebook labeled "Arrest Convict and Hang Obama."[5] Apparently, this page was allowed to remain online for at least a year or more.

Never before in our nation's history has a President been so grossly disrespected.

---

[1] Sarah, "Bill O'Reilly Thinks the 2nd Amendment is a License to Murder, So Accept it," October 2, 2015, http://www.addictinginfo.org/2015/10/02/bill-oreilly-thinks-the-2nd-amendment-is-a-license-to-murder-so-accept-it-america-video/

[2] Oh, Inae, "Jeb Bush on Oregon Mass Murder—'Stuff Happens,'" Mother Jones, October 2, 2015, http://www.motherjones.com/mojo/2015/10/jeb-bush-reacts-oregon-massacre-stuff-happens

[3] http://www.dailykos.com/story/2015/10/06/1428342/-Ben-Carson-Never-saw-a-body-with-bullet-holes-more-devastating-than-loss-of-gun-rights?detail=facebook

[4] Anomaly, "Organizer of Protest While Obama Visited Oregon Shooting Victims' Families Is A Convicted Felon," FreakOut, October 9, 2015.

[5] "Conservative Facebook Group Advocates Hanging President Obama," http://www.ifyouonlynews.com/politics/conservative-facebook-group-advocates-hanging-president-obama/

And the problem for the GOP is that rank and file Republicans are on the side of the zealots. This wouldn't be a problem if the most moderate Republicans were also the most active.

> In reality, the opposite is true. The most conservative voters are also most likely to vote in all elections, including primaries. Of the 37 percent of Republicans who agree with the Tea Party, 49 percent say they always vote in nomination contests, compared with 22 percent of moderate and liberal Republicans. In other words, hard-right conservatism is where the enthusiasm is.[1]

Does this mean, as Wagner-Pacifici posits, that we need a "metaphorical Hostage Rescue Team to periodically rescue us hostages of social life from ourselves and each other"?

For that matter, what does "metaphorical" signify in this excerpt?

Having based her work allegorically on the literary narrative, what Wagner-Pacifici seeks is to interpret (or re-interpret) the collective human "story." Without context, any advice is meaningless. Hence, the start of her book consists of a series of quotes, the first of which captures perfectly the pleading within her work:

> In every case the storyteller is a man who has counsel for his readers...
> After all, counsel is less an answer to a question than a proposal concerning the continuation of a story which is just unfolding.
> To seek this counsel one would first have to be able to tell the story.[2]

The use of the word "story" is, in itself, significant. From it, the reader may infer that things aren't "working" for those in power based on the soft and fuzzy version of why Americans love their country, i.e., because America is a classless society where anyone with a will to work has unlimited potential for upward social mobility. Even the rich admit that our unprecedented income inequality has created a "caste society" from which there is no escape.

The export of jobs to other countries has long created a nativist backlash, which worries the rich so much that NSA surveillance targets more than potential terrorists. People who oppose an integrated global economy are studied as an equal threat.

Not even *The End of Poverty*, written by renowned economic technocrat Jeffrey Sachs, has helped to alleviate fears that we have fallen into a bottomless well without a life preserver. Perhaps in a nod to present conditions, Wagner-Pacifici seeks a new "story" to calm those who are treading water.

Meanwhile, more water is pouring into the well.

---

[1] Ibid.
[2] Quoted from Walter Benjamin, Wagner-Pacifici, p. 1.

IS IT 1775?

On or about the anniversary of the historic ride of Paul Revere, "Is it 1775?" appeared in my Twitter feed. Given its confrontational nature and revolutionary value, this is obviously not what Wagner-Pacifici seeks in terms of our human "story," and yet it is part of our heritage that cannot be ignored.

If we are driven to seek the truth and promote understanding of the world in which we live, we must do so as practical people and accept that there are reasons why some things came to be. Knowledge rather than rhetoric is the key to unlocking our biases, which we should strive to do if telling our human "story" is not to be rendered pointless. This means applying reason to a hotbed of conflicting emotional actors, the most militant of which believe that a revolution is the cure for a troubled America.

If so, it should be a revolution of the American mindset—intellectual and bloodless—to make us *think* about what we think.

I will therefore focus on the history of Corporate Governance and the resurgence of white supremacy, eschewing the lamb's wool of a "story" in favor of naked truth.

CHAPTER 2. THE AMERICAN TRUTH

The goals underlying Corporate Governance as well as white supremacy and the history they share begins with North-South divisions proceeding through the Civil War and post-war Reconstruction, up to and including the Stock Market Crash of 1929, the presidencies of Herbert Hoover and Franklin Delano Roosevelt, The Great Depression, and the outcomes of World War II.

THE "ENDOWMENT" OF WHITE PRIVILEGE

Just as the Pilgrims who came to the New World believed that their vision of manifest destiny was instilled by their Creator, to be fulfilled as an endowment for God's chosen people, white supremacists today venerate that belief and are striving to resurrect it in the world they will leave to their children. Employing the symbols, language, and trappings of America's revolutionary heroes, they engage in more than theater. The America they venerate is one that drove out the Spanish as well as the British, and one that went on to seize new frontiers including Mexican territory while in the process of exterminating and ultimately exiling Native Americans (who had proven under the Spanish that they preferred death to slavery—when they did not die of disease anyway.) Believing blacks to be subhuman, whites justified their enslavement.

Because blacks were owned, their "blackness," at least initially, did not threaten male Southern whiteness. Slave owners who had intercourse with black women bred out their "blackness" to raise slave values. This perspective changed completely with black emancipation.

The Civil War, which officially ended slavery, was an attack on many fronts, only one of which was property. The North confronted a Southern aristocracy whose concept of nobility was built on a racial foundation, i.e. white gentility, stemming from the leisure bought with repression. In this, the South saw its predecessor as European nobility.

The so-called "knights" of the Ku Klux Klan were not named so by accident.

DEPENDENTS AND EMPTY PROMISES

The razed earth policy pursued by the Northern army ensured that the South would not recover without Northern assistance. In part, this meant turning a blind eye to rise of Jim Crow, the Southern code of conduct that created a united front for mistreatment of former slaves, as a sop to Southern pride. Indeed the transition to free-market labor had a distinctly punitive cast—via economic means of social engineering no blacks would be permitted to face whites on even ground.

As free blacks migrated to manufacturing cities, they found the "enlightened" North to be shockingly without pity. Like President Lincoln's promise to provide former slaves with the gift of "a mule and an acre," Northern propaganda on slavery proved virtually empty. It did not mean that the North welcomed a large demographic shift. Instead, four out of five blacks remained in the South,[1] where Reconstruction redressed the economic "inefficiency" of providing food, shelter, and medicines for blacks (as slaveholders had done) while also preventing the South from fixing commodity prices to the detriment of the North.

As such, black unemployment, black voter suppression, and the mass racial violence that marked the era of Jim Crow persisted from 1890 well into 1960.[2] In the South, governments and law enforcement either ignored or encouraged Jim Crow, which was undergirded by the following beliefs:

> Whites were superior to blacks in all important ways, including but not limited to intelligence, morality, and civilized behavior; sexual relations between blacks and whites would produce a mongrel race which would destroy America; treating blacks as equals would encourage interracial sexual unions; any activity which suggested social equality encouraged interracial sexual unions; if necessary, violence must be used to keep blacks at the bottom of the social hierarchy.[3]

---

[1] Kennedy, David M., *Freedom From Fear: The American People in Depression and War, 1929–1945* (New York: Oxford University Press, 1999) p. 15.
[2] "What Was Jim Crow?" Jim Crow Museum of Racist Memorabilia, http://www.ferris.edu/jimcrow/what.htm
[3] Kennedy, David M., p. 15

Nationally, racism manifested in redlining: "the practice of denying, or increasing the cost of services such as banking, insurance, access to jobs, access to health care, or even supermarkets to residents in certain, often racially determined, areas." Redlining entailed the practice of delineating the area "where banks would not invest." Redlining "most frequently discriminated against black inner city neighborhoods. Through at least the 1990s this meant that banks would often lend to lower income whites but not to middle or upper income blacks." In contrast, reverse redlining occurred "when a lender or insurer [targeted] minority consumers, not to deny them loans or insurance, but...to charge them more, which they had ample opportunity to do as late as 2007-2008 during the subprime mortgage craze."[1]

The civil rights movements of (1896–1954) and (1954–1968) fought economic discrimination as well as desegregation. Employment, however, remained an intractable issue, prolonged by the Stock Market Crash of 1929 and the ensuing Great Depression. As an unprecedented period of economic contraction that spread beyond America to include much of Western Europe, it affected all workers and was a non-conducive environment for blacks to press their rights during nationwide misery. Since there were no jobs for whites, the futility of fighting them was obvious.

This, for some, was, and is, the *value* of recession—a tool of behavioral modification *par excellence*.

A RETURN TO "MORAL" LIFE

In the words of President Hoover, Treasury Secretary Andrew Mellon "had only one formula. Liquidate labor, liquidate stocks, liquidate the farmers, liquidate real estate." As Mellon preached to the president, "It will purge the rottenness out of the system. High costs of living and high living will come down. People will work harder, lead a more moral life."[2]

The so-called "rottenness" in the system was, and always is, the nature of expectations. In times when no one has any and, in fact, is even afraid to, families will cling together, they will once again fill the church pews, and instead of daring to press for rights they will suffer without complaint as long as the measure of suffering is prominently widespread. This form of "chastening" on the heels of the Roaring Twenties when feminine sexuality, represented by the modern flapper who dressed in flashy sequins and frequented illegal speakeasies, like the failure of Prohibition, which gave

---

[1] "Redlining," Princeton.edu, http://www.princeton.edu/~achaney/tmve/wiki100k/docs/Redlining.html
[2] Kennedy, David M., p. 51.

birth to organized crime, were unwelcome developments and insults to propriety.

Prohibition, although seemingly a moral issue, was also a financial one, since, in the first case, the political "wets" of the time were largely Southern Democrats defending their regional industry. In the second case, immigrant communities had swelled to claim their own neighborhoods, such that:

> The nation's population had nearly doubled since 1890, when it had numbered just sixty-three million souls. At least a third of the increase was due to a huge surge of immigrants. [T]hrough...New York's Ellis Island, opened in 1892, streamed in the next three decades almost four million Italian Catholics; half a million Orthodox Greeks; half a million Catholic Hungarians; nearly a million and a half Catholic Poles; more than two million Jews; half a million Slovaks; [and] millions of other eastern Slavs. The waves of arrivals after the turn of the century were so enormous that of the 123 million Americans recorded in the census of 1930, one in ten was foreign born and an additional 20 percent had at least one parent born abroad.[1]

These immigrants were "disciplined" the hardest when liquor was unavailable to blunt life's rough edges and wages dropped even lower. To eliminate *every* advantage painfully created for ethnic communities, ethnically-founded banks were the very first to go under during The Great Depression.

Having been used as a substitute for the abundance of black labor (and even skilled white labor), much the same way that scabs were employed to break the power of unions (against the unlikely prospect that blacks might fight their repression harder, when anyone could see that such efforts would only backfire in the dog-eat-dog environment employers had created), the immigrants had no need to be told when they were no longer wanted, nor any means to protest it:

> Huddled on the margins of American life, immigrants made do with what work they could find, typically low-skill jobs in heavy industry, the garment trades, or construction. Isolated by language, religion, livelihood, and neighborhood, they had precious little ability to speak to one another and scant political voice in the larger society. So precarious were their lives that many gave up altogether and went back home. Nearly a third of the Poles, Slovaks, and Croatians returned to Europe; almost half the Italians; more than half the Greeks, Russians, Rumanians, and Bulgarians.[2]

Nevertheless:

---

[1] Ibid., p. 14.
[2] Ibid.

> Old-stock Americans continued to think of the foreigners who remained in their midst as alien and threatening...Some of that anxiety found virulent expression in a revived Ku Klux Klan, reborn in all its Reconstruction-paraphernalia at Stone Mountain, Georgia, in 1915. Klan nightriders...directed their venom as much at immigrant Jews and Catholics as blacks...By the early 1920s the Klan claimed some five million members [whose] nativist sentiment...found statutory expression in 1924, when Congress choked the immigrant stream to a trickle.[1]

Spurring this tide of nativism was the fact that white blue-collar workers without job security felt that neither the present nor the future offered the prospect of job advancement or social mobility:

> They worked feverishly when times were good, when the mills were roaring and the forges hot, in order to lay something away against the inevitable moment when times would turn bad, when the factory doors would swing shut and the furnaces be banked. The unpredictable perturbations in their lives constantly disrupted relations among family members and left little opportunity for social or civic involvement, or even for trade union organization. This precarious, disconnected, socially thin, pervasively insecure way of life was the lot of millions of Americans in the 1920s. They had a periodic taste of prosperity but precious little power over their conditions of work or the trajectories of their lives.[2]

Moreover, "carrot and stick" economics were not the only problems facing American workers:

> Manipulating ethnic and racial fears was...one among...several tools that management used to suppress workers' organizations. The most fearsome of these tools was the "yellow-dog" contract, which bound individual workers, as a condition of employment, never to join a union. Employers also relied on friendly judges to issue injunctions prohibiting strikes, picketing, the payment of strike benefits, and even communications between organizers and workers. In 1917, the Hitchman doctrine [resulting from the case of *Hitchman Coal & Coke Co. v. Mitchell*] made yellow-dog contracts enforceable at law. In effect, it rendered illegal almost any effort to organize a union without the employer's consent.[3]

As it also happened, increased mechanization and productive simplification ended the need for skilled labor, further decreasing wages and eliminating positions. Only white-collar workers seemed to be immune from

---

[1] Ibid.
[2] Ibid., p. 24
[3] Ibid., p. 26

uncertainty. According to David Kennedy, they had careers, not jobs. As such, market "discipline" had to be much deeper for the liquidation of labor to reach white-collar workers. It also had to reach into Western Europe where trade unionization and unemployment insurance—derided as socialism and opposed by the AFL (American Federation of Labor) as late as 1929[1] were already long-established as the mark of civilized countries progressively superior to our own.

THE STOCK MARKET CRASH IN PERSPECTIVE

The hysterical accusation that the average, common family was accessing the stock market via easy credit to engage in speculation (rather than respectable business) up to 1929 has been disproved by modern scholars. It is however important that the myth *was* believed.

In his 1931 essay, Only Yesterday, Frederick Lewis Allen portrayed ordinary Americans as "legions of slap-happy small stockholders, drunk with the dreams of the delirious decade suddenly wiped out by the Crash and cast en masse into the gloom of depression."

In the words of David M. Kennedy:

> This picture...is grossly distorted. Allen probably relied on an estimate by the New York Stock Exchange in 1929 that some twenty million Americans owned stocks...The chief actuary of the Treasury Department calculated that only about three million Americans—less than 2.5 percent of the population—owned securities in 1928, and brokerage firms reported a substantially lower number of 1,548,707 customers in 1929.[2]

Those who were horrified by the greedy expectations of small-change Americans seeking to rise above their station used the market to burst the speculative bubble with both speed and vitriol, wiping out millions of dollars on paper by virtue of mass collective selling. They only realized their error of judgment when completely respectable businessmen were driven to ruin and suicide.

To dispel another myth, the stocks which were thought to be "overvalued" showed spectacular dividend payments leading right up to the crash:[3]

- In the first nine months of 1929, 1,436 firms announced increased dividends. In 1928 only 955 announced an increase.
- In the first nine months, cash dividends were $3.1 billion, up from $2.4 billion in 1928 (a 29 percent increase).

---

[1] Ibid., p. 25.
[2] Ibid., p. 40.
[3] Bierman, Harold Jr., *The Causes of the 1929 Stock Market Crash: A Speculative Orgy or a New Era?* (Westport, CT: Greenwood Press, 1998) p. 10.

- In September 1929 dividends were $399 million compared to $278 million in 1928, an increase of 44 percent.
- The dividend payout was 64 percent in September 1929.

Thus the market rebounded, wobbled, and crashed again as the wealthy warred with each other over how deeply they dared to devalue before they resumed buying.

In any case, the stock market "failure" which reflected this devaluation was not, in fact, a failure, as stocks sold en masse were subsequently repurchased for a fraction of their former worth, representing a windfall in terms of actual assets.

As noted by Didier Sornette:

> [T]he stock market is not a "casino" of playful or foolish gamblers. It is, primarily, the vehicle of fluid exchanges allowing the efficient function of capitalistic, competitive free markets.[1]

In other words, stock market investors know *exactly* what they're doing, even if they act on perceptions that have no real foundation. This is and isn't a problem, and one that is recurrent. On the one hand, stock market panics which are driven by "uppity" behavior, whether it concerns an overly rosy (and therefore dangerous) perspective on the part of commoners bucking their station or governments claiming moral "superiority" regarding progressive policies, anyone can be subjected to market discipline within a scant number of hours. On the other hand, huge financial windfalls, realized through temporarily devalued assets (bought with increased purchasing power) are, and will always be, a self-motivating reward system. The only actual problem is the lack of self-discipline for stock market movers and shakers. Like rats that are trained to push a reward button, the temptation to hit that button and receive satisfaction induces frenzied behavior that manifests in humans as a constant drive for the ultimate payoff: the ownership of everything in a perfectly chastened society.

The question is, "How do the movers and shakers acquire actionable information?"

Enter the Federal Reserve and the nation's banking system, which always knows exactly who is borrowing and why.

Just as Wall Street has its own lingo to hide the stock market's nature, Fed watchers understand explicitly the language of banking interest. Nor is this any wonder, since America accepted as its mission the task of ritualizing business cycles before The Great Depression.

---

[1] Sornette, Didier, *Why Stock Markets Crash: Critical Events in Complex Financial Systems* (Princeton, NJ: Princeton University Press, 2004), p. xiii.

THE ECONOMIC MAINSTAYS PERVADING AMERICAN LIFE

"Voting" via the stock market allows politically-minded investors to shape and reorganize businesses, government policies, and labor markets. Instilling the business cycle, central banking does the same.

As I wrote in From Conflict to Crisis:

> The term "business cycle" refers to the regular alternation between "boom" and "bust" phases of economic behavior or, more simply, between times of success and failure. It may be claimed that no one benefits from a period of failure. The typical characteristics of bankrupted businesses, high unemployment, low sales and plummeting prices, drastic budget cuts and reduced productivity are reliable indications that people on the losing end suffer hardship and sacrifice. The idea that this is unavoidable or inevitable has more to do with who benefits than any so-called law of the economy, although ritualized business cycles and indoctrination on the subject have been unqualified successes in terms of public acceptance, not that the public has other options.[1]

This is why:

> The most important aspect of American economics is the tension between "old money" and "new," because old money (representing an affluent minority, usually expressed as 2% or less of the U.S. population) benefits the most on the business cycle's downturn whereas new money, along with new inventions and ideas, commonly grows to compete on the business cycle's upswing.[2]

> The business cycle's downturn is a political commitment to favoring old money because it raises the cost of borrowing from banking institutions at a time when recession causes widespread disruption for businesses dependent on borrowing and induces bankruptcies, downsizing, business takeovers, sales and mergers. Even under economic liberalism, old money is generous to a point. The imposition of business cycles limits the degree of economic expansion while ensuring that all significant growth depends on old money, whether it is through bank borrowing, investments or the issuance of stock. All three mediums serve as a vehicle for the conditional distribution, growth and protection of old money. Old money isn't adverse to new, as long as its own benefits outweigh new money's gains. The problem has always been to prevent *liberal policies* [emphasis

---

[1] Haskin, Jeanne M., *From Conflict to Crisis: The Danger of U.S. Actions* (New York: Algora Publishing, 2012), pp. 33-34.
[2] Ibid.

added] from uncontrollably translating into independent political or economic power, not to mention overthrow.[1]

Because:

> [A] society that is reared on competition as the only source of sustenance or purpose of existence (in accordance with Social Darwinism, survival of the fittest, and the theory of Natural Selection) will have continual challenges to authority and fundamental instability if it doesn't set certain functions *outside* the arena of battle and preserve positions of privilege for those who would otherwise resort to *unacceptable* competition to topple and ruin the system. [2]

In other words, the "boom"-"bust" cycle is a constant war of attrition. Rather than a "trickle down" economy, it is one that "bubbles up" allowing an ever-increasing share of wealth and intellectual property to be siphoned off from society into the hands of the privileged.

THE GREAT DEPRESSION

In cyclical terms, the lead-up to The Great Depression was similar to the events that followed World War I: a "boom" period of conspicuous consumption later chastened by recession, during which American recidivism on free trade and immigration marked a return to isolationism. The difference in The Great Depression is presidential action and the ascendancy of progressives.

As early as 1909, Herbert Hoover wrote, "[T]he time when the employer could ride roughshod over his labor is disappearing with the doctrine of *laissez faire* on which it is founded."[3] As secretary of commerce:

> [Hoover] not only supported the cause of labor but also urged closer business-government cooperation, established government control over the new technology of radio, and proposed a multibillion-dollar federal public works fund as a tool to offset downswings in the business cycle. As president, he meant to be no passive custodian. He dreamt the progressive generation's dream of actively managing *social change* [Emphasis added.] through informed, scrupulously limited, government action. "A new era and new forces have come into our economic life and *our setting among nations of the world*," [emphasis added.] he said in accepting the Republican presidential nomination in 1928. "These forces demand of us constant study and effort if prosperity, peace, and contentment shall be maintained.[4]

---

[1] Ibid., pp. 36-37.
[2] Ibid., p. 32.
[3] Kennedy, David M., p. 11.
[4] Ibid.

As it turned out, this would largely be left to Hoover's successor.

Taking charge immediately, FDR focused on reassurance, relief, and recovery. Under a Keynesian economy, which regarded government expenditure as a necessary economic stimulus, FDR oversaw the initiation of a welfare state that became a warfare-welfare state with the engagement in World War II that put America back to work.

THE RIGHT TO HOLD A JOB

During World War II, the refusal to employ black labor demonstrated the resilience of racism, up to the point of stupidity. Railway owners declined to hire blacks, even if it meant running fewer trains when the demand for mass transportation was a national imperative.

Taking his cue from British analyst William Beveridge, who found nothing more demoralizing than a man whose labor was not wanted, FDR attempted to impose a constitutional amendment guaranteeing every citizen the right to gainful employment (which would have made race irrelevant). This was shot down in the legislature, both because the wartime economy had produced a labor deficit (which was resolved by hiring white women) and because FDR was increasingly (and alarmingly) perceived as a runaway president or "dictator." He had, after all, tried to impose a federal income tax of 100% on all income over $25,000, which was overturned by the legislature.

In the international sphere, FDR's many achievements included the launch of the Marshall Plan for the reconstruction of Europe, and laying the critical foundation for the United Nations, international finance, and currency regulation. In other words, he and his Brain Trust exploited their wartime momentum to stampede over everyone—but particularly conservatives and isolationists—whose forebears had fought and defeated President Woodrow Wilson's support for the League of Nations.

The all-important difference? The cornerstones of global re-organization were, from start to finish, American creations: established for America's purposes and eventually its greatness.

LIBERAL "TRAITORS"

Because internationalism opened the door for industries to circumvent collective bargaining by exporting production and exploiting global labor, this was naturally seen as a betrayal of American workers.

Under successive presidents pursuing free trade agreements and other liberal policies, there would, of course, be others. In the meantime, America seemed to recapture its "whiteness" in the war against the former Soviet Union, suggesting that "whiteness" is not merely a matter of race but also one of belief—a core value system which is diametrically opposed to anti-religion, socialism, and state collectivism.

For those who resented FDR and the costs of World War II, whether construed in terms of taxes, the loss of American lives, or the burgeoning growth of the warfare-welfare state via the Executive Office, one thing was clear: that the state must be "reconditioned," even if it meant suffering the repulsive costs of transition and America's humiliation, which necessarily predicted enough government excess to turn the public against it, including:

The Vietnam failure.[1]

The North Korean stalemate.

Stagflation.

Unending recession.

The disappearance of the middle class.

The looming fiscal cliff.

Unbridled immigration.

Failure in Iraq.

And so on.

If it seems, in the present, as if President Obama has done his share of serving the wealthy by: bailing out the bankers with more debt to be borne by the public; eschewing health care reform in favor of a deal with private insurers for a disease management system; extending protection against liability to genetically modified seed inventors via executive order and failing to honor his promise regarding GMO labels; engaging in secret negotiations for the Trans-Pacific Partnership that will more fully open the floodgates to corporate penetration while stripping national sovereignty from participating countries; and allowing Wall Street to create another bubble economy that is meant to be burst in tandem with the 2016 presidential election, the point must be restated: Enough government excess will turn the public against it.

As it has.

---

[1] In this case, the CIA was directly implicated. Quoting from Wikipedia's "The Vietnam War": U.S. officials began discussing the possibility of a regime change during the middle of 1963. The United States Department of State was generally in favor of encouraging a coup, while the Defense Department favored Diệm. Chief among the proposed changes was the removal of Diệm's younger brother Nhu, who controlled the secret police and special forces, [and] was seen as the man behind the Buddhist repression and more generally the architect of the Ngô family's rule. This proposal was conveyed to the U.S. embassy in Saigon in Cable 243. The Central Intelligence Agency (CIA) was in contact with generals planning to remove Diệm. [The generals] were told that the United States would not oppose such a move nor punish the generals by cutting off aid. President Diệm was overthrown and executed, along with his brother, on 2 November 1963. When he was informed, Maxwell Taylor remembered that [President] Kennedy "rushed from the room with a look of shock and dismay on his face."

And as it will, motivating the Tea Party (which does not understand that all of these things were achieved for the business community to further promote Corporate Governance) to become even more radical in attacks against the government, even to the point of violent overthrow.

But with or without revolution, there will be Irreversible Reformation.

GOOD THINGS COME TO THOSE WHO WAIT

Ironically enough, FDR was accused of a second-rate mind yet he grasped "The Great Game" perhaps better than most. In 1933, when FDR was *urged* to become a dictator by his former political mentor Al Smith and respected columnist Walter Lippmann:

> [T]he affable sphinx of Hyde Park gave little clue about his reaction...Even his closest advisors...the members of the fabled Brain Trust, marveled at Roosevelt's capacity for what Tugwell called "almost impenetrable concealment of intention." [A]ttentively scrutinizing his chief during the electoral campaign (when it was said that FDR and Herbert Hoover each seemed to be reading the lines of the other), [Tugwell] remarked to Moley that Roosevelt had the mobile and expressive face of an actor. His features were utterly responsive to his will, finely molding themselves to his constantly shifting purposes of persuasion, negotiation, or obfuscation, never ceasing to charm but never opening fully...[1]

> [In 1933] John Maynard Keynes [had] issued an open letter to the newly inaugurated Roosevelt in the New York Times, whose two opening sentences of the more than 2,500-word manifesto defined the stakes and posed revolution as the price of failure of severely altering capitalism as it was practiced. Keynes was no radical. He urged the new president to work "within the framework of the existing social system," that is, to reform capitalism without allowing it to be abandoned or abolished.[2]

> [Joseph Kennedy said] "In those days I felt and said I would be willing to part with half of what I had if I could be sure of keeping, under law and order, the other half." Kennedy, like many (but hardly all) of his elite colleagues, knew that capitalism had to be bridled if it was to survive. "I knew that big drastic changes had to be made in our

---

[1] Kennedy, David M., p. 111.
[2] Pulver, Matthew, "Why conservative billionaires have started talking like Bernie Sanders: 'We are creating a caste system from which it's almost impossible to escape," Salon, http://www.salon.com/2015/08/11/why_conservatives_ billionaires_have_started_talking_like_bernie_sanders_we_are_creating_a_caste_ system_from_which_its_almost_impossible_to_escape/

economic system," he later told Joe McCarthy. "I wanted [Roosevelt] in the White House for my own security."[1]

It was later revealed that when in 1938 a year-long recession threatened the gains made against the Depression, as conservative Democratic legislators urged severe cuts in public works and farm aid, Roosevelt feared revolution. "The president remarked that this would mean calling out the troops to preserve order," wrote a cabinet member in his diary. "It might even mean a revolution, or an attempted revolution."[2]

This is where we stand today. With the recovery of the working man's economy still all too fragile, conservatives see the money-machine of Wall Street signaling the Federal Reserve that it should raise interest rates because they're ready to bet on the downside. The bitter medicine of recession is about to be re-administered, and the question for the wealthy is what they want the fallout to look like. Do they want someone like Bernie Sanders, whose openly populist platform would, like Roosevelt's, most gently save capitalism? Or do they want Tea Party radicals, who, from a need to ravage America, would impose IMF-style Structural Adjustment without the "benefit" of a bailout to crush the working poor while hunger stalks the destitute?

[Like] Kennedy, Roosevelt and Keynes—today's most prominent businessmen are urging another radical reformation of capitalism so that truly radical change doesn't come....They seem to [concede] that "the most obvious choice is our government" to guide and enforce the change. "But the current Congress has been paralyzed."[3]

Why? Because it's crazy to believe that capitalism can be saved by far-right radicals without shocking the rest of the world and indeed our own populace. Their openly stated plans for economic and racist brutality would require a war without to downplay their war within. They fail to see that progressivism, like liberalism, was a tactic for FDR—a stop-gap measure on the road to Irreversible Reformation of the United States and the world.

For FDR and his Brain Trust of wealthy academic elites to lay the groundwork for Corporate Governance while fighting fascism, communism, and ultimately totalitarianism required representation by genuine believers to staff real institutions: a real United Nations, with all its many divisions, a real IMF. The new system had to be real in every sense, or none of the world would believe it, nor would it serve its purpose. Paths had to be provided for

---

[1] Ibid.
[2] Ibid.
[3] Ibid.

people to be used as they wished. But also as they *didn't* and never realized they would be. As unaware propaganda, they lived their roles as they were meant to—with careers of inestimable worth representing America's goodness and, above all, freedom of choice.

It didn't matter in the meantime if Irreversible Reformation proceeded at a creep. Its proponents never doubted that it would take the leaps and bounds we are witnessing today.

This is the great leveler that few understand in American politics: Underlying FDR's liberal policies was an ethic so *conservative* that its successors have stuck to their goal of Irreversible Reformation, regardless of their course but never heedless of the costs. Having waited for the day when the state itself could be chastened, their reward will be privatization of services and assets controlled since the New Deal's formation—the last frontier to be conquered and the reason it was maintained.[1] Those who brought this about have all been public servants at one time or another, working within institutions that each have living memory of what it means to be conservative in order for each generation to work patiently and relentlessly toward the inevitable End Game, not as conspiracists but in fellowship, sharing a camaraderie that the world knows little of.

---

[1] Although the argument may be made that politicians before now feared to tamper with Social Security, their profligate spending of Social Security revenues in exchange for worthless government IOUs shows that Social Security has been steadily undermined with privatization as the long-held goal.

CHAPTER 3. STAYING AHEAD OF THE FORCE CURVE

Because the American "story" is one of stop-gap measures under a liberal banner that was not so much duplicitous as a matter of purposeful packaging (since it allowed and even needed people to be nothing but themselves) the extension of rights and benefits according to political need—as the necessary palliative to take away something more—means that we can't be certain such rights will be permanent or that the benefits will be lasting. In the context of "The Great Game" only one thing is guaranteed: that the government will act to stay ahead of the "force curve" against uncontrolled reactions, both predicting and preventing outcomes that would diminish its enormous advantage.

This chapter will look at how this is managed.

THE METHODS AND EVOLUTION OF BEHAVIOR MODIFICATION

In the transition from empire to nation to dreaming of ways and means for absolute privatization, it is clear that conservative focus can be summarized in two words as "behavior modification" employing the following tools:

- History as Knowledge: It is only what we learn that fulfills the imperative to categorize typologies.
- History as Instruction: In turn, what we know allows us to formulate theories as to why events occurred and how they can be replicated.
- Government à la Carte: Having the means to pick and choose what defines the structure of government is consistent with the knowledge and instruction we inherited from history.
- Mavericks in Experimentation: Tinkering with knowledge and instruction

both in and outside the state allows us to correct, develop, and/or adapt our institutions to limit, reverse, or advance observable outcomes.

• Successors in Assimilation: Refugees from different countries can be absorbed into the state, first as a source of labor, which is grateful for substandard wages, and then as a source of potential or, more importantly, *ideas* to ensure that innovation will remain an American stronghold as American education produces increasingly dogmatic thinkers due to over-pedantic teaching, conceptual compartmentalization, and the slide toward indoctrination that shores up the privileged but throttles critical thinking.

• The Logic of the "Invisible" Empire: In *From Conflict to Crisis*, I explained that the so-called "invisible hand" of free-market competition is, in fact, entirely visible via the methods of modern banking, manipulation of the stock market, and "on again, off again" regulation/deregulation. Yet, the fiction continues to "work" because action at a distance makes these institutions untouchable. Due to institutional protectionism and deliberate obscurity, social peace is secured at the cost of the losers— just like everything else.

• Gaming the World System: Because "tinkering" with theories and typologies in and outside the state can produce observable outcomes, it is inevitable that the "tinkerers" will seek predictability within a pre-established arena of what is and is not acceptable in asymmetric relations, where comparative advantage (and not equilibrium) is both the initial and final condition.

• The Phases of Revolution: As the three keys to the kingdom of de-nationalization under the re-centralization of economic containment, these include "the good wars," the privatization of religion, and implementing wars of attrition. In the first case, history, like science, must have an agreed point of beginning as the "truth" by which we are guided, or that point at which laws are established, thereby seating the Hague and what it stands for in international relations as the force behind social progression. In the second case, religion in the West was internalized as a countermovement to Marx, who held that religion was the "opium of the people," persuading them to accept injustice and inequality in this life to be rewarded in Heaven, when the good life is here for the taking if we have the courage to build it. The concomitant conception, which meant much at the time (and still does for those who are hopeful), was, of course, the American Dream. In the third case, wars of attrition are launched in every conceivable way to de-legitimize the nation, not just as a concept but by root-and-branch annihilation.

Each point that I noted (and explain further below) requires looking at earlier history to understand where we derived our knowledge of how to manipulate societies, the point being that banking and market mechanisms are not at all mysterious. As learned from our predecessors, their application in practice was simply a matter of creating continual crises whereby, over time, social engineering would be tolerated for lack of other options.

HISTORY AS KNOWLEDGE

All social science is based on observation, whether conducted through the study of history or the application of philosophy (what the mind perceives as cause and effect, as well as what is just). Most Western politics, ethics, mathematics, sociology, and economics are owed to Greek civilization, ignoring in the process that much of early Greek knowledge was acquired from the Persians.

From Aristotle, we inherited the concept that some minimal level of schooling is required for common citizens to learn what is useful to the state, i.e., the laws of the government, one's place in society, and how to comport oneself as a patriot. From Socrates, we learned that one must question oneself exhaustively on whether our knowledge is sound or illusory. If sufficient learning is lacking, one is exhorted to seek out leaders with the requisite expertise to excel where others cannot, whether it be in teaching, government, or the ideal model of citizenship. From Sophocles, we derive our critique of Sophistry, or that school of thought which teaches that knowledge is not knowledge when submitted to dialectic reasoning. By reducing any line of thought to its smallest constituent parts, and reducing those in turn to what can and cannot be known, the perceptions of the thinker are proven to be unreal. From Pythagoras, we learned to apply "the real" to mathematical models (now known as axioms—or mathematical statements of proof). The Pythagorean Theorem, consistent with Plato's forms (or projections of the ideal), is not just simplistically elegant—it was the first thing to be proved as the achievement of pure science.

In this period, Rome was no match for Greece in intellectual growth, but Greece was no match for Rome in the military arts. Where Greece colonized and occupied, thereby Hellenizing its territories, Rome conquered then levied tribute on independent cultures, and allowed them to grow, aided by Rome's construction of roads and other critical infrastructure, which suited Rome in turn by supporting its distant garrisons and providing direct, expedient means to dispatch armies to those who rebelled.

With the advent of Christianity, world leaders learned that Christians were peaceable people and martyrs for their own cause, such that the spread of Christianity was the means to reduce rebellion in far-flung conquered territories. At the same time, mistreatment of Christians in non-Christian territories provided justification for outside intervention.

In time, Christian monarchs persuaded papal authority that consolidation, and not expansion, of power through God-given sanction over the people they ruled would prevent further encroachment by the non-Western world. More importantly, by effecting decentralization, the monarchs gained independence and soon turned their attention to applying the lessons of Greece and Rome to their own administrations.

This marked the beginning of the Greco–Roman compromise.

HISTORY AS INSTRUCTION

If we turn to Great Britain between the 16th and 18th centuries, the monarchy's main concern was to earn more than it spent, since this had been a perpetual cause for territorial wars between European powers. Thus mercantilism, under which seafaring merchants supplied goods for resale and manufacture, produced an export orientation as well as a voracious interest in formal colonization.

Because a continual supply demands continuous control when the objective is one of asset seizure as opposed to importation (since the former supplies goods at the cost of the empire's victims—thereby maximizing profits and also the merchant's investment) the colonies of Great Britain suffered both military dominance and cultural penetration.[1] Like Rome, which conquered, Great Britain established outposts and provided infrastructure to police the subject people and promote resource extraction.[2] But, like Greece, which Hellenized as a means of assimilation, Great Britain also imposed order through colonial administration.

By the late 18th century, the rise and protection of the manufacturing sector became a source of contention, which above all else, expanded the Age of Reason. As philosophers applied themselves to every conceivable issue from ontology (the source or origin of things) to the etymology of thought, to freedom from taxation, they spawned a forward-looking justification for the onset of capitalism.

GOVERNMENT À LA CARTE

In the midst of Britain's changes the Pilgrims had fled to the New World. As the colonies grew successful, a conflict with Britain over newly levied taxes produced a groundswell of resistance that was sufficient to launch

---

[1] Claiming that its mission was to civilize its colonies, Great Britain, like other empires of course did no such thing, relying instead on massacres as the most expedient means to eliminate resistance.

[2] Unlike Rome, Britain never intended for the colonies to prosper.

and conclude a successful revolution. Explicitly rejecting the monarchy, America's prominent thinkers deliberately formed a government to protect and uphold the cause of the revolution, understanding as they did that it endowed legitimization via *laissez faire*—the concept that a free economy was also a fair economy, such that the government should leave it alone. Theoretically self-regulating, a laissez faire economy left business to those who conducted it. American institutions, both federal and state, evolved very much in line with Britain's Greco-Roman compromise, albeit with one distinction. Taking seriously the lesson of the Peloponnesian War (which, according to Thucydides, was that Sparta attacked and defeated Athens from fearing that "Athens had grown too big") Americans grasped the need for other nations to invest in its "frontiers."

If paths were provided for transnational collectives to own, control, and grow wealth through American institutions, the likelihood of *more* war on U.S. soil was one we might never face. Thus, America gained a stock market as well as a central bank. The former insured that the obsession of the privileged with conquering "new frontiers" as the means to grow their wealth ahead of everyone else would be met and maintained by an ability to create them through constant innovation in the "products" representing frontiers. At the same time, this laid the foundation for transnational "herd control." "Voting" via the stock market allowed politically-minded investors to shape and reorganize businesses, government policies, and particularly labor markets. Central banking did the same.

MAVERICKS IN EXPERIMENTATION

During the decline of the Ottoman empire, the government tried everything to shore up its dwindling resources, from tax-farming (which proved efficient but also threatened the ruler since it produced a self-interested class that, during calls for reform, could agitate for itself) to debasement of its currency (which produced runaway inflation and, on the empire's periphery, a black-market economy to trade for European currency). Likewise, political liberalization produced runaway modernization and, in particular, materialism, ensuring that religious conservatism would reemerge as a counterweight. The government strove for financial stability, and was at times successful (if only in relative terms). Finally, it succumbed to territorial dismemberment and recentralization in the form of a modern nation.

From this, the idea that economic crises could actually be *induced* to replicate the occurrence of (and alternation between) liberalism, materialism, consumerism, and religious conservatism, was both a novel concept and one that had solid roots.

SUCCESSORS IN ASSIMILATION

The rise of the Ottoman Empire owed much of its success to allowing religious freedom to conquered populations via a head-tax system and incorporating their children into the Ottoman armies. The former prevented the Concert of Europe from turning conquered Jews and Christians against their Ottoman rulers. The latter ensured that their liberation could not, and would never, be realized through the vengeance of their young.

Likewise, the U.S. "melting pot" offered stability, not insecurity.

It was not until World War II that U.S. internment of the Japanese-Americans signaled broader U.S. consciousness of the "encroachment" of "non-white" Americans. Although Japanese-Americans tended almost overwhelmingly to be shopkeepers and merchants with no motive and no potential to undermine U.S. objectives, their arbitrary internment provided a prominent example of civil militarization and allowed their assets to be seized, both of which were goads to white American patriotism (as well as militant white separatism). From then on, despite post-war regret (and financial reparations redressing the internment), more Americans have been steered toward at least a subconscious fear of "the enemy within." This, and fear of being outnumbered, since both blacks and Hispanics are largely spurned by Republicans is, by and large, the reason for militant negativity in the immigration debate, which moderates reject.

THE LOGIC OF THE "INVISIBLE" EMPIRE

The term "Corporate Governance," employed by academics (and herein attributed to transnational conglomerates) seldom makes an appearance outside the ivory towers of elite schools and think tanks, nor will it enter the public debate unless it is couched in the knee-jerk language of "uncertainty for employers" who need "liberty" and "freedom" to create jobs for the unemployed. That such words are misleading is the understatement of eras.

Modern corporations, which utilized government aid to the fullest, are now sitting quite comfortably on trillions in internal capital.

In December 2000, a study compiled by Sarah Anderson and John Cavanaugh of the Institute for Policy Studies revealed that fifty-one of the world's 100 largest economic entities were actually corporations. Only forty-nine were countries. In terms of gross domestic product (GDP), they are ranked below as follows (with corporations in italics):[1]

---

[1] http://www.corporations.org/system/top100.html

Rank	Country/Corporation	GDP/sales ($mil)
1	United States	$8,708,870.00
2	Japan	$4,395,083.00
3	Germany	$2,081,202.00
4	France	$1,410,262.00
5	United Kingdom	$1,373,612.00
6	Italy	$1,149,958.00
7	China	$1,149,814.00
8	Brazil	$ 760,345.00
9	Canada	$ 612,049.00
10	Spain	$ 562,245.00
11	Mexico	$ 474,951.00
12	India	$ 459,765.00
13	Korea, Rep.	$ 406,940.00
14	Australia	$ 389,691.00
15	Netherlands	$ 384,766.00
16	Russian Federation	$ 375,345.00
17	Argentina	$ 281,942.00
18	Switzerland	$ 260,299.00
19	Belgium	$ 245,706.00
20	Sweden	$ 226,388.00
21	Austria	$ 208,949.00
22	Turkey	$ 188,374.00
23	*General Motors*	$ 176,588.00
24	Denmark	$ 174,363.00
25	*Wal-Mart*	$ 166,809.00
26	*Exxon Mobil*	$ 163,881.00
27	*Ford Motor*	$ 162,558.00
28	*DaimlerChrysler*	$ 159,985.70
29	Poland	$ 154,146.00
30	Norway	$ 145,449.00
31	Indonesia	$ 140,964.00

32	South Africa	$ 131,127.00
33	Saudi Arabia	$ 128,892.00
34	Finland	$ 126,130.00
35	Greece	$ 123,934.00
36	Thailand	$ 123,887.00
37	*Mitsui*	$ 118,555.20
38	*Mitsubishi*	$ 117,765.60
39	*Toyota Motor*	$ 115,670.90
40	*General Electric*	$ 111,630.00
41	*Itochu*	$ 109,068.90
42	Portugal	$ 107,716.00
43	*Royal Dutch Shell*	$ 105,336.00
44	Venezuela	$ 103,918.00
45	Iran, Islamic Rep.	$ 101,073.00
46	Israel	$ 99,068.00
47	*Sumitomo*	$ 95,701.60
48	*Nippon Tel & Tel*	$ 93,591.70
49	Egypt, Arab Republic	$ 92,413.00
50	*Marubeni*	$ 91,807.40
51	Colombia	$ 88,596.00
52	*AXA*	$ 87,645.70
53	*IBM*	$ 87,548.00
54	Singapore	$ 84,945.00
55	Ireland	$ 84,861.00
56	*BP Amoco*	$ 83,556.00
57	*Citigroup*	$ 82,005.00
58	*Volkswagen*	$ 80,072.70
59	*Nippon Life Insurance*	$ 78,515.10
60	Philippines	$ 75,350.00
61	*Siemens*	$ 75,337.00
62	Malaysia	$ 74,634.00
63	*Allianz*	$ 74,178.20

64	Hitachi	$ 71,858.50
65	Chile	$ 71,092.00
66	Matsushita Electric Ind.	$ 65,555.60
67	Nissho Iwai	$ 65,393.20
68	ING Group	$ 62,492.40
69	AT&T	$ 62,391.00
70	Philip Morris	$ 61,751.00
71	Sony	$ 60,052.70
72	Pakistan	$ 59,880.00
73	Deutsche Bank	$ 58,585.10
74	Boeing	$ 57,993.00
75	Peru	$ 57,318.00
76	Czech Republic	$ 56,379.00
77	Dai-Ichi Mutual Life Ins	$ 55,104.70
78	Honda Motor	$ 54,773.50
79	Assicurazioni Generali	$ 53,723.20
80	Nissan Motor	$ 53,679.90
81	New Zealand	$ 53,622.00
82	E.On	$ 52,227.70
83	Toshiba	$ 51,364.90
84	Bank of America	$ 51,392.00
85	Fiat	$ 51,331.70
86	Nestle	$ 49,694.10
87	SBC Communications	$ 49,489.00
88	Credit Suisse	$ 49,362.00
89	Hungary	$ 48,355.00
90	Hewlett-Packard	$ 48,253.00
91	Fujitsu	$ 47,195.90
92	Algeria	$ 47,015.00
93	Metro	$ 46,663.60
94	Sumitomo Life Insur.	$ 46,445.10
95	Bangladesh	$ 45,779.00

96	*Tokyo Electric Power*	$ 45,727.70
97	*Kroger*	$ 45,351.60
98	*Total Fina Elf*	$ 44,990.30
99	*NEC*	$ 44,828.00
100	*State Farm Insurance*	$ 44,637.20

More recently, Business Insider has found that Yahoo is more profitable than Mongolia, with an annual revenue of $6.32 billion; Visa is bigger than Zimbabwe, with an annual revenue of $8.07 billion; eBay is bigger than Madagascar, with an annual revenue of $9.16 billion; Nike is bigger than Paraguay, with an annual revenue of $19.16 billion; Consolidated Edison is bigger than the Democratic Republic of Congo, with an annual revenue of $13.33 billion; McDonald's is bigger than Latvia, with an annual revenue of $24.07 billion, Amazon.com is bigger than Kenya, with an annual revenue of $34.2 billion; Morgan Stanley is bigger than Uzbekistan, with an annual revenue of $39.32 billion; Cisco is bigger than Lebanon, with an annual revenue of $40.04 billion; Pepsi is bigger than Oman, with an annual revenue of $57.83 billion; Apple is bigger than Ecuador, with an annual revenue of $65.23 billion; Microsoft is bigger than Croatia, with an annual revenue of $62.48 billion; Costco is bigger than Sudan, with an annual revenue of $77.94 billion; Proctor and Gamble is bigger than Libya, with an annual revenue of $79.69 billion; Wells Fargo is bigger than Angola, with an annual revenue of $93.249 billion; Ford is bigger than Morocco, with an annual revenue of $128.95 billion; Bank of America is bigger than Vietnam, with an annual revenue of $134.19 billion; General Motors is bigger than Bangladesh, with an annual revenue of $135.59 billion; Berkshire Hathaway is bigger than Hungary, with an annual revenue of $136.19 billion; General Electric is bigger than New Zealand, with an annual revenue of $151.63 billion; Fannie Mae is bigger than Peru, with an annual revenue of $183.83 billion; Conoco Phillips is bigger than Pakistan, with an annual revenue of $184.97 billion; Chevron is bigger than the Czech Republic, with an annual revenue of $196.34 billion; Exxon Mobil is bigger than Thailand, with an annual revenue of $354.67 billion; and Wal-Mart is bigger than Norway, with an annual revenue of $421.89 billion. Wal-Mart therefore would rank as the world's 25th largest "country."[1]

As high-powered conglomerates, these transnational actors are, in fact, successors-in-waiting to the services and assets controlled by the nation state.

---

[1] "25 US Mega Corporations: Where They Rank If They Were Countries," Business Insider.

The state, however, has to be undermined before it can be dissolved.

For one who has never experienced the gist of elite curriculums, it may seem "unreal" that they project the nation state as the new source of all "evil," going so far as to claim that from the time of the Korean War, the U.S. has sought international sanction as a matter of window-dressing to achieve imperial aims. But where the nation state is "evil," tribalism (studied with equal vigor) is the province of "Hell" itself.

Thus, moving the world past tribalism to forming the nation state is but a phase in the revolution toward achieving Corporate Governance by transnational conglomerates as the means of social atomization and political reorganization. In the process, transnational actors will hijack the repressive means of the state (i.e., the military and all levels of law enforcement from the NSA and the CIA to state and local police, all of which may participate in a "rapid reaction" force, designed to minimize global armies in emasculation of their subject states).

GAMING THE SYSTEM

To maneuver into position, corporations first sought vertical integration (control of the supply chain related to production) and then horizontal integration (manufacturing expansion to include new product lines suited to their means of production) through corporate buy-outs, mergers, and so forth. What they sought in real terms, however, was *bionomic* integration, or the ultimate control of their environment as a whole.

The term "bionomic" refers to ecological nesting, or the ways in which facets of the environment interact with our lives. Rather than being simply issue-centered, bionomic integration necessarily requires both access to, and influence over, legislative bodies (including the Executive office), which are staffed by self-interested actors who either require conflicting tradeoffs or are increasingly too costly to place and maintain in office.

In sum:

> The "old" America mastered the economic machinery that encouraged men to build and then robbed them of what they built. The losers became powerless and there was nothing for them to lash out against, nor did they feel sorry for any who shared their misery. The small pool of assets reserved for the commoners passed from hand to hand in a game of musical chairs while the chatter of the stock market, vivid and often hysterical, instilled ignorant unease that could be tweaked into full-blown fear with a run on the national currency—or any nation's currency. Inflation was the watch-word and the Federal Reserve was the boogeyman.

Inevitably, we could have gone the way of Germany, where lack of confidence in the government led to the rise of the Nazis. The alternative was Athens, which was destroyed in the war with Sparta because it became "too big." Unsustainable debt offered a third alternative. America could behave as big as it liked because it owed money to everyone. In the process, it enlarged [its] economic machinery so it spread throughout the world.

What followed were economic crises, carefully coordinated to exert maximum damage while displaying minimal force. That's where the story stops. Now that the dying American dream is no longer believable, the U.S. government will have to be dissolved. Both because it's expensive and because it's no longer needed.[1]

THE USE OF GAME THEORY TO PRODUCE ACCEPTABLE OUTCOMES

"Game theory" (also called interactive decision theory) employs "mathematical models of conflict and cooperation between intelligent rational decision-makers" to "deduce a set of equilibrium strategies for each player such that, when these strategies are employed, no player can profit by unilaterally deviating from their strategy. These equilibrium strategies determine...a stable state in which either one outcome occurs or a set of outcomes occur with known probability."[2] Prerequisites for co-operational game theory are: 1) identifying the players, 2) identifying the information and actions available to each player at each decision point, and 3) the payoffs for each outcome. In those situations where players are assumed to be confrontational, game theory provides both a normal and extensive form.

The extensive form is used in situations where information is imperfect and the game is inherently volatile, albeit not as much as implied by the normal form. As explained:

The extensive form can be used to formalize games with a time sequencing of moves. Games here are played on trees [where] each... node [on the vertex] represents a point of choice for a player. The player is specified by a number listed by the vertex. The lines out of the vertex represent a possible action for that player. The payoffs are specified at the bottom of the tree. The extensive form can be viewed as a multi-player generalization of a decision tree. The extensive form can also capture simultaneous-move games and games with imperfect information. To represent it, either a dotted line connects different vertices to represent them as being part of the same information set

---

[1] Haskin, *Ageless* (Artema Press: Chattanooga, TN, 2013), pp. 107-108
[2] "Game Theory," Wikipedia, http://en.wikipedia.org/wiki/Game_theory

(i.e., the players do not know at which point they are), or a closed line is drawn around them.[1]

The normal form, in contrast:

> [I]s usually represented by a matrix which shows the players, strategies, and payoffs. More generally it can be represented by any function that associates a payoff for each player with every possible combination of actions. When a game is presented in normal form, it is presumed that each player acts simultaneously or, at least, without knowing the actions of the other. If players have some information about the choices of other players, the game is usually presented in extensive form.[2]

Because the normal form accommodates the most volatility, when an extensive-form game proves too limited to be useful it can be transformed to normal. However, the problem in translation is that this produces "an exponential blowup in the size of the representation, making it computationally impractical."[3]

In other words, the extensive form allows for a certain margin of freedom regarding the *unknown*, whereas the normal form is necessarily more expansive because it allows for the *unknowable*. Of course, the bias in game theory is that equilibrium—which may be viewed as the prevention or defusing of a conflict in the interest of attaining a stable state—is actually just the foundation *from which other events may proceed.* A stalemate, for example, may be viewed as a stable state. So might an impasse or, for that matter, détente. In either case, there is seeming equilibrium, and this, crucially, is where participants in a standoff will either stand or fall based on what comes after.

Historically inspired by "zero-sum" transactions, or "lose–lose" situations, game theory attempts to corral the participants within the overarching parameters of a pre-defined outcome. A key component of the system is that the parties must act in concert. There must be mutual concessions or some other concerted movement, the point being that neither party is allowed to act unilaterally. Thus, the payoff incentives must match the parties' actions in terms of mutual gain.

Implicitly, however, an equilibrium state is neither the start nor the finish, unless you believe that asymmetric relations are both mutually beneficial and can be maintained in a stable state. The point being that to maintain an enormous advantage is the expected final state. This defines the militant standoff, since the party that possesses a monopoly of force expects

---

[1] Ibid.
[2] Ibid.
[3] Ibid.

to subdue the other actor(s), dispose of the situation, and pass it down the chain for "behavioral modification."

THE INFLUENCE OF LITERATURE

Corporate Governance also defends itself through the appeal of popular literature, the most famous of which portrays the battle between communism and capitalism as one in which liberalism inevitably leads to socialism. I have argued that liberalism is a *conservative* stop-gap measure (albeit seen as the opposite for those whose lives revolve around liberalism).

To be sure, Ayn Rand protests taxes and redistribution, but she does so in much the way that conservatives and isolationists did at the end of World War II—as the cause for ever more national excess to push the state toward extremism and costly overextension, until the nation becomes so hated that it will be its own undoing.

This marks the misunderstanding of Corporate Governance by most white supremacists. Whereas the former employed liberalism as the necessary "foot in the door" for Irreversible Reformation (the ultimate ownership of all assets and organizations controlled by the nation state), the latter embraced enmity in light of seeming betrayal, never realizing that the goal of Corporate Governance is to deliver the privatization of *everything*—which in effect will replace the state with a neo-feudal technocracy.

The new "rulers" of society will be transnational conglomerates whose gross domestic product (GDP) already rivals or surpasses that of small to mid-sized countries. Thus, ownership of national assets and control of government services can only vault them to greater power. Their "reign" will be technocratic both because industry has raised the bar for employment with sophisticated technologies requiring highly specialized skill sets and because economic marginalization and social engineering will continue to be controlled by central banking and Wall Street "voters."

Whereas Corporate Governance would eliminate the government, white supremacists need it to vent their wrath upon their "enemies." Of course, the saddest thing is that they really have no enemies. Instead, they are enemies unto themselves, filled with a bitter vitriol that no Americans ever earned.

ANTI-COMMUNISM

When a government is viewed as the overt source of control in every aspect of life, it causes destruction by slow suffocation. What is allowed is what serves the state. What is prohibited is *life*.

It was in this sense that Ayn Rand wrote what is arguably her greatest work, *We the Living*, a critique of the Soviet Union and its elimination of opposition through the simple means of credentialing access to everything via service to the state.

Originally titled *Airtight*, Rand wrote in her working journal for *We the Living*:

> [Dictatorship] crush[es] [a] whole country and smother[s] every bit of life, action, and air... [It] makes the atmosphere choking, airtight.[1]

The same is also true of transnational conglomerates because employers have (or will have) access to every person's credit score, social media, health records, and (if the FBI is accessed) infinitely more as the means to credential access to jobs, without which the majority of the world can not, and will not, survive.

That Ayn Rand was blind to this (or rather did not care) can be inferred from *Atlas Shrugged*, which is the justifying philosophy for corporate emancipation from empathy, morality, community and loyalty. Because Rand understood tragedy only in terms of how it affected inventors and entrepreneurs—the movers and shakers of history—their moment in the sun is not when they give most to man, but when, led by John Galt, the greatest inventor of all time, they withdraw the means of modernity and leave for a private sanctuary to wait out the death of taxes, redistribution, and the world.

To wit:

> John Galt is Prometheus who changed his mind. After centuries of being torn by vultures in payment for having brought to men the fire of the gods, he broke his chains—and he withdrew his fire—until the day when men withdraw their vultures.[2]

Although Rand understood the destructive power of the socialist revolution, she expected too much in her own day and age: for a largely non-secular audience to make the same leap required by Communism—rejection of religion as man-hating mysticism—albeit in defense of individualism rather than a totalitarian state. She paved the road to emancipation from what bound men in community long before they could abandon society with the chaos that she advocated. In so doing, she glimpsed the truth—that only a relentless and shining example could defeat what she so hated and turn it against itself in order to make it a convert beyond anyone's will to change.

---

[1] Rand, Ayn, *We the Living* (New York: Signet, 1996,) vi.
[2] Rand, Ayn, *Atlas Shrugged*, (New York: Signet, 1996)478.

AN ANTI-BIBLE BEFORE ITS TIME

That capitalists should be exalted and obligated only to voluntary contracts is the essence of individualism, the antithesis of communism, and the basis of seeing one's life as an end in itself. In presenting this as a truism, Ayn Rand knowingly gave Western civilization what the Soviet Union extorted by force from the Intelligentsia—its unmitigated romanticism— its own metaphor, complete with an atheistic messiah and pastoral deliverance—an anti-Bible, so to speak. Her choice of a fictional venue was deliberate—more direct than a parable and certainly not veiled as allegory. The last would have been too complicated for the readership she needed (but had no respect for) if her work was to take root in a broad and meaningful way.

This decision is nontrivial.

As the Cassandra of apocalyptic socialism, Rand's goal was to warn the West against the malignant creep of dictatorship.

Not surprisingly, this results in a form of "man-worship,"[1] first expressed by Kira in *We the Living* upon meeting Andrei Taganov, a Communist GPU officer and Rand's anti-hero:[2]

> A: "You're going to say, as so many of our enemies do, that you admire our ideals, but loathe our methods."

> K: "I loathe your ideals...For one reason, mainly, chiefly and eternally, no matter how much your Party promises to accomplish, no matter what paradise it plans to bring to mankind. Whatever your other claims may be, there's one you can't avoid, one that will turn your paradise into the most unspeakable hell: your claim that man must live for the state."

> A: "What better purpose can he live for?"

> K: "Don't you know that we live only for ourselves, the best of us do, those who are worthy of it?"

> A: "Don't you know...that we can't sacrifice millions for the sake of the few?"

> K: "Can you sacrifice the few? ... Deny the best its right to the top— and you have no best left. What *are* your masses but millions of dull, shriveled, stagnant souls that have no thoughts of their own, no dreams of their own, no will of their own, who eat and sleep and chew

---

[1] Rand, Ayn, The Fountainhead, (New York: Signet, 1996) ix.
[2] Rand, Ayn, We the Living, 89-90.

helplessly the words others put into their brains? I loathe your ideals... because I know no worse injustice than the giving of the undeserved. Because men are not equal in ability...And because I loathe most of them."

A: "I'm glad. So do I... Only I don't enjoy the luxury of loathing. I'd rather try to make them worth looking at, to bring them up to my level."

It is the loathing of the masses that necessarily connects them, for on no other basis can Andrei be brought to see the light, as he does when Kira confesses that she has used him all along to save Leo, her anti-revolutionary lover, whom Andrei has just arrested. In that moment, the reader must fall in love—not with Leo, who has thus far been the hero, but with Andrei, the anti-hero, for his extraordinary kindness in the face of scorn and betrayal. Because Kira has become the only light in his dark life, Andrei must be her convert. He speaks her words to power before taking his own life as a shining act of defiance, which mirrors Kira's own end with a plain and powerful message: Execution and suicide are two sides of the same coin—the only currency in a dictatorship with which freedom can be bought.

THE FAR-RIGHT REVOLT

By now, the reader should understand that a "win" for Corporate Governance must be one of total victory. If transnational conglomerates have the means to extract everything from society—if they garner more than our intellect while instilling insecurity to make a mockery of free will—then they will never stop spreading and siphoning until violence becomes unnecessary because their victims will self-eliminate. Above all, this collective machinery will not, and *can never*, stand still because doing so would be the death of it.

Totalitarianism, in other words, is still totalitarianism, even if it's upside-down (controlled by corporations rather than the state). And the most effective means of defeating it is not a strategy of containment but one of controlled implosion.

In the former Soviet Union, this meant allowing a government that was feared, violent, and universally hated to run its course of self-destruction, aided by an arms race that made it deathly parasitic.

This, however, is also the far-right strategy for defeating the American left.

With or without revolution, it intends to overthrow the established order, and pushing the state toward extremism is the surest way to do it.

Chapter 4. Echoes of Yugoslavia

When *From Conflict to Crisis* was published in 2012, I pointed out the dangers of pushing economic reform too far too fast, based on the lessons of former Yugoslavia, which resembled our U.S. multiethnic society in too many ways to miss. Far from being a country that broke apart at its barbarous roots, Yugoslavia fought a war to escape Stalin's influence, much like the American Revolution severed colonial rule. Yugoslavia then fought a civil war to establish Tito's Partisans as the dominant ruling group. Its homegrown militia was incorporated by right into the government system as a backup to each republic's system of territorial defense, much as America's militias were recognized by the state. Everyday usage of weapons prevailed in Yugoslavia's outlying, rural areas (as it does in the United States) and was preponderant among Serbs, who, based on the census figures and proportionality system in place during Tito's rule, comprised a majority of the Army as well as the police.

COMMUNITY AND BROTHERHOOD: TOP DOWN OR BOTTOM UP?

As a popularly elected president, Tito was not a dictator, but he *was* authoritarian when it came to maintaining a nation of community and brotherhood.

Sound familiar?

America, America, God shed his grace on thee
And crown thy good with brotherhood from sea to shining sea...

First Lady Michelle Obama spoke out to children, urging them to challenge their parents over manifestations of racism. The President, meanwhile, proposed a new law to empower the U.S. Congress to regulate political speech (which should make any writer leery). Derided by the U.S. right as the imposition of "thought police," this initiative echoed one of the measures imposed by President Tito for Yugoslavia's very survival.

Citing from my fiction book *Unbreakable*,[1] the following conversation between Rosa, an American journalist, and Jovan, a Romanian mercenary, illustrates the arguments that defined the Yugoslavian war:

R: "I took time off a year ago to write a book about the war."

J: ["In Yugoslavia?"]

R: "Yes. I was in Croatia when it started."

J: "And what is your opinion?"

R: "That this war is much more complicated than most people believe. In part, I blame the U.S."

J: "In what way?"

R: "There was no more need to tolerate communism once the USSR crumbled, not even with an ally. But if we'd wanted to change Yugoslavia without harming its citizens we should have done it with something that worked. Not with such poverty and decline that people would kill for scraps or to control a piece of dirt."

J: "No one here will agree. The collapse of the USSR was living proof of failure and change was required."

R: "Of course. But the U.S. pushed too hard and asked for change too fast. If we hadn't passed resolutions to force free elections, the [federal] government might have survived."

J: "Which makes you responsible?"

R: "Partly. I'm well aware that demilitarization and nationalist politicians created a situation where rights disappeared and fears were prostituted to inspire separatism."

J: "Prostituted?"

R: "Yes. Old horrors and hatreds made good press for warmongers who needed moral and social decay."

J: "Perhaps. But people wanted to buy what they sold."

---

[1] Haskin, Jeanne M., *Unbreakable* (Chattanooga, TN: Artema Press, 2013), pp. 26-27

R: "Which just proves my point. No form of hate-speak was allowed under President Tito. He knew it was destructive, so anyone who spewed it would have been imprisoned."

J: "Then peace was artificial and your argument is false."

Embedded in this conversation are many sides of truth:

That economic collapse produces a war for spoils, aided and abetted by massive political breakdown (both of which were engineered from outside Yugoslavia by international lenders and the U.S. political right) as opposed to ethno-nationalism (which arose from within Yugoslavia) once society was atomized and alienated politically.

Because all economic collapses:

[initiate] a ritual of purification against encroachment by other cultures...The greater the economic contraction, the "purer" must be the nation.[1]

Here, I disagree with Leonard Zeskind, who wrote in *Blood and Politics* that militant white nationalism does not rise or fall according to business cycles or changes in society, but rather remains consistent as a deeply personal world view.[2] That such views may remain consistent throughout one's own lifetime does not mean it has mass appeal in the absence of a sense that society is doomed, whether it is caused by a protracted economic recession and fear of no recovery (ongoing at this moment)—where fear is the one quality that can consistently be manipulated—or fear that one's government is not just godless but "demonic" with plans for martial law and genocide.

In short, mass ethno-nationalism is in-group protectionism against perceived threats in the present and exacerbated fear of the future, both of which are conducive to out-group sacrifice and perceptions of victimhood.

For Randall and Vicki Weaver (who were targeted by the government in the standoff at Ruby Ridge):

It has been pretty well established that [they] were loosely affiliated with or sympathetic to the Christian Identity movement, which holds, among other off-center beliefs, that the true descendants of the tribes of Israel are the modern nationalities of Europe, that today's Jews are impostors, and that Yahweh has fierce punishment planned for sinful America and its Babylonian Occupational Government. Christian

---

[1] Haskin, *From Conflict to Crisis*, p. 3.
[2] Zeskind, Leonard, *Blood and Politics* (New York: Farrar, Straus and Giroux, 2009) Kindle Edition.

Identity believers claim to live by Old Testament laws, to be the true heirs of Israel.[1]

Apparently this view has more popularity than the writer I quoted realizes. For example, in an interview on Fox News, Ann Coulter asserted: "Well, Christians believe that they are perfected Jews."

"RESPECTABLE" ETHNIC CLEANSING

In a Yale class on international diplomacy, the ethnic cleansing in Yugoslavia was being taught, even then, as a means to avoid war by "group relocation."

This projected ethnic cleansing as a "reasonable" goal of diplomacy, but it also sanitized U.S. history for anyone familiar with The Trail of Tears, one of the most horrendous and heartbreaking trials imposed on Native Americans by white Christian America as the seeming inevitable end to the long war of attrition waged to persecute their "otherness" and banish them from society.

To rub salt in the wound, Native Americans were forced into exile with food that could literally kill them (and obviously was meant to, since the Army never lifted a finger to provide fresh provisions as they passed through cornfield after cornfield during their arduous journey):

> The rations...issued...consisted of damaged pork, damaged flour, and damaged corn, with salt...not regularly issued. The provision was so bad that, on distributing it to the party, many would not receive it. The corn appeared to have been shelled in the green state, and had been mildewed. A part of the corn was weevil-eaten. Some of the corn was so much injured that horses would not eat it. The flour was sour, but occasionally a barrel of it could be used...The pork was so bad that Dr. Walker told me that if the emigrants continued to use it, it would kill them all off. It gave those who ate it diarrhea...many of our poor people died in consequence of it.[2]

Returning to the comparison with Yugoslavia, American war strategists were both prepared and eager during the war to create a protective corridor through which Bosnia's Muslims could escape as refugees. The reason this did not take place was that few of Yugoslavia's neighbors wanted them. Even when condemnation of Serbian concentration camps provoked the Serbs to offer the Muslims freedom if other countries would take them, many thousands of prisoners died in mass executions because the world would not open its doors to them.

So much then for "respectable" ethnic cleansing...

---

[1] Bock, Alan W., "Ambush at Ruby Ridge," Reason.com, October, 1993, http://reason.com/archives/1993/10/01/ambush-at-ruby-ridge/3

[2] Jahoda, Gloria, *The Trail of Tears* (New York: Random House, 1975), p. 171.

THE ROLE OF THE PARAMILITARIES

Because the Yugoslavian federal government collapsed mainly from without, it is worth noting that the country's privileged position in international relations as a bulwark against expansion by the former Soviet Union became null and void with the collapse of the USSR. For a nation that fought a war to be free of Soviet influence, Yugoslavian identity was defined by the common goal of opposing the USSR. However, Yugoslavia as a *concept* also had to be fought for, via a civil war.

In the wake of the Soviet meltdown, Yugoslavia found itself stuck with plants and equipment that were decrepit and outdated, offering little promise for economic gain. What Yugoslavia *did* have in abundance were arms depots and territorial defense systems, as well as a massive Army comprised mainly of Serbs. In the ensuing ethno-national war, the fiercest battles took place over arms control. Even the belated (and mutually distrustful) alliance between Bosnia's Muslims and Croatia required the Muslims to disarm.

Throughout, the Muslims were robbed of their assets, herded across minefields, deported in box trucks and buses, subjected to tortuous internment, and slain with egregious violence.

In the process, the many paramilitary organizations that arose on the Serbian side reenacted the role of shock troops and committed the worst of the slaughter, leaving the Army to mop up after.

As the author of *The Turner Diaries*, William Pierce, who wrote under the pseudonym Andrew Macdonald, projected that American paramilitary groups would fulfill this same function.

According to this excerpt:

> [Earl Turner], a thirty-year-old electrical engineer turned guerrilla fighter...and a few thousand members of an Organization survive a dragnet aimed at violators of a draconian Cohen Act gun control law. They launch an uncoordinated guerrilla war aimed at destabilizing the System. Turner's four-person "unit" murders and robs unsuspecting Jews and blacks, blows up the FBI headquarters building, and kills a Washington Post editorial writer...They live in clandestine safe houses, manufacture new weapons, and survive by their wits... Eventually, guerrilla skirmishes grow into a full-scale war between small enclaves of white people and the disintegrating remains of the multiracial United States government. When the Organization finally gains control of Southern California, it drives the black and Latino population into the desert, kills off all Jews, and terrorizes the remaining white population into submission through the public hanging of white "race traitors." A nuclear war destroys Israel and China, neutralizes the Soviet Union, and leaves radioactive deserts smoldering in patches across the globe. The Organization imposes a

dictatorship on the white enclaves it controls, enabling it gradually to gain a military advantage over the remaining multiracial forces. The racists' victory in North America ultimately leads to victory in Europe and finally to complete eradication of all the nonwhite populations on the planet.[1]

This meshes extremely well with a report on the Alabama KKK, which found that:

> Leaders of the Klan claim their membership rolls include politicians, teachers, hospital staff and others, saying, "Most of the majority of our people are in the military. We all have our concealed weapons permits."

Going on, one of the men interviewed said:

> "There's going to be a great war—I won't call it a Civil War—it'll be anything but that. It'll be an uncivil war. You'll see a bunch of Americans getting killed and blown up."

He goes on to say:

> "It'll be a matter of time, we gonna take America back."[2]

While the documentary presents a chilling look underneath the hoods of the KKK, what's more chilling is the fact that there is very little difference between the official KKK agenda and that of the GOP/Tea Party. Right wing political leaders have softened the message, to make it more palatable to voters.

The KKK agenda includes:
1. "The recognition that America was founded as a Christian nation."
2. "The recognition that America was founded as a white nation."
3. "Abolish all affirmative action programs."
4. "Put American Troops on the Borders and Stop the Flood of Illegals."
5. "Abolish all anti-gun laws and encourage every adult to own a weapon."
6. "Drug testing all welfare recipients."
7. "Privatization of the public school system."
8. "Restoring individual freedom to Christian America."
9. "Sovereignty of the states."
10. Outlaw abortion.
11. Outlaw homosexuality.

---

[1] Zeskind, Leonard.
[2] Morris, Randa, "Alabama KKK Rolls Include Politicians, Teachers, Medical Professionals, Military," September 28, 2015, http://www.addictinginfo. org/2015/09/28/alabama-kkk-rolls-include-politicians-teachers-medical-professionals-military-video/

And this is not a complete list.

But it agrees with Dominion theology, the primary objective of which is to claim a Christian nation subject to Biblical teaching.

It also agrees with the agenda of Augustus Invictis, a so-called libertarian who is making a bid for the Senate. According to Adrian Wyllie, ex-chairman of the party:[1]

> Mr. Invictus has repeatedly vowed that it is his destiny to start a second civil war in America. In a 2013 memo to his colleagues, he wrote, "I have prophesied for years that I was born for a Great War; that if I did not witness the coming of the Second American Civil War, I would begin it myself."

He has described himself as an American fascist, and even his campaign logo is nearly identical to that of Benito Mussolini. He has displayed swastikas in his published campaign materials. He has expressed support for a eugenics program, which would sterilize, euthanize or forcibly abort "the weakest, the least intelligent, and the most diseased."

> Many of his supporters are known members of Neo-Nazi and white supremacist groups, such as American Front, Vinelanders, and Stormfront, and he has been recruiting them into the Libertarian Party.

> In a private, face-to-face meeting with Mr. Invictus, I asked him directly, "Do you actually intend to kill millions of people and start a civil war?" His answer to me was, "It's my religion."

THE U.S. COMPARISON

If we now look critically at America, condemned buildings and the boarded-up wrecks of entire towns and cities stand silent testimony to the scars, scabs, and wounds of de-industrialization. Today's economy is based overwhelmingly on services, and the only real owners of property, plant and equipment are transnationals in biotechnology, pharmaceuticals, and agriculture. Looming over all is our national defense industry, which means you can bet your life that none of America's assets will ever be up for grabs. Unlike what destroyed Yugoslavia, there will be no war for "spoils." Instead, there can only be in-group, out-group wars over territorial boundaries encompassing natural resources and who will have homes and jobs.

---

[1] Downes, Nathaniel, "Crazy Fascist With Deluded Manifestos Runs For Florida Senate," October 5, 2015, http://reverbpress.com/politics/augustus-sol-invictus-florida-senate-fascist/

TAKING BACK "REAL" AMERICA

In the Yugoslavian comparison, I also focused on militant white separatism within the United States, noting that the Christian Exodus movement has coalesced into intra-state separatism as well as state separatism and plans for mass relocation with the goal of territorial takeover.

When groups refute authority on the slippery slope to separatism, there is a literal vote of no confidence through a refusal to pay taxes, the establishment of "common law" courts, abuse of the judicial system, and notices served on federal agencies, oftentimes with violence. The tendency to accumulate weapons (that become truly military), and attempt to claim jurisdiction over the towns, cities and states these groups already occupy signals a need to control the environment against the encroachment of the government and its "pollution" of society with anything deemed "liberal," thereby redressing such long-time grievances as state and federal taxes, unsustainable national debt, racial integration, equal employment opportunity, political correctness, income redistribution, and the new marriage equality.

The sense that "big government" has forced these things on Americans was also voiced in Yugoslavia, i.e., that Tito repressed the people to hold the country together, denying their desire for change.

Yet, for months after Tito's death, efforts were made to maintain that he was still alive, from fear that the bonds he policed would too rapidly come unglued.

It is this that motivates moderate and left-leaning Republicans to work with moderate and right-leaning Democrats on establishing Corporate Governance for transnational conglomerates. But Republicans do so in their own way, having created the Tea Party to co-opt white militant movements and channel the electorate's anger into beating down liberal Democrats. Now militant white movements are carefully couched in the language of "liberty" and "freedom" threatened by "religious intolerance."

In a political campaign, it may manifest much like this:

> [Jihanna] glared at the stage being wheeled onto the field, an eight-by-ten platform with a bunting of red, white, and blue. Matching cloth covered its backboard. Speakers flanking the stage connected to a standing microphone, where a middle-aged, sandy-haired man with plain, forgettable features appeared eager and earnest. Dressed in a thin jacket and blue jeans, he chose to ride the platform instead of ascending the steps, like the winner of a pageant, a president-elect, rather than a dark-horse candidate secretly backed by OWL.
>
> Though Americans knew little about his private past, even the newspapers in Moscow were acquainted with Stuart Ross. He'd served a brief stint as a congressman by stepping into the shoes

of his [intimidated] predecessor—a Republican who hadn't been "real" enough to lead Real America. Private militias and right-wing extremists had flocked to Ross, not because he walked their walk but because he spoke their language.

A reporter who'd counted the number of times Ross referred to "watering the tree of liberty" (a call for revolutionary violence), sealing the borders, ousting immigrants, and "Real America without apology" had been "disappeared" immediately.

Now Ross sang into the microphone, his image projected via the scoreboard, in case anyone missed the hand over his heart or the honest tears in his eyes. As "America the Beautiful" rolled forth in his vibrant tenor, the audience joined in, deeply touched and happy to, although Ross was only a figurehead conditioned to pull their strings, push their buttons, and make them weak.

When Ross detached the microphone, [he] walked with it to the backboard. With a flourish, he tore down the curtain to expose a black and red banner that read:

DEMOCRACY IS THE MEANS BY WHICH THOSE WHO ADORE AUTHORITY AND CRAVE THE SECURITY OF SERVITUDE CAN USE THEIR SUPERIOR NUMBERS TO ENSLAVE THOSE WHO WISH TO BE FREE.[1]

This wasn't political posturing.

"We will have safety," Ross exhorted, stalking the stage with the microphone, "security, and morality. America is not, and was never born to be, a godless abomination but this is what they've made of it." He paused, reflectively, to let the crowd decide what was meant by "they," an all-encompassing term that could have meant the ACLU, corrupt servants of government, or everyone and anyone, whatever the flavor of prejudice. Ross pointed to the front-row seats, acknowledging his supporters. "Let the Commandments be our guide as we enrich the lives of our elderly! Let us come together to heal them and improve the lives of all with unprecedented support for the giants of modern medicine. Let us cast out foreign elements to take back Real America!"[2]

This approach is so predictable that I could recite its screed in my sleep.

Meanwhile, transnational conglomerates have atomized society by refusing to employ the long-term unemployed, those with poor credit histories, and, far more importantly, post-combat veterans with specialized skills for which they seemingly have no use.

Yet.

---

[1] This is a recurrent post on Facebook.
[2] Haskin, Ageless, (Chattanooga, TN: Artema Press) pp. 8-10.

CHAPTER 5. THE PRISONER'S DILEMMA OF WHITE SUPREMACY

> From the first moment of quickening when Thought raised its voice to Energy, it saw that Energy was vast, limitless, and asked, "Where then am I?" To which Energy replied, "In the place where we [converge]."
>
> Wanting more of this Energy to expand the realm of Thought was, and is, the relentless force behind conquest of the host. Thus the battle raged, from Time immemorial, for what is Time but Energy, given that thought—and therefore man—might live.[1]

For each of us, human thought has value. Explicitly, it defines the human state.

From it, we derive ideas that determine the course of our lives. Whether it concerns far-right imperatives or those of white supremacists, both of them at the time of this writing are determined to annihilate alternatives to their prejudicial mindsets as they project these onto the world.

As minorities, both groups are asymmetrically disadvantaged in democratic societies. Creating, maintaining, and advancing their collective interests necessarily excludes the interests of other groups.

To shape the world in their image, they must choose between:

- expansion from a minority to a majority
- accumulating disproportionate power as a minority;
- abolishing democracy in favor of a minority-ruled society; or
- decreasing the majority to become a non-minority

Notably, these are the "corners" of the prisoner's dilemma, wherein there are four possible outcomes during interrogation: that X and Y will both tell the truth;

---

[1] Haskin, Ageless, p. 122.

that X will lie and Y will tell the truth; that Y will lie and X will tell the truth; or that both X and Y will lie. Since neither white supremacists nor far-right activists wish to admit to b), c), and d) as being either a matter of practice or goals that they hope to achieve, both groups are faced with a conundrum. To exist peaceably (or non-peaceably) within a democratic society, a) is the only "lie" available to each.

In other words, absorbing the majority into their ranks and thereby polluting their cause is the wish of neither the far-right nor those who believe in white supremacy.

The fact that these groups are converging means we must examine their "truths," as well as the fiction that hides them, to expose the tremendous destructive potential they pose with respect to our world.

THE CONVERGENCE OF RIGHT AND MIGHT

As I developed an alternative to contemporary game theory, I viewed the realization of far-right goals and the growth of militant white movements as historically related threads,[1] each pressing against the boundaries imposed by democratic society—the former from above and the latter from below— sometimes touching at points of interest until white supremacy became a cohesive force capable of forming a wedge. Driven upward by core believers, this wedge connected with the world of the privileged, at which point their threads converged.

In the process, at least part of society was dragged along in its wake due, in the main, to the standoff at Ruby Ridge and the siege of the Branch Davidians, from which martyrs emerged to elicit the public empathy that had thus far eluded white supremacists.

EMPATHY AS POWER

Restating the options of the far-right and white supremacists, the limitations of a democratic society require that they choose one or more of these options to shape the world as they wish:

- expanding from a minority to a majority (inclusive–expansive)

---

[1] As argued by Leonard Zeskind: [G]rowing parts of the [white nationalist] movement want to carve out a new territory free entirely of black people, Jews, and a host of others they regard as undesirable....A secondary thread...reaches over to...the Christian right...[It] is necessary...to trace those points at which the two converge...[since] white nationalists share many of the obsessions that motivate religious and cultural traditionalists. They both believe that feminists, gay men, and lesbians are destroying the (white) nuclear family. And they share the notion (with many outside their immediate ranks) that middle-class white people—men in particular—are actually victims in contemporary society, without adequate political representation.

- accumulating disproportionate power as a minority (militant–exclusive);
- abolishing democracy in favor of a minority-ruled society (totalitarian–exclusive); or
- decreasing the majority to become a non-minority (terrorist–exclusive)

If we argue that incitement of public empathy for militant white movements in the wake of Ruby Ridge and the Branch Davidian siege satisfied the criteria for (b) in the immediate present, then we are left to debate whether (c) and (d) are their final objectives,[1] noting in the process that militant white supremacists have agonized over their own race in changing their public face.

Having grown from a foundation of whites-only militant groups spouting theories of racism and virulent anti-Semitism to a politically savvy, cohesive, and more self-aware collective, their whites-only leaders now target "liberal elites" (or those who lead the ignorant "sheeple") and therefore levy blame on moderate Republicans as well as Democrats. "Real" whites-only Americans must fight the "corrupt liberal elite establishment" by any means necessary, even if it requires temporary alliances with the movement's contemptible enemies (to be disposed of afterward).[2]

Thus, readers of this book should not mistake its arguments for agreement of any sort with whites-only pragmatists. Contrarily, this book was written to say that a marriage of convenience between groups who share nothing other than hatred of anything liberal will have very different meanings assigned to such a relationship, whether or not it culminates in divorce—if such will even be possible[3]—once control of the state protecting the privileged is wrenched out of their hands.

It is in this spirit that I conducted my work on the standoff: as the means to deter such a union and steer us back to the political center from which we can tell our leaders, "Wrong way, go back."

In Evelyn Schlatter's words:

> All Americans are faced with shifting cultural and social situations, economic anxieties, and increased globalization. We need

---

[1] According to Leonard Zeskind, two political trends, mainstreaming and vanguardism, compete for supremacy within the white nationalist movement. "[M]ainstreamers believe that a majority (or near majority) of white people can be won over to support their cause, and they try to influence the existing structures of American life. Vanguardists think that they will never find more than a slim minority of white people to support their aims voluntarily, and they build smaller organizations of highly dedicated cadres with the intention of forcefully dragging the rest of society behind them."

[2] Zeskind, Leonard.

[3] If there is a divorce, it can only be a violent one, bringing to mind the specter of Trotskyism.

to remember that we are all part of this American community and that solutions to our problems, whether real or perceived, do not lie in conspiracy theories, scapegoating, or rage...I can understand why some of us turn to these approaches for answers. However, all of us have a greater responsibility to one another as fellow Americans and, ultimately, global citizens, to address real inequalities in our social and cultural institutions and hierarchies and find workable, community based solutions. It will require that we look at ourselves, at our core beliefs, and put our history under a microscope. It will also require us to look at the beliefs and stereotypes many mainstream Americans hold and how they can be used in an extremist context. It will be an uncomfortable and, most likely, painful process in some respects. But to ignore the extreme right—to ignore the parts of this country's history that have encouraged this ideology—is to allow it to grow and spread unchecked. The consequences of that, I'm afraid, do not bode well for a united America.[1]

NEW FACE BUT SAME OLD RACE

Regardless of whom they target, the resilient characteristics of militant white movements are racist and anti-Semitic theologies in which the U.S. government is either portrayed as the Beast of biblical infamy or the Babylonian Occupational Government—one which is run by Jews (who are not really Jews and therefore God's chosen people but instead pretenders who oppose the "true tribes of Israel"). For militant white separatists, the latter are "really" represented by white Christian America, white Western Europe, white South Africa, and white Australia. As such, Armageddon (which has been said to be imminent many times throughout the last millennium) has arrived once again to trouble the Christian universe, demanding a fight to the death.

Quoting again from Evelyn Schlatter:

> Since the late 1970s, this country has witnessed a plethora of home-grown so-called white supremacist groups whose members seek to restore the power of white men, segregate races into specific geographic regions of this country, and bring about the downfall of the federal government, which, they believe, is controlled by a secret, powerful cabal of Jewish families and white race traitors. According to these groups, the ultimate goal of "ZOG" (Zionist Occupied Government) is to bring the United States to its knees economically, integrate it with a "New World Order," and place its opponents in concentration camps. The white race, proponents believe, is the last

---

[1] Schlatter, Evelyn A., *Aryan Cowboys: White Supremacists and the Search for a New Frontier 1970–2000* (Austin, TX: University of Texas Press, 2006), p. xi.

line of defense against this conspiracy, and they contend that the day of reckoning—the "showdown"—in which ZOG begins its final campaign against them, is upon us. To prepare for this penultimate battle, members of white supremacist groups run secret paramilitary camps, build secluded compounds, conduct survival skills seminars, stockpile food, collect impressive arsenals that include some of the latest military hardware, and spread the word via publications, gun shows, fax machines, phone lines, shortwave radio, and the Internet.[1]

Although biblical histrionics are disdained by the elite, the far-right has an audience to play to. Thus ticking off option (d) "decreasing the majority to become a non-minority," as the last remaining objective of militant white supremacists, does not place them at odds with the privileged and the elite—who achieved (b) and (c) long before militant white movements acquired public empathy—because (d) is the far-right's last imperative—their own End Game of wreaking and inciting terrorism.

TERROR-INCITING CAPITALISM

Predatory capitalism (or that which relied on coercion, persuasion, bargaining, and formal indoctrination to achieve market penetration and leverage foreign direct investment while wreaking devastation on the majority of the populace) was, believe it or not, the "soft sell" for terror-inciting capitalism. Where the former was the preferred method for dealing with the "white" world, it was only a half measure on the road to massive destabilization of the remaining "non-white" world. Therefore, it is not difficult to explain why countries all over the globe, from Sudan to Syria to Pakistan to Thailand, are being destroyed from within by non-secular, non-white militants. Framing this in the language of "culture war" or the "clash of civilizations" merely masks the visceral treatment extended through Corporate Governance to the predominantly non-white world.[2]

A year ago, Americans recoiled in horror from the massive slaughter of Iraqi innocents at the hands of radical Islamists, never realizing that we gave them the keys to the killing fields. By demolishing national armies and replacing them with constabularies incapable of defending civilians, we denied the Iraqi government a monopoly of force and created a power vacuum.

Too, it is now known that ISIS, the terror group in Syria, was a creation of the Pentagon badly gone awry.

---

[1] Ibid., pp. 6-7.
[2] As Holly Sklar has pointed out, there is not just an underdeveloped Third World but also a suffering Fourth World, for which far-right plans are not inconsistent with the argument just made.

Why?

For decades Islamic bankers have bent over backwards to subvert Islamic teachings expressly prohibiting *riba* (interest, compound interest, and anything else perceived as usury). Islamic theologians even cooperated to help articulate the conceptual contortions circumventing Islamic law. But now the teaching of Prophet Mohammed—that the wealthy must aid the poor in the spirit of true charity, duty, and self-sacrifice—is a resurgent and pressing concern consuming the Islamic world.

To stamp it out once and for all (since economic control requires the infiltration of Western banking institutions wherein egalitarian ideals must be fought at any cost), terror-inciting capitalism must use the enemy's own sword.

Through internecine wars pitting all against all, Islamic nations will fall...

Their wealth will be freed for distribution to the West. Oh yes...and then there's oil.

CODE WORD: LIMITED GOVERNMENT

Whereas militant white movements revere the founding of America and remain tightly bound to the U.S. Constitution (or, more truthfully, to parts of it),[1] Irreversible Reformation projects a far more limited nation— one that avoids "foreign adventures" in the words of President Obama, even though the CIA "adventured" all over Syria, and the encirclement of Russia manifested in joint military exercises throughout the former eastern bloc. Together, neo-isolationism and theatrical saber rattling cater to the mindsets of both militant white movements and far-right conservatives, persuading them in the process that plans to limit the reach of the state will accommodate their need to remain inward-looking until government minimization becomes a *fait accompli*. But instead of leaving the far-right to flounder in a new era of corporate technocracy organized along the lines of neo-feudalism, more likely than not corporate leaders (who have no further need for political wranglers) will reserve nominal positions at unjustifiable salaries for those who board their neo-feudal train instead of making a last gasp effort to derail it at the outskirts of Washington.

In the words of Gilbert Mercier, the new feudalism will resemble the old feudalism in that:

> The feudal system of the Dark Ages was the social and economic exploitation of peasants by lords. This led to an economy always marked by poverty, sometimes famine, extreme exploitation and wide

---

[1] According to militant white supremacists, the Thirteenth, Fourteenth, and Fifteenth Amendments are contracts with illegitimately privileged groups (as opposed to sovereign rights), all imposed by Congress and martial law.

gaps between rich and poor. The feudal era relation of a serf to his lord is essentially identical to the relation of a so-called Wal-Mart associate to an heir of the Walton family...A powerful network of oligarchs worldwide seems to be pursuing the objective to set back the social clock to before the era of Enlightenment so as to return us to the Dark Ages of lords and serfs: a new era of global slavery to benefit Wall Street's "masters of the universe." Compared to the Middle Ages, today's servitude is more insidious: the International Monetary Fund (IMF), World Bank, and many private banks operate like mega drug dealers. The IMF and World Bank do so with countries, while the banks do so with individuals. Once Greece, Detroit or John Doe is addicted to its fix—loans in this case—the trick is done. After a while, money must be borrowed even to service the debt.[1]

As for militant white supremacists, they will make natural shock troops (or neo-knights, if you prefer).

In return, they will have what they wished for.

Their so-called Holy War.

PROVOCATION AND DISINFORMATION

To demonstrate that such a threatening convergence between Corporate Governance and militant white supremacists could never have been predicted (or even understood) without the public empathy that arose from Ruby Ridge and the branch Davidian siege, I must argue Ruby Ridge, first as the defense team and then as the prosecution—albeit in a way that the prosecution never envisioned. I will therefore use sympathetic sources to initially frame the case before revisiting the issues to show how the power of empathy produced a sea change in public relations via a suspect history that underscores its allure as well as its continuing danger.

---

[1] Mercier, Gilbert, "Back to the Dark Ages of Feudalism," http://www.counterpunch.org/2014/06/02/back-to-the-dark-ages-of-feudalism/

CHAPTER 6. THE BIONOMIC LOGIC OF U.S. MILITANT STANDOFFS

Based on bionomic logic (a theory for predicting actions and reactions in the context of their environments), the diagrams in Appendix A and the crossover between them are provided there for readers to explore their relative value and:

1. decide for themselves how they impact perceptions of militant white movements;

2. provide recommendations for responses to militant standoffs; and

3. suggest proactive measures to identify those actors most likely to commit retributive violence.

If we start, therefore, by defining the environment as one in which sociology and political-behavioral economics are equally important and psychologically influential, then the reverse is also true: that the psychology of militant separatist groups leads them to create alternative societies (and, in fact, entire polities) in opposition to their treatment as "economic units" in the Community of Consumerism, which, when contrasted with "life, liberty, and the pursuit of happiness," is a meaningless, faithless void.

THE PSYCHO-SOCIAL DEVELOPMENT OF MILITANT SEPA-RATIST GROUPS

Whether applied to individuals, groups, societies, or nations, it should be noted from the outset that attitudinal characteristics (used in psychological profiling), such as hostile, aggressive, passive-aggressive, and pacifistic, evolve throughout the "life cycle," primarily and sometimes lastingly in response to threatened belief systems.

Drawing on child psychologist Erik Erikson's stages of maturation, the typical "life cycle" (which can easily be applied to groups, societies, and nations throughout their historical evolution) ranges from when children and adolescents are most malleable and trusting, to the turbulence of teenage years (when experimentation and/or rebellion are part of conscious self-definition), to varying degrees of retrenchment during early adulthood (wherein life "outside the nest" and exposure to responsibility requires learning and rationalization, assessments and decisions, and, once again, the self is malleable concerning external relations). By then, we typically make life choices, such as what to study in college, whether to join the military, to participate in an internship, or seek out gainful employment. In the process, we may choose partners: friends, lovers, spouses, but also institutions, such as fraternities, sororities, private clubs, civic associations, political parties, activist groups, and organized religions. Then advanced maturation induces self-referential judgment, and the tendency to challenge authority (recalled from our teenage years) emerges somewhat differently as another turbulent period but one of cognitive dissonance—a struggle within oneself to rationalize heuristics (perceptual "rules of thumb" that, by now, are ingrained in the psyche as shortcuts for making decisions) when faced with opposition (or a world that doesn't comport with one's pre-established beliefs).

TYPOLOGIES AND STEREOTYPES

As Wagner-Pacifici has noted, law enforcement agents tend to frame responses to conflict (and to view conflict itself) through typologies and stereotypes. The Branch Davidians, for example, were viewed as a cult under the sway of David Koresh, a charismatic leader. Their "programming," so to speak, or intellectual "conditioning," was not an offense against nature but (since we are raised to compete as children in support of a capitalist system) an offense against the state, which monopolizes our world views as well as the means to police them.

Does the state not provide a two-party system for political inclusion? Does it not encourage civic participation in matters of local importance? Does it not provide venues for those with international concerns?

In short, the government's *normative* view of what does and does not contribute to the maintenance, growth, and stability of Corporate Governance dovetails (and is meant to) with the obsession to pigeon-hole people who are either for or against transnational conglomerates via actionable stereotypes.

In this way, cult members become hostages to be rescued and, more importantly, deprogrammed, not because they *are always* dangerous—

depending on whether they are offensive or defensive—but because they deviate from the paths provided for society and therefore challenge monopoly world views. Most threateningly, they are *ordinary* people for whom "deviant" behavior is not so very irrational, repellant though it may be.

Quoting from Leonard Zeskind, who describes the overarching movement of militant white nationalism (in a way that also applies to militant white separatism, wherein apocalyptic "cults" are a broad-based phenomenon rather than a sub-development):

> [T]his is not a story of paranoids or uneducated backwoodsmen with tobacco juice dripping down their chins, the "extremists" of popular imagination. As a movement white nationalists look like a demographic slice of white America: mostly blue collar and working middle class with a small number of wealthy individuals. Doctors, lawyers, and Ph.D.s are among the leaders.[1]

Quoting also from Evelyn Schlatter:

> I want to make very clear that the personal reasons people have for joining white supremacist groups are myriad. Those who have participated and who are still participating in groups or the movement as a whole come from a variety of backgrounds and households. Most, however, join because they feel somehow "displaced" or "disenfranchised" from society at large. It's a subjective perspective and depends on the person involved. What is apparent, however, is that the movement is largely male.[2]

In other words, the labels, traits, and powerful characteristics that analysts ascribe to those who withdraw from society to build competitive polities are a reflection of the fear and revulsion that people rebelling against the government invoke as *individuals*—in the true sense of the word—with the power to oppose monopoly world views and in no way support them.

American exceptionalism is founded on the concept of rugged individualism. Yet, those who resist being hammered into the mold of well-behaved consumers become miscreants and criminals, not always contrary to evidence but sometimes out of proportion to the threat they actually pose.

Thus, "anyone who is a minority of one," either alone or in aggregation, "must be convinced that he is insane" because a minority of one can never be right if millions can never be wrong.[3]

This naturally begs the question: "What do the millions now believe?" If the "pursuit of happiness" is tangibly, demonstrably, and systemically

---

[1] Zeskind, Leonard.
[2] Schlatter, Evelyn A., p.2.
[3] Fromm, Erich, quoted loosely from George Orwell's *1984* (Signet: New York, NY, 1981), p. 264.

impossible, then that is the real threat pushing ever more of America away from Corporate Governance toward the movement of white supremacy.

THE DENIAL OF HAPPINESS

In tandem with life's phases, Maslow's hierarchy of needs defines the physical, emotional, and intellectual criteria for healthy human beings, which, in order of priority or fundamental necessity, begin with food, safety, and shelter, followed by acceptance and a broader sense of belonging, with both selflessness and self-actualization as the overarching goals and sources of true contentment. Once met, each of these achievements may remain fairly consistent or they may be subject to constant turnover, but happiness is denied us when abstract calculations in behavioral economics reduce every citizen to a functional working unit as opposed to a feeling person.

For example, a criticism leveled at far-right Republicans is that they champion innocent life until that life is born but thereafter lose focus on helping to raise that life. Instead, parents must bring up their children at the mercy of the market, where cutthroat competition makes them "efficient units."

Never treated again as a person, the economic "unit" becomes caught in the vicious circle of "the lock and key dilemma."

Why?

Instead of applying the age-old method of "carrot and stick" manipulation (Pavlovian conditioning), the carrot makes its appearance only *once* in a meaningful way as the key that turns the lock to make people desperate achievers. For example, an individual may be raised in a fully supportive household and then sent on to college with positive expectations. In this case, the "carrot," or promise of a bright future, is the availability of student loans. After accepting the carrot, the student becomes indebted and learns, upon graduation, the meaning of debt peonage—that every thought and action must be pressed into service as the means to pay it off. He or she is now an "economic unit" on the merry-go-round of debt that never stops taking or turning.

The Community of Consumerism can function no other way. It lives, breathes, and feeds via abstract calculations that constantly narrow the range of benefits required for pacification of each "economic unit."

Once reduced to a non-person, the victim is forced to wage an internal war from every possible angle, only to ask again and again when denied opportunity at every turn, "What was my original sin?"

If the crisis is one of faith or a crushing fear of the future (which affects parents even more than their children), this has incredible resonance for those who are predisposed to religion. It may also be equally resonant for post-combat veterans who relied heavily on trust and structure to perform heinous jobs under life-altering conditions. Upon discharge into a ruthless economy overseen by a "corrupt" or "immoral" government, they may feel that society has spurned or betrayed them.

That said, it is worth quoting a Facebook post[1] from Marine Corps veteran Brandon Raub which inspired intervention from the FBI, Secret Service, and local police, leading to Raub's arrest, a ten-day imprisonment, and a mental health evaluation:

The Truth

by Brandon J Raub on Friday, November 11, 2011 at 10:00 am

America has lost itself. We have lost who we truly are. This is the land of the free and the home of the brave.

This is the land of Thomas Jefferson.

This is the land of Benjamin Franklin.

This is the land of Fredrick Douglas.

This is the land of Smedley Butler.

This is the land John F. Kennedy.

This is the land of Martin Luther King.

This is the land where the cowboy wins. This is the land where you can start from the bottom and get to the top. This is the land where regardless of you race and ethnicity you can succeed and build a better life for you and your family. This is the land where every race coexists peacefully. This is the land where justice wins. This is the land where liberty dwells. This is the land where freedom reigns. This is the land where we help the poor, and people help each other. This is land where people beat racism.

The Federal Reserve is wrong. They have designed a system based off of greed and fear. They designed a system to crush the middle class between taxes and inflation. This is wrong, and it is unjust. It is wrong.

We have allowed ourselves to be deceived and seduced by the powers of the printing press. It is not a good system. It discourages saving: the foundation for all stable economic activity. The Federal Reserve is ar-

---

[1] Raub, Brandon, http://americanoverlook.com/highly-respected-marine-thrown-in-jail-after-making-this-post-on-facebook-about-obama-3/59231

tificially manipulating interest rates and creating phony economic data.

This thing has deceived our entire nation.

They created it in 1913. They also created the income tax in 1913. They encouraged the growth of debt so they can tax you on it. There is interest on the debt. Your government is in bed with these people. They want to enslave you to the government so that they can control every aspect of your lives. It is an empire based on lies. They operate on greed and fear.

There is a better way. It's called freedom. Freedom is called a lot of things. But there is a true meaning. It means very simply that you have the right to do whatever you want as long as you are not infringing on the freedoms of other people.

I firmly believe that God set America apart from the other nations of the world. He saved a place where people could come to escape bad systems of government. This system we have created works. It really works.

There is evil going on all around the world. The United States was meant to lead the charge against injustice, but through our example not our force. People do not respond to having liberty and freedom forced on them.

Men and Women follow courage. They follow leadership, and courage. Our example has paved the way for people all around the world to change their forms of government.

Force is not the way because liberty is a powerful concept. The idea that men can govern themselves is the basis for every just form of government.

We can govern ourselves. We do not need to be governed by men who want to install a one world banking system. These men have machine hearts. Machine and unnatural hearts.

They have blocked out the possibility of a better world. They fear human progress. They have monopolies on everything.

This life can be free and beautiful. There are enough resources on this earth to support the world's population. There are enough resources on this earth to feed everyone. There is enough land for everyone to own their own land and farm, and produce their own energy.

These people have been hiding technology. There are ways to create power easily. There is technology that can provide free cheap power for everyone. There are farming techniques that can feed the entire world.

The Bill of Rights is being systematically dismantled. Men have spilled their blood for those rights.

Your sons and daughters, your brothers and sisters, and Americas best young men and women are losing their limbs. They are losing their lives. They are losing the hearts. They do not know why they are fighting. They are killing. And they do not know why.

They have done some extraordinary acts. Their deeds go before them. But these wars are lies. They are lies. They deceived our entire nation with terrorism. They have gotten us to hand them our rights. Our Rights! Men died for those rights!

September Eleventh was an inside job. They blew up a third building in broad daylight. Building 7.

Your leaders betrayed you.

You elected an aristocracy. They are beholden to special interests. They were brainwashed through the Council on Foreign Relations. Your leaders are planning to merge the United States into a one world banking system. They want to put computer chips in you.

These men have evil hearts. They have tricked you into supporting corporate fascism. We gave them the keys to our country. We were not vigilant with our republic.

There is hope. BUT WE MUST TAKE OUR REPUBLIC BACK.

This is a carefully-drawn expression of the world as Raub sees it—a situation of betrayal. It is a cry for help, but it is also a rallying call.

In instances where people are unwilling or incapable of giving their fears peaceful expression, hyper-agitation cannot be sustained forever. The body's natural defenses—to fight or flee the situation—may function or dysfunction—depending on the crisis and whether there is intervention.

For a visual portrayal of how this works in practice, please refer to the models provided in Appendix A. For now, there will be an analysis of the webs involved in Leaderless Resistance (which replaced cell formations as a more resilient and impenetrable mode of militant organization) and the relationships between them.

INTRA-WEB, INTER-WEB, AND OUTSIDE RELATIONS

Intra-Web Relations

Combative	Shared combat experience allows a core group of activists to both usurp and subordinate the structure of the regular U.S. military. In the former case, specialized battle skills which have been increasingly oriented toward small-scale rapid reaction forces provide the group with confidence as well as competence. In the latter case, the need to defend and assert the group's core beliefs necessarily subordinates those of the U.S. military.
Altruistic	The knowledge that all combat veterans are willing to fight and die for each other is the most altruistic and therefore binding commitment of any militant separatist group.
Suicidal	Suicide is preferable to betrayal of the group.
Sanctioned	Members of a group may kill one of their own from fear of being betrayed.

INTER-WEB RELATIONS

Non-cooperative	Different militant separatist groups need only be non-cooperative in efforts to prevent the state from penetrating their network.
Evasive	Thus different groups will protect each other by spreading lies, disinformation, and sometimes projecting their own views onto otherwise innocent people, or simply evading the truth.
Non-neutral	The projection of non-neutrality both affirms and propagates government distrust.
Supportive	There is nothing to prevent militant groups from exchanging financial support. However, they tend to avoid this by bartering and sharing weapons and supplies, connections and information.

Outside Relations

Neutral	The importance of neutrality should not be understated. Whether on the part of legislators who empathize to some extent with militant separatist groups' withdrawal from a world that is corrupt, or those who fight corruption in empathy with such groups, the lack of an overt commitment to them or connection with them allows legislators to garner support from voters and political donors who fear or are opposed to militant separatist groups.

In other words, different degrees of extremism are not undesired by militant separatist groups. Instead, they serve as insular buffers for ultramilitant groups.

BUFFERS AND "FELLOW TRAVELERS"

Although empathy differs with respect to the three blocks defining societal penetration, insistence on "the real" helps rather than hinders.

Indeed, it is a prerequisite to honest, trusting relations, providing something *reliable* in a world that seems without honor or values.

Simultaneously, such groups leave little to chance. As noted by Leonard Zeskind:

> An electronic stress test specialist [runs] a buzz box, looking for informants. Code names, false identification, and elaborate communication systems [become] de rigueur.[1]

To expand in the present day, militant separatist groups must navigate carefully through society, cautiously probing and testing until they believe with absolute certainty that each individual absorbed in their core identity would rather die than betray their ideals.

One reliable way to achieve this is via the venue called "swap meets"—gun shows, usually hosted in outdoor environments, where "like calls to like" and deals between buyers and sellers (typically "off the books" for non-financial gain) allow weapons to change hands without criminal background checks. It is also an information exchange, where casual encounters open up space for recruitment, or different groups "bump elbows." Then overtures are made to determine who can be trusted to either enter one's own group or function as a separate support group. As noted, support may range from mutual sympathy or cross-affirmation of ideals to the ability of moderate

---

[1] Zeskind, Leonard.

groups to "run interference" between groups that are more extreme and the hated outside world.

THE PROTECTION OF PHYSICAL BOUNDARIES

When individuals are attached to identities (rather than typologies), it allows the focus on group formation to become person-centered and self-referential with different degrees of attachment both possible and probable for each individual. Because exposure to the outside world first instigates attachment to the world, then agitates against it, there is a need to erect boundaries that enforce and reinforce alternative belief systems.

Thus, militant white separatists resort on the one hand to territorial aggregation, where they are able to stockpile weapons, food, and other supplies while securing a safe haven. On the other hand, theological immersion is the staple of daily life and the only path to salvation.

Chapter 7. The Standoff at Ruby Ridge

Let's review Wagner-Pacifici's method and what it does and doesn't offer pertaining to an analysis of Ruby Ridge. In her words:

> [W]hat does it mean to...want to theorize about what happens when things could literally go one way or the other? In some sense, this is the opposite of what the comparative-historical sociologist and the ethnomethodologists have...set out to do, that being to theorize the emergence or order, of regularity, and shared meaning. It also differs...in aiming its...light at which I call the "midro" life of the analytic object, the level where macro structure and micro interaction are *both* "in the picture"... As well, such a project differs from...current preoccupations with trying to decipher patterns in apparent chaos...though it shares with them the desire to keep up with that which is emerging out of the past into the present. Finally...the emphasis is *not* on predicting the outcomes of contingent action (though the outcomes are not irrelevant). The *focus*...is on charting or describing the coming together of diverse elements, individuals, institutions, and languages, in a moment of action and interaction. It is the charting of a process in the present...[T]o theorize the moments just before and as a social interaction takes its definitive form...to highlight rather than bracket the insight that reality is a moving target and that theory has to keep moving to try and keep up with it.[1]

Wagner-Pacifici does tread where comparative-historical sociologists and ethnomethodologists have trod before her in characterizing the standoff as a *conflict* of meaning. This results in the admission that there is indeed the capacity to "freeze" a situation—that such situations, in fact, occur naturally as the "eye

---

[1] Wagner-Pacifici, p. 2.

of the storm" before action and reaction intervene to break an impasse. Moreover, what she seeks as her final outcome is readily recognizable as that which negotiators, analysts, and theorists have sought all along, which is to say "common ground," or the means "to get a foot in the door."

It is likewise a foregone conclusion that the parties in a standoff will be committed to "different situations," just as such situations have emotional, attitudinal, and tactical components in terms of their "conflict of meaning."

Wagner-Pacifici is therefore at her strongest when asserting that the *unknowable*, rather than the *probable*, opens up new vistas for conflict resolution (even if this outcome is not her final objective). It is to say that nothing is predetermined unless we inject our biases and goals (which influence our actions) into the "eye" of the standoff.

FREEZING THE MOMENT

Looking at Ruby Ridge, there were frozen moments, just as there are in all standoffs. The challenge is to recognize when they became manifest and to seize them as opportunities to take stock of the emotional, attitudinal, and tactical components for each side in the conflict, regroup in ways that are cognizant of biases and preferences, and proceed with the understanding that no course of action is necessarily set in stone but instead can be altered in part or in whole to achieve common ground.

To that end, frozen moments can also be *created*.

THE RUBY RIDGE DEBACLE

In the case of Randall Weaver, he and his wife Vicki had some interaction with the Christian Identity movement as well as Aryan Nation before they built a cabin in a remote area of Idaho, where they lived with their home-schooled children, apart from "immoral" society. A paid informant of the BATF (Bureau of Alcohol, Tobacco, and Firearms) who had infiltrated Aryan Nation became acquainted with Weaver and asked him to break the law by selling him two sawed-off shotguns, which Weaver reluctantly did. Once the BATF paid informant was "outed" by a member of Aryan Nation, the BATF decided to cut its losses by threatening Weaver with arrest and confiscation of his assets in order to coerce him into informing on the group(s) with which he had interacted.

Weaver refused.

Exercising deceptive caution, BATF agents served an arrest warrant on Randall Weaver by posing as stranded motorists whom Randall and Vicki stopped to help. The court notice of Randall's hearing was mailed to his attorney, who then sent a letter to Randall, albeit with a different date.

When Weaver failed to appear in court, the Judge issued a bench warrant, at which time BATF agents discovered the lawyer's error and asked the Judge to suspend the warrant. If Weaver appeared on the later date, it would still allow them to press their case. Instead, the court convened a grand jury which indicted Randall Weaver without knowledge of the mixed up dates. The BATF was then forced to take action; however, they remained cautious. Neighbors were paid to become informants and BATF agents, acting like ordinary citizens, made unsuccessful efforts to engage with the Weaver family.

The turning point occurred when three U.S. marshals neared the Weaver cabin, and the Weavers' dogs responded. Sammy (Randall's thirteen-year-old son) and family friend Kevin Harris followed the dogs to a trail where the marshals were discovered. Here, the narrative diverges, to provide different accounts:

> [Marshal] Cooper told the jury that as the boys passed their concealed spot, [Marshal] Degan crouched on one knee and yelled, "Stop, U.S. Marshal!"—whereupon Kevin fired his .30-06 rifle from the hip and shot Degan in the chest. But Idaho State Police Capt. David Neale testified that shortly after the battle, [Marshal] Roderick told him that he, Roderick, had fired first, wounding and then killing Sammy's dog, Striker. And although the government initially claimed that Degan was killed by the first shot of the battle, seven shells from his gun were found near the deputy marshals' hiding place. What is certain is that the dog was shot in the rear end (suggesting that he was running away) and then killed by a second shot. Sammy Weaver, who was running toward the cabin, wheeled around, yelled something like "you shot my dog, you son of a bitch," fired a couple of rounds, and started running again. He was shot twice—first wounded in the elbow and then killed by a bullet in the back. Kevin fired his .30-06 at the marshals and believed he had hit Degan, though he insists the marshals started shooting first and he was firing in self-defense after Sammy was hit.[1]

> The law ordinarily permits the use of deadly force by law-enforcement officers only when the officers or others are in imminent danger of death or serious bodily injury. But in writing the "rules of engagement" for the siege to follow, [Richard] Rogers, [commander of the FBI's Hostage Rescue Team] ...seemed to be under the impression that a fierce two-way gun battle was going on even as he wrote. So he decided that any armed adult outside the Weaver cabin should

---

[1] Bock, Alan W.

be subject to "shoot-to-kill" sniping, whether or not that person was menacing anyone.[1]

According to another source:

After the death of [M]arshal [Degan], the FBI was called in. A source of continuing fierce debate across America is: Did the FBI set out to apprehend and arrest Randy Weaver and Kevin Harris—or simply to kill them? Unfortunately, the evidence from the Justice Department report is damning in the extreme on this count. The report noted, "We have been told by observers...that law enforcement personnel made statements...that the situation would be 'taken down hard and fast.' [A] member of an FBI SWAT team from Denver "remembered the Rules of Engagement as 'if you see 'em, shoot 'em.'" The report concluded that the FBI Rules of Engagement at Ruby Ridge flagrantly violated the U.S. Constitution: "The Constitution allows no person to become 'fair game' for deadly force without law enforcement evaluating the threat that person poses, even when, as occurred here, the evaluation must be made in a split second...The Constitution places the decision on whether to use deadly force on the individual agent; the Rules attempted to usurp this responsibility."[2]

Then:

On August 22, the day after the shootout, Randy Weaver left the cabin for the little outbuilding that held his son's body. As he raised his arm to unlatch the door to the shed, he was shot by a sniper posted on the mountainside. The bullet entered his right shoulder area and exited near his armpit. He and Kevin Harris,[3] who was also outside, ran for the cabin. Vicki Weaver stood in the doorway, yelling for the two to hurry, cradling baby Elisheba in her arms. She was unarmed. As Kevin Harris tumbled into the house, another shot from the sniper went through the glass window and entered Vicki Weaver's temple, killing her instantly. The bullet and fragments of Vicki's skull went on to injure Kevin Harris's arm and torso, breaking a rib and puncturing one of his lungs. The sniper, Lon Horiuchi, was a West Point graduate armed with state-of-the-art sniping equipment and trained to be accurate to within a quarter inch at 200 yards. He claims he missed Kevin and hit Vicki by accident. But Bo Gritz, the former Green Beret commander who eventually negotiated Randy Weaver's surrender, said that after he became a negotiator the FBI showed him a psychological profile of the family prepared for the Marshals Service before the siege that described Vicki as the "dominant member" of

---

[1] Ibid.

[2] Bovard, James, "Ruby Ridge: The Justice Report," The Wall Street Journal, June 30, 1995, p. A14. http://www.stormfront.org/ruby.htm

[3] Sara was also with her father and Harris.

the family. "Vicki was the maternal head of the family," Gritz told the *Spokane Spokesman-Review*. "I believe Vicki was shot purposely by the sniper as a priority target....The profile said, if you get a chance, take Vicki Weaver out."[1]

As for the trial that followed the siege:

> Ron Howen, the assistant U.S. attorney...secured a 10-count grand jury indictment of Randy Weaver and Kevin Harris in September... Although no evidence was presented to tie the Weaver family to neo-Nazi activities, the full panoply of right-wing anti-Zionist, anti-Semitic beliefs was trotted before the jury. Spence objected, saying the prosecution was attempting to "demonize" his client, but the prosecution was allowed to spend several days describing conspiracy theories, interlocking groups, and violent activities.[2]

As noted by Tim Lynch, Director of the CATO Institute's Project on Criminal Justice:

> The FBI told the world that it had apprehended a band of dangerous racists. The *New York Times* was duped into describing a family (two parents, three children)[3] and one adult friend as "an armed separatist brigade." The Department of Justice proceeded to take over the case, charging Weaver and Harris with conspiracy to commit "murder." Federal prosecutors asked an Idaho jury to impose the death penalty. Instead, the jury acquitted Weaver and Harris of all of the serious criminal charges...When Weaver sued the federal government for the wrongful death of his wife and son, the government that had tried to kill him twice now sought an out-of-court settlement. In August 1995, the U.S. government paid the Weaver family $3.1 million. On the condition that his name not be used in an article, one Department of Justice official told *The Washington Post* that if Weaver's suit had gone to trial in Idaho, he probably would have been awarded $200 million.[4]

EXPLAINING THE INEXPLICABLE

As shown, the crime that Weaver committed (selling sawed-off shotguns a quarter of an inch below the legal limit) was actually a minor one that carried a stamp fine of two hundred dollars. Moreover, his defense was one of entrapment.

---

[1] Bock, Alan W.
[2] Ibid.
[3] There were actually four children: Sammy, Sara, Rachel, and Elisheba.
[4] Lynch, Tim, "Remember Ruby Ridge," CATO Institute, http://www.cato.org/publications/commentary/remember-ruby-ridge (Originally published in National Review Online, August 21, 2002.

As to why Weaver was chosen for an antagonistic standoff, it is worthwhile to note that once the BATF informant's cover was blown, the Bureau's expenditure for militant group infiltration had to yield *something* by way of justification. In fact, an essential point of due process is to draw out the number of opportunities the judicial system has to gain willing cooperation in whatever it sought to begin with. Too, any militant organization is only as strong as its weakest link. Since Weaver had only limited interaction—short of full indoctrination under, and incorporation into, the core structure of militant, separatist groups—it is logical to assume that BATF agents thought he could be "turned" more easily than anyone else, co-opted through coercion, and used to greater effect.

However, a cost-to-benefit analysis should convince any reader that the difference between paying a two hundred dollar fine and betraying armed separatist group(s) to which Weaver was sympathetic was, from the start, a no-brainer. Weaver would gain more from silence, not from fear of retribution *but for the tangible reinforcement of a shared belief system.*[1]

INTERPRETING GOVERNMENT TIMING

Because the Branch Davidian siege was already underway during Randall Weaver's trial, there are six facets of governmental action which need to be discussed. The first is how the BATF and the FBI Hostage Rescue Team could, and did, act differently, so as not to repeat the mistakes (with the same culpability) that occurred at Ruby Ridge. The second is that the Branch Davidian case was an opportunity for the state to prove by association (while Weaver was on trial) the irrational, intractable, and ultimately suicidal nature of all militant separatist groups. It was for this reason that the prosecution trotted out the full panoply of white supremacists, neo-Nazis, conspiracy theorists, zealots, and other fringe groups, attempting to prove that they were mutually supportive and networked, such that no group, however small, could be seen as innocent in the conspiracy as a whole. The third facet, conversely, is that Waco was put on trial as part of the Weaver trial. For those who were watching both cases, the prosecution's stance was both forward- and backward-looking, from a need to prejudice public opinion as Waco was pushed to conclusion. The fourth facet, which was certainly no secret since it received plenty of press, was the contrast of saving women and children after Vicki Weaver's death. A fifth facet depended on Waco as a distraction (and example of positive government action) for those who had yet no interest in the case of Ruby Ridge. The sixth, and perhaps most

---

[1] Also avoiding, in the process, the prisoner's dilemma because emphatic silence remains the safest course.

important facet, is that the timing of Waco, Texas, foreclosed on telling the human "story" in Randall Weaver's case.

THE SELF-FULFILLING PROPHECY

From the perspective of law enforcement, militant groups create their own prisons (and opportunities for martyrdom) via the self-fulfilling prophecy that disobeying the law and refuting legal authority will result in law enforcement. All that remains is to prepare for the standoff, where naturally both sides create a potential for violence. As a militant white separatist, Weaver was prepared to meet force with force. However, the agencies dispatched to deal with him were trained in overwhelming force, since their privilege as government agencies is to possess a *monopoly* of force.

This asymmetric relationship is both proper and problematic, as it underscores the reasons for federal overreaction.

GOVERNMENT EXTREMISM

On the one hand, a nation cannot stand without the means of public defense. Although the authority of the government rests on the consent of the governed through the democratic process, the will of the many eclipses that of the few,[1] just as the needs of the many outweigh those who refute the law and its authority. As paramilitary intermediaries between the government's monopoly of force and the revolutionary militia that was raised to secure that end, contemporary militant groups do not perceive themselves as anomalies. On the other hand, the militia had to be formed to start the revolution. The formation of a national army to incorporate the militia could only happen after.

In present-day America, the anomaly of which I speak has its roots in military enlistment followed by military discharge, disenchantment with the nation, and withdrawal into secretive groups. These groups are not "militia" but potential paramilitary formations, both capable of war (as a result of their formal training) and recruiting, training, and aiding like-minded people who join them.[2]

It should therefore be obvious why infiltrating such groups to gather information is a government priority. If a backward link exists between

---

[1] More realistically, this will only continue to work as long as the perception of the majority can be manipulated by the few.

[2] Hence, Janet Napolitano (Secretary of the Department of Homeland Security) issued a public warning that post-combat veterans returning to society with dangerous, specialized skills and different views of the world could pose a threat to U.S. stability. She was then forced to apologize due to patriotic backlash.

these groups and the regular, enlisted military,[1] then it raises the threatening prospect that a monopoly of force for government defense may, in fact, be an illusion, to be sustained by secret association until such time as paramilitary intermediaries have the means and the opportunity to overthrow the established order.

THE SIGNIFICANCE OF FALLOUT

Since confrontational standoffs[2] already involve a crime or at least a perception of guilt, negotiation is a stop-gap measure to disarm, defuse, and dispose of the situation, specifically excluding the fallout. What happens next, after the hostages are rescued and the guns confiscated, becomes the work of the justice system. It also becomes subject to interpretation by the media, bystanders, critics, and analysts within the agencies responsible for the standoff. More lastingly (and importantly) it becomes another landmark case for those who sympathize with resistance to authority and the reason the standoff took place.

Thus, the need for a new palliative (or pacification device) can be inferred from Wagner-Pacifici's own way of summing up her work:

> Ultimately, this study aims to suggest some strategies of rescue, though perhaps not of final reconciliation.[3]

WE WILL BE FOREVER HAUNTED

For its part the F.B.I., as represented by Director Louis J. Freeh, who appeared before the U.S. Subcommittee on Terrorism, Technology and Government Information on October 19, 1995, the Ruby Ridge tragedy left the agency remorseful and respectful. In the statement given by Director Freeh, he made it plain that the F.B.I. would never forget the incident, saying:[4]

> Ruby Ridge has become synonymous with tragedy, given the deaths there of a decorated Deputy United States Marshal, a young boy, and the boy's mother. It has also become synonymous with the

---

[1] In fact, *A Force Upon a Plain*, written by a journalist who covered white militant separatist groups many years ago, noted that recruitment for at least one group originated in the U.S. Army.

[2] This could refer to any conflict, since Wagner-Pacifici views all citizens as "hostages" of society. That she interprets this correctly, allows her to admit that society is a construct, subject to constant refinement, without ever challenging who has the right to refine it.

[3] Wagner-Pacifici, p. xii.

[4] "Opening Statement of Louis J. Freeh, Director, Federal Bureau of Investigation, Before the Subcommittee on Terrorism, Technology and Government Information, Committee on the Judiciary, United States Senate, Washington, DC," October 19, 1995.

exaggerated application of federal law enforcement. Both conclusions seem justified.

At Ruby Ridge, the FBI did not perform at the level which the American people expect or deserve from the F.B.I. Indeed, for the F.B.I., Ruby Ridge was a series of terribly flawed law enforcement operations with tragic consequences.

We know today that law enforcement overreacted at Ruby Ridge. F.B.I. Officials promulgated rules of engagement that were reasonably subject to interpretation that would permit a violation of F.B.I. policy and the Constitution—rules that could have caused even worse consequences than actually occurred. Rules of engagement that I will never allow the F.B.I. to use again.

There was a trail of serious operational mistakes that went from the mountains of Northern Idaho to F.B.I. headquarters and back out to a federal courtroom in Boise, Idaho. Today there are allegations that a cover-up occurred—allegations that, if proven, shake the very foundation of integrity upon which the F.B.I. is built.

Although I was not F.B.I. Director when the Ruby Ridge crisis occurred, I am sincerely disappointed with the F.B.I.' s performance during the crisis and especially in its aftermath. These hearings have only served to confirm that belief. The F.B.I. has, however, learned from its mistakes there. I have changed almost every aspect of the F.B.I.'s crisis response structure and modified or promulgated new policies and procedures to address the flaws and shortcomings apparent from the F.B.I.'s response. I am committed to ensuring that the tragedies of Ruby Ridge never happen again...

...As I have stated many times before, Vicki Weaver's death was tragic but accidental. I fully appreciate the fact that three children have been left without a mother as a result of what occurred at Ruby Ridge. On behalf of the F.B.I., I wish to express my regret and sorrow for Mrs. Weaver's death. Moreover, the F.B.I. fully supports the settlement with the Weaver family that the Department of Justice negotiated. For the F.B.I., the settlement does not bring any sense of closure to the stark tragedy of Vicki Weaver's death. Rather, her death will always be a haunting reminder to the F.B.I. to take every possible step to avoid tragedy, even in the most dangerous situations.

CHAPTER 8. THE PROSECUTION OF RUBY RIDGE

> Actions and reactions that splinter moments of impasse cre-
> ate lines in the door of glass through which adversaries face off.
> Sometimes this "door of glass" is perfectly transparent, such that
> both sides are aware of the other's perceptions and actions; some-
> times it is semi-transparent, so that each side has only limited
> knowledge of the other's perceptions and actions; and at times
> it is so opaque that each side only sees its own reflection, which
> means that they are blind to the other's needs and perceptions.
> Each of these conditions can be the "fault" of one side or both. But
> violence commits both sides to the incredibly daunting task of
> keeping the glass intact so that those who do surrender can still
> open and walk through the door once death has affected them all.

Since the defense never mounted a case in the Randall Weaver trial, relying instead on the prosecution to bungle its presentation via the contradictions of witness after witness, we can start by reviewing the statements of the surviving U.S. marshals involved in the first spate of violence.

Citing from the team's 542-page report[1] (with my comments in italics):

> Marshal Roderick: Roderick...decided to take Cooper and Degan closer to
> the house to collect more data...Sensing their presence, the Weavers' dogs
> began barking...Randy came running out of the cabin, followed by Kevin
> Harris, Sammy Weaver, Sara Weaver, and Rachel Weaver. All of them
> were armed...Rather than taking defensive positions...the Weavers began

---

[1] Lohr, David, "Randy Weaver: Siege at Ruby Ridge," ‹crimelibrary› http://www.
crimelibrary.com/gangsters_outlaws/cops_others/randy_weaver/22.html

jogging down the driveway...Roderick then saw a large Labrador retriever running toward his position, followed by an armed Kevin Harris.

Marshal Cooper: Cooper...reportedly saw Randy Weaver coming... from the cabin, approximately 40 feet away from his position behind some brush. When Randy first noticed Cooper, he appeared shocked... Cooper assumed that Roderick and Degan were covering Randy (*This places Cooper in the rearmost position, facing off with Harris,* with Roderick and Degan in the forefront, apparently facing Randall) and...turned his attention to Harris and the dog, which were still behind him and yelled out, "Back off, U.S. Marshals," fearing that he had been set up for an ambush...When the dog caught up to Cooper, it began growling and snarling...Cooper decided not to shoot [it], as he did not want...to invoke a firefight between himself and Harris. After circling Cooper a few times, the dog ran past him...headed towards Roderick's position. Cooper left the trail and dove behind a rock approximately 15 feet behind Degan.

Marshal Roderick: [Randy] Weaver...screamed something unintelligible. Roderick yelled, "Stop! U.S. Marshal"...Roderick could not tell if Weaver continued up the trail or if he ran into the woods. (*This last is important.*)

Marshal Cooper: [Cooper] saw...Harris and Sammy...walking directly in front of Degan [who squatted] behind a stump, facing up the trail. When Harris and Sammy stepped out into the clearing...Degan...raised his weapon and [yelled] "Stop! U.S. Marshal," Cooper then stood up... and repeated the phrase [at which time] Kevin Harris...fired at Degan with a 30.06 rifle. Cooper...saw Degan fall back, realizing [he'd] been shot. Cooper then fired a three-round burst at Harris [who] dropped to the ground "like a sack of potatoes." (*This is an obvious misperception, as Harris probably dropped to avoid becoming a target before finding a tree stump for cover.*) Cooper...could not tell if Sammy had a gun, because of trees blocking his view, so he did not shoot at Sammy. Cooper did not realize that Degan had returned any fire before being shot.

Fact: In preparation for the mission, the marshals acquired three .223 caliber M16 rifles, a .223 caliber M16A2 Colt Carbine, a "sniper" rifle, a shotgun, and a "suppressed" .9mm NATO Colt Carbine. In addition, the team members brought their own personal service weapons... Marshal Degan carried one of the..M16s...Roderick had an M16; and Cooper had the "suppressed". 9mm...they did not bring the sniper rifle with them.[1] Since it was later learned that Degan backed up several

---

[1] "Ruby Ridge," Wikipedia, http://en.wikipedia.org/wiki/Ruby_Ridge

paces and fired seven rounds from his M16 (which investigators removed from the scene before putting them back to photograph a phony reenactment), that Marshal Cooper failed to notice Degan's movements, let alone the shots, is nonsensical to say the least.

Marshal Roderick: Roderick heard a shot from...a heavy caliber weapon...(*Presumably when Cooper fired at Harris and seemingly dropped him "like a sack of potatoes."*) [T]he dog stopped and Roderick shot [it]... Sammy called Roderick a, "son of a bitch" and shot two rounds at him. Roderick...dove behind a tree.

Marshal Cooper: [Cooper] began taking fire and heard Degan call out, "Coop, I need you."...Cooper then...fired a second three-round burst... to provide cover as he tried to get to Degan. Following these...shots, Cooper saw Sammy run out of view. When Cooper reached Degan... he...had been [shot] once in the chest. He was lying on his left side... lost consciousness and died. Cooper then radioed...Roderick.

Because the surviving marshals were not separated for questioning following the shootout, they had time and opportunity to coordinate their stories, albeit not in a way that helped them.

Now, turning to the statement of Randall Weaver,[1] which was dictated to Sara (where my comments are in italics):

Randall Weaver: "When I reached the first fork in the logging road, a very well camouflaged person yelled 'freeze RANDY,' (*According to the marshals, Randall wore camouflage also*) and I immediately said 'f—k you,' and retreated toward home 80–100 feet. I realized...that we had run smack into a ZOG/NEW WORLD ORDER ambush. I stopped to see if I was being followed....I heard a gun shot and Striker [the dog] yelped...I started yelling for Sam and Kevin to return home...I also fired my shotgun once into the air to draw attention to myself praying that would help. (*But Randall—a former Green Beret and loving father—didn't take up a position to help?*) I replaced the empty shell with a new one, jamming the shotgun. I drew my .9mm handgun and fired 3–4 rounds up into the air and I yelled again for Sam to return home. Sam responded 'I'm coming dad!' I then walked backwards up the hill toward home yelling to Sam and Kevin to come home. All the while I heard many shots ringing out from the direction of the ambush."

Fact: "The ballistics evidence presented at trial (and cartridge counts on the Marshals' guns performed by DUSM Mark Jurgeson) showed: Art

---

[1] Lohr, David.

Roderick fired one shot from a .223 M16, Sammy Weaver fired three rounds from a .223 Ruger Mini-14, Bill Degan fired seven rounds from an M-16 while moving at least 21 feet, Larry Cooper fired six rounds from a 9mm Colt submachinegun, and Kevin Harris fired two rounds from a .30-06 M1917 Enfield Rifle, for a total of nineteen rounds fired." [1] *Thus the rounds fired by Weaver were not accounted for at the trial because no one saw Weaver shoot. Yet Marshal Degan was apparently defending himself from someone if he fired seven rounds while simultaneously in motion, taking a total of 21 steps before he was shot in the chest. Importantly,* "the ballistics experts called by the prosecution testified on cross examination by defense that the physical evidence did not contradict either the prosecution or defense theories on the firefight...[Martin] Fackler testified that Roderick shot and killed the dog, Degan shot Sammy through the right elbow, Harris shot and killed Degan, and Cooper "probably" shot and killed Sammy. The 1993 trial jury accepted the defense theory of the firefight and acquitted Harris on grounds of self-defense." [2] *Then,* "in 1997—*four years later*— Boundary County Sheriff Greg Sprungl conducted an independent search of the "Y" and Lucien Haag confirmed that a bullet found in that search matched Cooper's gun and contained fibers that matched Sammy Weaver's shirt." [3] *In other words, a round probably covered by leaf mulch in a heavily-wooded area somehow retained fibers that weren't biodegraded over a four-year period?*

If we now turn to the statement dictated to Sara Weaver by Kevin Harris: [4]

> Kevin Harris: "Me...and Sam followed Striker through the woods until we came out on the road that forks off the one Randy was on. Striker reached the corner first, then Sam, and then me. A camouflaged... person...shot Striker. Sam yelled "You shot Striker, you son of a bitch!" And they pointed a gun at Sam. Sam opened...fire. I took cover behind a stump and Sam headed up the road toward home. It appeared...as though Sam had been wounded in the right arm. The men were still shooting at Sam (*These are the many shots that Randall heard ringing out from the direction of the ambush?*) so I shot one of the sons of bitches. After they killed Sam one of the Feds jumped out of the woods and for the first time declared he was a federal marshal. The Feds then grabbed their wounded and left. I...headed home up the road and spotted Sam's body laying [sic] in the road without a doubt shot in the back."

In a later statement to the FBI,[5] Harris said that he raised his rifle and fired at Degan after he saw that Sammy had been shot:

[1] "Ruby Ridge," Wikipedia, http://en.wikipedia.org/wiki/Ruby_Ridge
[2] Ibid.
[3] Ibid.
[4] Lohr, David.
[5] Ibid.

[Harris] heard Degan call out that he had been hit...[After Harris] fired at Degan, the shooting came to a halt for a few seconds before he heard another shot. Sammy "yelped," then was silent. Harris said he fired one more shot in front of a camouflaged man "to scare him." Harris remained behind the stump "approximately ten more minutes"...then retreated to the Weaver house.

Contrasting the statements of Randall Weaver and Kevin Harris with accounts provided by retired Lt. Col. James "Bo" Gritz, Gritz both contradicts and embellishes his stories, then ultimately tells the truth.

First, with respect to the initial shootout[1] (where my notes are in italics):

Gritz: Suddenly, a man in fatigues jumped up from some thick brush and shot one of the dogs. Samuel, not knowing who the intruder was... (*Really? The family believed for months that they would die in a government frame-up*) fired back...whereupon someone fired upon him, wounding him in the shoulder. (*In fact, Samuel was shot in the elbow.*) Samuel turned to run back home when he was hit in the back and killed instantly. Harris, after determining that Samuel was dead by taking his pulse (*Harris was able to take Samuel's pulse from where he crouched behind a stump for cover during a live shootout? Something Harris never even mentioned?*), turned and shot one of the intruders. As the shots were fired, two armed men in camouflage fatigues jumped in front of Randy Weaver and attempted to arrest him. (*According to Marshal Cooper's, Randall Weaver's, and Kevin Harris's testimony, Randall was confronted first and fired before the dog, Marshal Degan, and Sammy were shot.*) Weaver ran for the house, firing two (*Randall admitted to firing his shotgun once before it jammed and then firing 3–4 shots from his .9mm pistol.*) shots into the air as a prearranged signal for his son and Harris to return. Deputy Marshal William Degan...was also killed.

Now Gritz provides different accounts as to who contacted who, and whether he was asked or allowed to negotiate the surrender of Randall and Harris. In his first letter to *The Wall Street Journal*, which was posted on the Internet in 1998, Gritz wrote:

Initially, the FBI called me when Weaver wouldn't communicate with official negotiators. After wading through an army of bureau-rats, I was allowed on Weaver Mountain. In our first exchange, Randall (Pete to family and friends), told me the feds had killed Vicki and were keeping it a secret. He was also upset that the media was falsely labeling him a "white supremacist."[2]

---

[1] LaRosa, Benedict D., "Standoff in Idaho," http://www.constitution.org/col/san920910.txt

[2] Gritz, Bo, "I Was There," http://www.freewebs.com/jeffhead/liberty/gritz.htm

Then in his second letter to *The Wall Street Journal*, Gritz wrote:

> I had never known Randy Weaver before receiving a call from the FBI on 24 August 1992, in Phoenix, Arizona. They said I was a person, identified by friends and family of Randall, that he respected and might listen to. Weaver was a Green Beret demolition sergeant in the 70s, but did not go to Vietnam. I visited the Green Beret headquarters at Fort Bragg, N.C. several times during my tour of duty from 1964–1969. As a special operations commander actively engaged in guerrilla warfare, I shared trade craft and lessons learned with those who might be going over. Randy Weaver might have been at one of those sessions.[1]

In agreement, David Lohr reported:

> On Friday August 28, 1992, the FBI brought in Colonel Bo Gritz, in hopes that he might be able to negotiate with the Weaver family. *The Washington Post* at one time named Colonel Bo Gritz the "American Original" and *The Atlanta Constitution* had referred him to as a "Renaissance Green Beret". Decorated 62 times for valor during his combat service in Vietnam and elsewhere, Gritz became a prominent figure on the right-wing fringe after leading several unsuccessful commando-style missions to rescue alleged American POWs in Vietnam during the 1980s. He ran briefly for Vice President in 1988 and was currently running for president on the Populist Party ticket. Gritz was also the founder of several survivalist-oriented land developments, for the purpose of paramilitary boot camps. With close ties to both the anti-government movement and white supremacists, Gritz seemed to be the perfect nongovernmental negotiator...Randy Weaver was well aware of who Bo Gritz was and had often times referred to him as the original "Rambo," [As has been repeatedly pointed out, only Gritz himself believed he was the model for Rambo, which the director of the film denied.] so when Bo announced his presence outside the Weaver cabin, Randy agreed to speak with him through the door.[2]

However, Gritz told Benedict D. LaRosa:

> A month before the standoff, Weaver had written his old Special Forces commander from Fort Bragg, retired Lt. Col. James "Bo" Gritz (who is the Populist Party candidate for President), asking for his help. Weaver wrote to Gritz that he feared the government would destroy him and his family.[3]

---

[1] Ibid.
[2] Lohr, David.
[3] LaRosa, Benedict D.

And, according to Leonard Zeskind, Gritz was contacted by Pete Peters, a prominent white supremacist leader, before Gritz traveled to Ruby Ridge, where it turned out that the FBI had never made contact with Gritz, much less asked him to intervene:

> Peters was at that moment convening his annual summer Bible camp in Colorado...Everyone already knew that Weaver's son Sam and the federal marshal were dead, although they did not yet know that Vicki Weaver was also dead. Peters convened a late-night three-hour session of "Elders" to decide what to do. They issued a press release signed by someone not known by the media as an anti-Semite. That small decision indicated that Peters intended to speak out beyond the confines of the white supremacist movement. The Elders also asked campers to phone the Bush administration's U.S. attorney general's office in protest. Knowing that Bo Gritz was then en route to Idaho, Peters also wrote a letter to Randy Weaver and sent it to Gritz, asking that it be delivered to the family. "Dear Randy," it began, "Please know that the murder of your son has not gone unnoticed. Five hundred Christian Israelites from 40 states gathered at my 1992 camp in Colorado are right now praying for you and the Gideon situation you face." There is no evidence that Gritz delivered the letter or that it had any impact on the final outcome. Meanwhile, Gritz arrived at Weaver Mountain and...at first...read with great fanfare a multipage "Citizen's Warrant for Citizen's Arrest," at the behest of the protesters, then placed it under a rock at the FBI's barricades. The next day Gritz handwrote a personal note to the special agent in charge of the siege: "We aren't trying to make your task more difficult. We want to help. We believe that we can convince Randy to come out . . ." The FBI, stuck at an impasse, agreed to let Gritz try to negotiate directly with Weaver.

According to the account Gritz gave Benedict D. LaRosa:

> [He] arrived Tuesday, August 25, with Jack McLamb to negotiate a peaceful resolution to the standoff. Upon his arrival at the roadblock, Gritz spoke to an angry crowd of over 100 friends and neighbors of the Weaver family, calming them considerably. He asked to speak to the F.B.I. agent in charge, Gene Glenn. Glenn refused to see Gritz and his party or to allow him to negotiate with Weaver. On Friday, August 28, Gritz, McLamb, Isbell, and criminal investigators Eric Lighter from Hawaii and retired. Lt. Col. John Salter from Montana attempted to serve citizens arrest warrants on Gene Glenn, and through him on F.B.I. Director William Sessions, Idaho Governor Cecil Andrus, and Director of the U.S. Marshal Service Henry Hudson for felonious abuse of office and failure to perform their duties. Gritz read the charges at the roadblock and asked the people mentioned or their representatives to

step forward. When no one did, he placed the document on a rock on the government's side of the roadblock. Although the county attorney told Gritz the warrants were of no consequence, within a half-hour Glenn had Gritz escorted to the top of the mountain to make contact with Weaver.[1] [No mention was made of the note containing Gritz's humble plea.]

Since the FBI had not solicited help from Bo Gritz, there is also the mystery of a tape they supposedly asked him to make. Quoting from Gritz's second letter to *The Wall Street Journal*:

> The FBI wanted me to make a tape recording (to be broadcast) over the telephone urging Weaver to surrender. I know Special Forces and knew such a puny effort was hopeless. Before being commissioned, I had walked in Weaver's boots as a demolitions specialist. *Randy could have fugas* (jellied napalm) *buried around his home in 55 gallon drums and homemade mines in the trees* [emphasis added]. A lot of people could die— especially when I learned they had shot his son, 13-year-old Sammy, in the back while he was running home. I told Randall on the tape that I would come to Idaho the next day. The FBI didn't play the tape.[2] [Author's note: Gritz was very specific regarding Randall's possible defenses. This issue will be important when we discuss the Weaver's neighbors.]

Then, after the Weavers' surrendered, Gritz pulled another stunt:

> While explaining the last stages of his negotiations to a group of protesters (and the press), Gritz stopped, raised his right arm in the typical Nazi salute, and said: "By the way, [Weaver] told me to... give you [guys] a salute. He said you know what that is." Certainly, a skinhead in the back of the crowd understood, even if Gritz then pretended that he didn't. The skinhead returned the Sieg Heil white power salute and then turned his thumb up.[3]

Finally, on the same Internet post where Gritz is described as "America's most decorated Special Forces soldier [who] is one of our foremost authorities on counterinsurgency and special warfare and an acknowledged expert in the area of field expedient explosives," Gritz seemingly had some difficulty "recalling" the ballistics and forensics evidence presented at the Weaver trial:

> Randall Weaver, his 16-year old daughter, Sara, and Kevin Harris came out of the cabin to look in on Sammy Weaver, shot in the back

---

[1] LaRosa, Benedict D.
[2] Gritz, Bo, "I Was There."
[3] Zeskind, Leonard.

the day before...by U.S. Marshal Arthur Roderick. [1] [In fact, Roderick shot the dog.]

Gritz then goes on to say:

Lon Horiuchi was the FBI Hostage Response Team (HRT) sniper who killed Vicki Weaver. The Department of Justice report says he shot her by "accident" after shooting Randall in the back. This is a blatant lie! The truth testifies of premeditated murder.

I...examine[d] Randall's wound. It was clear to see that he had been hit by a .223 caliber bullet fired from an M-16 rifle, not a 7.62 millimeter from Horiuchi's Remington 700 sniper rifle. The .223 entered his right upper back and emerged cleanly from the center of his arm pit. I examined Vicki Weaver, who lay in a puddle of body fluids at one end of the 30-foot squared 3/4 inch plywood and 2x4 cabin. Clearly a high velocity 7.62 mm. slug had struck her right face just in front of the lower ear–jaw line and exited just beneath the left jaw, tearing through the artery. The ugly wound almost completely destroyed the once beautiful face. I commented to Randall that it was obvious his bride was killed by a 7.62.

Lon Horiuchi is lying when he claims to have shot Randall in the back and then accidentally hit Vicki trying to get a second quick shot off as Randall ran into the cabin. Every sniper team has a back-up shooter (number two man) responsible for communication with the Command & Control unit and security of the number one sniper. This number two carries an M-16 with open (iron) sights. The number one man has a choice (of weapons), but the FBI standard is a Remington 700 bolt action using 7.62 "match" ammunition with a 10-power United States Marine Corps sniper telescope.

Lon Horiuchi testified in Court that he practiced, hitting a quarter inch target at 200 meters (yards). I lay in Horiuchi's sniper nest beside a pine on a hillside 200 yards from, and overlooking the cabin. He fired from a prone supported position and almost anyone with training could have hit the target from that range with a 10-power telescope— yet he missed—by more than 10 inches! Horiuchi testified under oath that he aimed his first shot at the base of Randall's skull for an instant kill. Weaver was standing stock still with his back directly facing Horiuchi, lifting up his right arm to unlatch the tiny shelter less than 200 yards away, but Horiuchi didn't fire the first round—number two DID! Horiuchi was zeroed in on Vicki Weaver, but she would have made a better target standing in the yard. The number two man aimed

---

[1] Gritz, Bo, "I Was There."

his M-16 offhand with iron sights at Weaver's head, but typically (ask any vet) missed by the margin stated. When Weaver didn't fall and the family ran for the cabin, Horiuchi hit his quarter-inch bull's eye target—as planned.

> The feds cremated both Vicki and Sammy, so no confirming autopsy is possible...It should come to trial, but probably won't, that I was the only "outsider" on the inside of what happened on Weaver Mountain. HRT Commander (Lon Horiuchi's boss), Dick Rogers, told me they "TARGETED VICKI WEAVER AS PRIORITY NUMBER ONE, SINCE THE PSYCHOLOGICAL PROFILE SHOWED HER TO BE THE MATERNAL HEAD OF THE FAMILY AND IT WAS THOUGHT SHE WOULD KILL THE CHILDREN BEFORE ALLOWING A SURRENDER."[1]

Apparently, Gritz could tell the difference between the rounds that pierced Randall and Vicki just by looking at the wounds, but his memory continued to fail him regarding evidence from the trial. Citing again from his first letter to *The Wall Street Journal*, Gritz wrote:

> The Media continues to report that Kevin Harris killed Marshal William Degan: THIS IS NOT TRUE! Kevin did in fact tell me through the cabin wall on the second day of negotiations that he shot Degan. When I asked him how he was certain, he said: "Well, he's dead and Sammy didn't do it." Degan, Roderick and Larry Cooper (armed with a 9mm silenced Colt sub-machine gun) were wearing camouflage and laying in prepared positions within a wooded area overlooking the trail at the "Y." Harris confirmed that he didn't actually "SEE" Degan, but he "...did fire one shot [In fact, he fired two.] from a bolt action 30.06 rifle at a spot where smoke and expended shell casings were coming from."

> During the Boise trial (July 1993), Gerry Spence proved from the trail of expended cartridges that William Degan, the most decorated Marshal in the U.S. Marshal Service's (USMS) 208 year history, ran in front of Larry Cooper trying to get a better shot at Kevin Harris. Not hearing the silenced Colt in the din of machine gun fire, Degan was killed. Cooper testified, "I aimed my weapon and pulled trigger. The target fell like sack of potatoes." Kevin was not hit and Degan died, albeit accidentally. [Author's note: If true, it certainly would have been noted that Degan was shot in the back.][2]

In fact, the evidence and testimony at the trial proved that Degan was killed by Harris, who was armed with a shotgun. If, however, Gritz would

---

[1] Ibid.
[2] Gritz, Bo, "I Was There."

like to have it his way, whether Degan was killed by a shotgun or a .9mm round, there was one man who stated that he harmlessly fired both.

Randall Weaver.

WORDS THAT WOUND

The question of whether the F.B.I. was aware of Vicki Weaver's death has been addressed in many ways—some straightforward, others laden with innuendo. As an example of the former, Patrick J. McGrail writes:

> For the next nine days, the FBI, unaware of Vicki Weaver's death, used the standard hostage negotiation tactic of appealing to the welfare of the women inside and begging Weaver to produce his wife. To Weaver, who assumed that the FBI knew that they had shot his spouse, it was a cruel and inhumane tactic.[1]

As noted by another writer, the Weavers tried yelling to federal agents that Vicki Weaver was dead. They therefore assumed that the F.B.I. knew this and used it as a cruel tactic. To wit:

> The psychological warfare became even worse the following day. "Good morning Mrs. Weaver," Fred Lanceley, an FBI negotiator, called out. "We had pancakes this morning. And what did you have for breakfast? Why don't you send your children out for some pancakes, Mrs. Weaver?" Following the statements made by the negotiator, the whole family began sobbing loudly. The phone, which had been placed outside the cabin door, rang continuously every 15 minutes as the negotiator continued yelling through the bull horn, at times stating that if they failed to come out, they were all going to die. A robot was soon deployed in an attempt to take a telephone inside the cabin by breaking out a front window. Randy was convinced that the robot would use tear gas on them and shouted, "You'd f—king better back off," and stated that he would shoot the robot if it came any closer. Following his statements, the robot retreated and a negotiator began speaking again, "Vicki, how's the baby?" he said. "Let me know if there is anything that can be done for the baby."[2]

According to Bo Gritz, the F.B.I. had equipped the cabin with listening devices and knew that Vicki was dead. He was therefore aghast to learn that a banner reading "Camp Vicki" had been erected at the command post,

---

[1] McGrail, Patrick J., "Sensationalism, Narrativity and Objectivity—Modeling Ongoing News Story Practice," p. 90. http://books.google.com/books?id=9xrlVC yngAoC&q=Randy+Weaver#v=snippet&q=Randy%20 Weaver&f=false

[2] Lohr, David.

not to rally support for the family, but in grotesquely triumphant cruelty. Yet, Gritz was fitted with a transmitter before he was sent to negotiate, indicating that there were no other devices employed at the cabin.

THE IMPEACHMENT OF BO GRITZ

Before the Ruby Ridge standoff, Gritz had become a presidential candidate on the Populist Party ticket. In so doing, he wanted to be seen as *the* all-American hero: a highly decorated veteran whose forays into Vietnam in search of American POWs (for which he received financing from Ross Perot, among others) made him the living manifestation of the military's motto "we will leave no man behind," even though said forays have been exposed via the Internet as both theater and sham.

He has been called out as a supposed "secret government agent," labeled a parasitic "pay-triot," and even laughed at for his "botched" suicide attempt (where one commentator suggested that if a Green Beret wanted to kill himself, he would certainly know how to do it). In seeming exasperation another writer asked, "Will the real Bo Gritz please stand up?"

Why?

Apparently he can't be the one-stop shopping center for everyone, let alone the patriot movement, not to say that he hasn't tried.

As a person of long-standing interest to the Southern Poverty Law Center and the Anti-Defamation League, his language, views, and actions have been documented as follows:

> Gritz' military demeanor and his far-fetched claims made him friends among the conspiracy-minded right, including Willis Carto, founder of the Holocaust-denial organization Institute for Historical Review and the now defunct Liberty Lobby, who encouraged him to run as the vice presidential candidate on the Populist Party ticket in 1988. While Gritz dropped out of the campaign shortly after learning that his running mate was to be former Klansman David Duke, he ran again on the same ticket in 1992, this time for the presidential slot, garnering 0.1% of the vote with his "God, Guns and Gritz" platform, which opposed everything from the federal income tax to the "New World Order."[1]

In 1994:

> ...contractors broke ground in a remote section of central Idaho that was to become a land development Gritz called Almost Heaven. He started the project, he said, out of disgust with both "an encroaching, ravenous, predator government" and the "grip of international bankers."

---

[1] Southern Poverty Law Center, http://www.splcenter.org/get-informed/intelligence-files/profiles/bo-gritz

He said that the isolated, like-minded community of separatists would be specially prepared for civil unrest and the onslaught of government: "I believe by 1996 you're going to see the noose tighten up around liberty's neck....For that reason we're training people, not to be paramilitary, but to live off the grid...so they can have a choice.... tyranny always wears a badge of authority."[1]

As for his religious beliefs, they have not been made public.

> Nonetheless, Gritz has upped the ante by enlisting God against the government and its supporters. He says: "I can assure you that if I was ever convinced that it was God's Will for me to commit an act of violence against the laws of our land, I would hesitate only long enough to, like Gideon, be certain. I would then do all within my power to accomplish what I felt he required of me....If God does call me into the Phinehas Priesthood [Author's note: This, in far-right parlance, denotes a person who'll use violence against those not committed to the superiority and "purity" of the white race]...my defense will be the truth as inspired by the Messiah."[2]

As noted by Leonard Zeskind:

> In his speeches, "intelligence briefings," burning of United Nations symbols, and other histrionics, Gritz continually flirted with the imagery, code words, and stock phrases of the [white supremacist] movement, all the while acting as if he weren't sending signals to his audience. At that point in his life, Gritz did not want to be known as anything other than a true American patriot, a fighter against evil conspiracies, and a brave candidate for president. And the successful negotiation of Weaver's surrender certainly gave his Populist Party candidacy a moment of fame. Gritz went back to electioneering, and he drew larger crowds...But the venues hadn't changed. He still rode the Christian patriot and survivalist circuit, primarily in the West. He told five hundred people in Nampa, Idaho, "We'll either take it with ballots in 1992, or we may be required to defend our rights with bullets in 1996."[3]

More ominously, Gritz wrote in his 1998 bulletin to supporters:

> "Do you see the sign, the scent, stain and mark of the beast on America today? ...Are you willing to submit and join this seedline of Satan? ...Look to those who are openly antichrist...[W]ho in the world is promoting abortion, pornography, pedophilia, Godless laws,

---

[1] Anti-defamation League http://archive.adl.org/learn/ext_us/gritz.html? LEARN_Cat=Extremism&LEARN_SubCat=Extremism_in_America &xpicked=2&item=5
[2] Ibid.
[3] Zeskind, Leonard.

adultery, *New Age* international banking, entertainment industry and *world publishing*? [Emphasis added.] Wherever you find perversion of God's laws you will find the worshippers of Baal with their roots still in Babylonian mysticism."[1]

Finally, citing from the Nizkor Project:

> Colonel James "Bo" Gritz, who deplored the deadly Oklahoma bombing but commented that it was a "Rembrandt—a masterpiece of art and science," is highly influential in the anti-government "patriot" movement. [He] opposes gun control and...urges supporters to resist any attempts by the Federal government to "take away their guns." [Gritz] leads survivalist, paramilitary training sessions, which he calls S.P.I.K.E. (Specially Prepared Individuals for Key Events). [Having] served for many years on the advisory board of the Liberty Lobby's Populist Action Committee...[he] is particularly fond of conspiracy theories, asserting that AIDS is a Federal conspiracy to ease population growth. He has also compared the U.S. government to the Soviet KGB and the Nazi Gestapo. He has expressed support for the white supremacist "Identity" movement, which preaches that Jews are "Satan's spawn" and that non-whites are "mud races." Gritz gives the distinct impression that he is preparing for a stand-off with the Federal government, stating: "The FBI knows me and the Special Forces know me...The last thing they want to do is tangle with me, because I'm trained in guerrilla warfare."[2]

During the worst of Ruby Ridge, Gritz became a prominent actor when he openly appealed to the public:

> On August 28, [he] issued a call for outraged citizens to converge on the Naples, Idaho area to demand the peaceful release of Randy Weaver and his family and avert further bloodshed. When news of Vicki Weaver's death reached the crowd, their anger became so intense that Gritz feared they would attack the police. McLamb asked several skinheads at the scene to stand between the police and the crowd. The skinheads cooperated. When they heard of Vicki's death, even the police officers at the roadblock appeared disgusted with the actions of the U.S. marshals in the Special Operations Group who had precipitated the violence, and were grateful for Gritz' influence in calming the crowd.[3]

---

[1] Ibid.
[2] The Nizkor Project, *Paranoia as Patriotism: Far Right Influences on the Militia Movement*, http://www.nizkor.org/hweb/orgs/american/adl/paranoia-as-patriotism/bo-gritz.html
[3] LaRosa, Benedict D.

Although Gritz was *not* an active participant in the cynical congregation that acted to seize the moment and propagandize Ruby Ridge in the aftermath of the trial, Gritz did recast the standoff, not once but many times with language that differed from story to story, leaning simultaneously toward denigrating law enforcement and projecting procedural impossibilities to exonerate the Weaver family. In this, he remained a "circus of one," juggling fact and fiction until they were one and the same.

NO HELP FOR THE PROSECUTION

I have, as a researcher, poked holes in the Weaver case by cross-referencing and dissecting contradictory statements made, in the main, by the political chameleon and anti-government negotiator Ret. Lt. Col. James "Bo" Gritz. This does not mean, in any sense, that I am unsympathetic to the plight of the Weaver family or that I disagree with those who have rightly condemned the extremism with which the government first attacked and then prosecuted Randall Weaver. Even if Randall did act to protect Samuel and Kevin (which was never alleged in court), there is no way to interpret that possibility as anything but defense. At no time did the Weavers actively "hunt" for federal agents, although they knew for months that their home was under surveillance. Instead, they took up protective positions whenever they left the cabin from fear of an invasion.

The last was consistent with the handwritten affidavit that the Weavers filed with the Boundary Court Clerk on February 28, 1985. "Claiming that persons around Deep Creek, Idaho were conspiring to endanger the Weaver family and to precipitate an attack on Randall Weaver's life" via forged letters and false statements submitted to legal authorities and prominent politicians, Randall "expressed fear that he would be killed or arrested for assault of a federal officer, if he tried to defend himself." He therefore gave "legal and official notice that [he] believe[d] [he] may have to defend [him] self and [his] family from physical attack on [his] life."[1]

To this, the government paid heed, but not as the Weavers had hoped. Instead of taking the fears of the family seriously, the affidavit was construed, like the letters later written by Vicki, as a threat to fight to the death. In the first case, the affidavit was filed as a threat-deterrent. In the second, Vicki's letters threw down the gauntlet. Having failed to distinguish between them and intervene on a small scale when the government still could have, federal agents finally mounted an assault that was no shoebox operation.

As noted by Benedict D. LaRosa:

---

[1] Lexis Counsel Connect, http://www.byington.org/carl/ruby/ruby4.1.html

When the F.B.I. took control of the situation Saturday afternoon, August 22, they imposed a news blackout and cordoned of an area 3 miles in radius from the Weaver home. All residents were evacuated. At least 200 heavily armed lawmen from the F.B.I., Bureau of Alcohol, Tobacco & Firearms, U.S. Marshall Service, and state and local police departments surrounded the Weaver home. They were supported by a National Guard command post, two M-113 Armored Personnel Carriers, three heavy trucks, 14 HUMVs, and two helicopters. Idaho Governor Cecil Andrus declared a state of emergency in the county where the Weaver home is located and an adjacent county, citing a danger to government buildings and a fugitive at large.[1]

And once the Weavers surrendered:

Snipers and camouflaged agents began crawling out of the woodwork...[A]s the Weavers noticed multiple armored carriers, helicopters flying overhead and a massive tent city at the base of the mountain, they could not believe their eyes. "All this for one family," Sara muttered as tears ran down her face.[2]

Yes, all of this, at the cost of one million dollars per day.[3]

THE MAKINGS OF THE NIGHTMARE

After his military discharge, Randall and Vicki married. Living in Iowa, which was then being inundated by Christian Identity evangelists, Randall worked at the John Deere plant in Waterloo, where a member of Aryan Nations popularized Richard Butler as an anti-Semitic leader who founded a compound in Idaho. Meanwhile, followers of James Ellison were exploiting the farm crisis to herd new recruits into the compound of the Covenant, the Sword and the Arm of the Lord on the Missouri-Arkansas border.[4] Since Montana, rather than Idaho or Missouri, was to be the Weaver's first choice of refuge, there is no evidence at this time that they were drawn to either leader, Richard Butler or James Ellison.

Instead, Randall and Vicki reacted in near panic to the Arab-Israeli war that followed Egypt's invasion of Israel in 1973.[5] Believing this war was the start of the End Times prophesied in the Bible, Vicki began an exhaustive search for knowledge that started with Hal Lindsey's *The Late Great Planet Earth*, which warned of a nuclear holocaust and the onset of Armageddon. Although the world would be wracked by violence and natural disasters

[1] LaRosa, Benedict D.
[2] Lohr, David.
[3] Ibid.
[4] Zeskind, Leonard.
[5] Lohr, David.

during "The Great Tribulation," God, according to Lindsey, would intervene via the "Rapture" to save his true followers. Moving on to *Atlas Shrugged*, Vicki embraced Ayn Rand's vision of apocalyptic socialism.[1] Then she read about the Great Illuminati ruling in Babylon, and the push for one world government by the Trilateral Commission and Council on Foreign Relations.[2] Subsequently, she and Randall adopted a conspiratorial world view linking them all together under a Zionist Occupied Government, referred to as "ZOG" by the anti-Semitic movement.

Although Vicki and Randall wanted no part of organized religion, believing that churches were in denial and therefore misleading their followers, they regularly met with like-minded radical Christians at the Cedar Falls Sambo's restaurant.[3]

According to Douglas Linder:

> Vicki pored over passages from her King James Bible, drawing lessons ranging from what to eat...to how to prepare for the "end time." In Matthew 24 she encountered the passage which reinforced her vision of their future: *Then let them which be in Judea flee into the mountains*...Randy began sleeping in a flak jacket with a loaded gun under his pillow. In an interview with a reporter for a Waterloo paper, they said they planned to build a house in the woods with a defensible 300-yard "kill zone" around its perimeter. They became increasingly isolated, as their radical beliefs caused them to lose former friends.[4]

By 1978, Vicki experienced recurrent visions of a mountaintop where she and her family would be safe. Vicki would also bear more children, who would be called Samuel and Rachel.[5] After being shown land in Montana, which proved to be too expensive, the Weavers found their mountain in Boundary County, Idaho.

ONE PART PURE HATRED

Quoting from *Guns in America*, edited by Jan E. Dizard:

> Self-reliance is Idaho's byword. The landscape fosters an American romance...that is equal parts Thoreau and manifest destiny—and one big part pure hatred of government. Up in the mountains of the panhandle, Idahoans bring those feelings to a high art. Local newspapers are filled with laments like the one that a husband and

---

[1] Linder, Douglas O., "The Ruby Ridge (Randy Weaver) Trial: An Account," 2010, http://law2.umkc.edu/faculty/projects/ftrials/weaver/weaveraccount.html
[2] Lohr, David.
[3] Linder, Douglas O.
[4] Ibid.
[5] Lohr, David.

wife, new to the state, sent to *The Clearwater Progress* in Kamia to complain about Federal policy on land use and schooling: "we eat the bitter bread of tyranny and the cake of oppression." For people like this, Idaho offers not only a landscape but a coherent politics, a world view: survivalism, tax protest, apocalypse, conspiracy theories. A woman in Kamiah urges you to investigate sightings of black helicopters, which, she has heard, are a sign that the United Nations is about to take over America's Armed Forces...And the publisher of *The Clearwater Progress*, Bill Glenn shows you the plastic security strip they're putting in $20 bills, and says this is a step toward one world government.[1]

In northern Idaho, the community of Coeur d'Alene divided on the issue of Richard Butler and his Aryan Nations compound. Some shared his views while others chose to ignore them. Those who opposed Butler by forming the Kootenai County Task Force on Human Relations in 1981 did so at personal risk. After a restaurant owned by a Jewish family was painted with swastikas, the activists protested—and one leader's home was bombed while he sat in his living room.[2]

Quoting again from *Guns in America*:

> Inevitably Butler seeded violence. In 1984 a group linked to the Aryan Nations and calling itself the Order went on a...spree of bank robberies...bombings and killings...The F.B.I. was "behind the ball" on the Order, recalled Wayne Manis, then the special agent in charge of the F.B.I.'s Coeur d'Alene office. But officials were far better organized when a second Order group with connections to the Aryan Nations began a crime spree in 1986, setting off several bombs in the Coeur d'Alene area and threatening greater destruction: bombs for gay discos in Portland, cyanide for the water supply of Los Angeles. "The F.B.I. did Order 1," says Tony Steward, the current president of the Kootenai County Task force. "Order 2 was F.B.I., A.T.F., Secret Service, the sheriff's office and the state police"...The F.B.I. was all over northern Idaho; they weren't going to be surprised again.[3]

This was the coming criminal backdrop that the Weaver family bought into when it found Vicki's mountain in 1983.

HOLY ROLLERS AND TACTICAL SOLDIERS

In Boundary County, the Weavers built a cabin, intending to raise chickens, garden, and live off the land. Vicki home-schooled their children while Randall armed the family for the coming of Armageddon. He bought

[1] Dizard, Jan E. ed., *Guns in America: A Reader* (New York: New York University Press, 1999), pp. 427-428.
[2] Ibid.
[3] Ibid.

two Ruger Mini 14 semi-automatics, a pump-action Remington shotgun, and plenty of ammunition.[1]

In the words of former friend Tony Brown:

> "The Weavers were a curious blend of religious holy rollers and tactical soldiers of God, plus reactionaries. They reacted to things around them. So you're on the defensive, things aren't going the way you want them to do. Which is why I dropped out of the egomaniac-driven society in Oregon and followed a path of my own. But Weaver believes the Bible tells people of the knowledge and that they should expound that knowledge to their brothers and sisters. Form a body of true believers. Part of their life was sharing with people what they thought. They weren't pushy, but they thought a remnant or small group of people would bring about a new kingdom. Over the sheep type...Randy thought everyone was in for higher taxes, more restrictions, erosion of rights till you were a slave. One thing that sets his mental tone, he was a believer in absolute truth. I think the truth is pretty relative to what you know, two ideas can coexist. He was an idealist. The mission's right, we're going to do it."[2]

Before the BATF ever met him, Randy drove to Butler's compound to attend an Aryan Nations annual conference in 1986 (while Order 2 was in full swing). Then in 1989, he brought the family along.[3] "His children played with other children while men in Nazi regalia talked politics and Butler distributed leaflets for "a nigger shoot" along with anti-Semitic pamphlets on how the Jews were enslaving white men.[4]

THE ROLE OF NEIGHBORS

Because some people tired of the Weavers' preaching, while others accused them of stealing, they made enemies as well as friends. Most importantly, a boundary dispute with neighbor Terry Kinnison and the letters Kinnison later forged using Randall's name had a lasting impact, as later shown at the Weaver trial:

> Kinnison wrote letters to the FBI, Secret Service, and county sheriff alleging Weaver had threatened to kill the Pope, the President, and John V. Evans, governor of Idaho. In January 1985, the FBI and the Secret Service started an investigation. In February, Randy and Vicki Weaver were interviewed for hours by two FBI agents, two Secret Service agents, and the Boundary County sheriff and his chief investigator. Although the Secret Service was told that Weaver was a

---

[1] Ibid.
[2] Ibid.
[3] Zeskind, Leonard.
[4] Dizard, Jan E., ed., p. 427-428.

member of the Aryan Nations and that he had a large weapons cache at his residence, Weaver denied the allegations and no charges were filed. The investigation noted Weaver associated with Frank Kumnick, who was known to associate with members of the Aryan Nations. Weaver told the investigators that neither he nor Kumnick were members of the Aryan Nations, and described Kumnick as "associated with the Covenant, Sword and Arm of the Lord." On February 28, 1985, Randy and Vicki Weaver filed an affidavit with the county courthouse alleging that their personal enemies were plotting to provoke the FBI into attacking and killing the Weaver family.[1]

Whether it was due to the Weaver's perception of a conspiracy against them or to place power in the hands of the locals (as Randall claimed in public), his views when he ran for Boundary County sheriff in 1988 were summarized in one sentence: "The Federal income tax is the most cunning act of fraud that has been perpetrated against Americans since the introduction of paper money and the credit system."[2] He also distributed "get out of jail free cards," promising that if he were elected anyone convicted of a nonviolent crime would "get a second chance."[3] Nevertheless, Weaver lost the primary and only collected ten percent of the vote.

THE THREAT PROFILE

According to the 452-page report that was obtained after the standoff via Lexis Counsel Connect, what federal agents failed to realize was that many of the Weaver's neighbors were more radical than they were. The Secret Service was told, for example, that Weaver had "rigged his driveway with bombs" from expecting the world to end in two years, when his home would be under siege. Due to a "paranoid defensive attitude," he was alleged to have an enormous "cache of semi and fully automatic weapons" collected for "survivalist purposes."[4] When Deputy US Marshal Dave Hunt asked Bill Grider about Randy Weaver: "Why shouldn't I just go up there... and talk to him?" Bill Grider replied, "Let me put it to you this way. If I was sitting on my property and somebody with a gun comes to do me harm, then I'll probably shoot him."[5]

For his part, Bo Gritz may have added to government fears by noting that Weaver was an expert in explosives who could have rigged the trees with homemade mines and buried 55-gallon drums of jellied napalm at points around his home.

---

[1] "Ruby Ridge," Wikipedia, http://en.wikipedia.org/wiki/Ruby_Ridge
[2] Dizard, Jan E., ed., pp. 434-435.
[3] Lohr, David.
[4] Lexis Counsel Connect, http://www.byington.org/carl/ruby/ruby4.1.htm
[5] "Ruby Ridge," Wikipedia, http://en.wikipedia.org/wiki/Ruby_Ridge

In any event, the SOG team set forth its findings before the standoff in a Law Enforcement Operations Order, "which portrayed the situation as exceedingly difficult and Randy Weaver as 'extremely dangerous and suicidal.' The team concluded that the Weavers had been looking for a war with law enforcement and that Randy had most likely established numerous fortifications and defensive positions on his property. It is also concluded that since Randy was a former Green Beret, he had probably placed booby traps or command-detonated explosive devices throughout the property.[1]

THE TYRANT'S BLOOD SHALL FLOW

During Randall's arraignment, he was told that if the court found him guilty he would probably be required to pay the cost of the trial. Believing he would lose his home for having failed to turn informant,[2] Randall decided to stay on his mountain, making a moot issue of whether he received notification of the proper date of trial. As Vicki noted in letters to family, they were not going to play along with a "frame-up."[3] She began writing letters to government agencies about the "Beast One Order," stating "The tyrant's blood shall flow" and "Whether we live or die we will not obey you... war is upon our land."[4] She also wrote to the Aryan Nations, explaining, "We cannot make deals with the enemy. This is war against white sons of Isaac [sic]. We have decided to stay on this mountain. You could not drag our children away from us with chains." While the family prepared for war, neighbors and friends from Aryan Nations kept them in fresh supplies.[5]

WHO WAS IN CONTROL?

If, as contended by Bo Gritz, Vicki was the maternal head of the family and therefore the priority target of the F.B.I., we should ask how the F.B.I. arrived at this conclusion. On the one hand, it is true that Vicki wrote what can be considered incendiary letters to the Governor and other officials. On the other, the Threat Profile, when considered in investigation, noted that the report centered on Randall and was prepared by an agent who didn't even know him, such that he referred to Randall as Mr. Weaver throughout. As for the information the F.B.I. had gathered, none of it, aside from the initial interview by the F.B.I. and the Secret Service over the threatening letters written by Terry Kinnison, was considered first-hand knowledge, nor was the Threat Profile a "living document" because the F.B.I. agents never revised

---

[1] Lohr, David.
[2] Ibid.
[3] McGrail, Patrick J.
[4] Lohr, David.
[5] Zeskind, Leonard.

it. Instead, the information they gleaned from informants was added to the file without question, providing a body of allegations for which the F.B.I. had no way of knowing whether they reflected the facts.

Drawing at the same time on the posited characteristics of escalating tensions that affect internalization, such as a belief in mystical visions, meaningful signs and portents, Vicki readily described her visions and the family acted on them by moving to Weaver Mountain.

It is, however, important to make the distinction between belief in conspiracy theories—which, albeit grounded in some truth, may be called misperception due to irrational connections made between world events and literature (whether it is popular fiction, the Bible, or yet more conspiracy theory) and delusional perspectives, such as elevated narcissism and a sense of grandeur. Based on research only, the Weavers admitted to the former, but also displayed, in part, the latter, not from psychological breakdown but as if God had thrown them a lifeline. As noted, nervosa of the kind they suffered—the fear that The End was coming, but organized religion couldn't, or wouldn't, face it—led to a survivalist mindset. This may also be true of perfectly rational people. As a measure of pain avoidance, we naturally want to know how to avoid a crisis, how to be saved should it occur, and to spare other innocent people from being destroyed in the process. This is a form of empowerment that also produces balance.

Randall and Vicki can be seen as co-dependents with a stable configuration offset only in part by Vicki's instability, which is reflected in the things she wrote., i.e., "That war is upon our land," and "Whether we live or die, we will not obey you," to which she added, "You could not drag our children away from us with chains."

Thus, her externalization is equated to Randall's internalization—the fear that he was being set up by neighbors to be killed by federal agents—a fear that was very *rational* because it was grounded in *actions* that caused Randall to file of a defensive affidavit with the clerk of Boundary County.

Finally, because Randall's internalization and externalization are perfectly in proportion, Randall was prepared for violence as the most rational means he could think of to save himself and his family.

There is also no support for Gritz's allegation that Vicki was listed in the Threat Profile as the F.B.I.'s priority target. The words, "If you get the chance, take Vicki Weaver out," would have been damning in court, yet they were never voiced.

THE DEFENSE THAT WAS NEVER MOUNTED

The attorney for Kevin Harris believed that his client would make a sympathetic witness, as a good kid who had intended to do no harm. Gerry

Spence, on the other hand, had to soberly consider whether Sara Weaver would be too honest and admit that she stole from neighbors, referred to African Americans as "niggers," and frequently wore swastikas. As for Randall, Spence had told Weaver up front that he would only defend his family on the condition that Randall did not try to proselytize his beliefs. For Spence, there was no need to put his racist, government-hating client on the stand because, first and foremost, Randall was not charged with murder. Secondly, and decisively, the government was doing his job for him by unraveling its own case. Announcing that the defense waived its right to present any witnesses, Spence rested his case.[1]

HONEST OUTRAGE VERSUS POLITICAL OPPORTUNISM

During the Ruby Ridge standoff, neighbors, strangers, and people with or without agendas gathered without distinction to become united in protest. As reported by Leonard Zeskind:

> A twenty-four-hour vigil of movement activists and neighbors began, quickly growing to a permanent presence of almost two hundred men, women, and children standing nose to nose with the FBI at the barricades. Aryan Nations members gathered from Canada, Montana, and, of course, Idaho. Skinheads traveled from Las Vegas, Utah, and Oregon. Identity believers from throughout the Northwest joined with unbelievers to bear witness against federal agents. A camplike cook kitchen fed the protesters, who formed bonds across ideological lines. They cried with grief at the news of the deaths and screamed with rage at each newly arrived federal agent. They held aloft a bevy of homemade signs: DEATH TO ZOG... F.B.I. BURN IN HELL. But also more temperate pleas: KIDS KILLED TOO. TELL THE TRUTH. STOP. COME WALK WITH US. THE WEAVERS TODAY! – OUR FAMILIES TOMORROW. And an even more remarkable sign that read REMEMBER KENT STATE. RED SQUARE. TIANANMEN SQ. MY LAI. RUBY RIDGE...Some understood that their presence at the foot of...Weaver Mountain was acting as a brake on further bloodshed...Violent or nonviolent, enraged or prayerful, the protest represented a break with the movement's past practices. It brought together mainstreamers and vanguardists alongside non-movement people who were concerned about the immediate situation, but not sympathetic to the movement's final goals.[2]

Those who had gathered at Ruby Ridge understood implicitly what Jim Oliver expressed explicitly:

---

[1] Linder, Douglas O., "The Ruby Ridge (Randy Weaver) Trial: an Account," 2010, http://law2.umkc.edu/faculty/projects/ftrials/weaver/weaveraccount.html
[2] Zeskind, Leonard.

> [W]hy had the BATF picked Randy Weaver to set up as an informer? He was a man devoted to family, a man with no criminal record, a veteran who served his country with honor. It was Weaver's beliefs that made him an ideal target. His unorthodox religious and political views were far outside mainstream America. He was a white separatist. *And, Randy Weaver was little, a nobody.*[1] [Emphasis added.]

The same writer goes on to say, whether it pertains to one or all of us:

> [T]hat the United States government is supposed to serve its citizens, not entrap them, not defame them, not falsify evidence against them and absolutely not kill their children.[2]

Finally, Alan Bock spoke to the heart of the problem for militant white movements: that the BATF, in league with law enforcement, was succeeding all too well with defeating the spree of robberies and murders that were terrorizing northern Idaho in the wake of the Weaver standoff. By the time of the Weaver trial, Bock sounded like the voice of reason, arguing both sides:

> If you talked to some of the self-styled patriots who hung around the Boise courthouse, you would hear all kinds of scary theories. The Weaver operation was just a dress rehearsal for Waco, which was part of a government campaign to shut down, intimidate, or terrorize minority religious groups and political dissenters. Now and then, you'd hear that the real problem was Zionist control of the government. An ironworker hanging around the Naples General Store...saw it this way: "All these federal agencies—IRS, DEA, BATF, FBI, FDA—have too many agents trained in paramilitary tactics. They get itchy to see if the training really works, so every so often they have to target some poor sap."[3]

> Certainly [Bock contends] the BATF, which Reagan and Bush... budget cutters recommended abolishing, seems to be an agency in search of a mission...It currently carries out a mix of licensing, regulatory, tax-collection, and law-enforcement functions that could easily be handled by other agencies, if they are necessary at all. It's doubtful that the republic would be any poorer if the BATF ceased to exist.[4]

In other words, remove the agency that deals with them and militant white movements will be left to live in peace. The presumption that they

---

[1] Oliver, Jim "The Randy Weaver Case," *American Rifleman*, a publication of the N.R.A., http://www.lawfulpath.com/ref/weaver.shtml.
[2] Ibid.
[3] Bock, Alan W.
[4] Ibid.

want to is pressed as a foregone conclusion, when evidence to the contrary has been mounting year by year.

For evidence, I refer the reader to Appendix B, where "Terror from the Right," a report of hate crimes compiled by the Southern Poverty Law Center and printed in this book with their permission, factually supports the argument that "Leaderless Resistance" is very much alive.

"WE CAN'T LET THIS DIE AND GO AWAY"

On September 19, 1992, Louis Beam sponsored another gathering in Spokane, Washington, two hours from Ruby Ridge, where his first order of business was to distribute a wanted poster for citizens' arrest of U.S. Marshals, FBI agents, and agents of the ATF.[1]

Beam had been part of the protest at the foot of Weaver Mountain. Now he was ready to launch a post-Ruby Ridge campaign in Naples, Idaho, the town closest to Ruby Ridge, where the locals were heartbroken over the violence and willing to join with Beam in pressing for justice. It was to become a nationwide movement as Beam moved on to Colorado, where a much more purposeful gathering, comprised of the militant faithful, allowed Beam to resurrect his essay on "Leaderless Resistance," with the result that a vigilante group, calling itself the Divine Ways and Means Committee noted for the record that it would carry out "directives from God." Another group, the Sacred Warfare Action Tactics (SWAT) Committee clove to leaderless resistance, saying "Whatever resistance is done should be done without an earthly leader. Because we have been INFILTRATED as a nation."[2]

Meanwhile, Chris Temple, from United Citizens for Justice maintained that the crisis at Ruby Ridge represented a strategic moment:

> As horrible as the murders of Sam and Vicki Weaver had been...the killings provided a great opportunity. "All of us in our groups," Temple told the assembly, ". . . could not have done in the next twenty years what the federal government did for our cause in eleven days. . . what we need to do is to not let this die and go away."[3]

To do this:

> Temple argued for a new kind of unity, not just among white supremacists but between white supremacists and others— particularly their cousins on the Christian right who were neither biological (racial) determinists nor explicitly anti-Semitic. "We need to remember the Muslim's saying that my enemy's enemy is my friend.

---

[1] Zeskind, Leonard.
[2] Ibid.
[3] Ibid.

You know, we've got a common goal . . . to restore Christian government in this land so that our people, the descendants of Abraham, Isaac and Jacob— and any strangers that live among us, until we take care of that problem— so that everyone can live their lives free of fear."[1]

Because "strangers" in conspiracy parlance represent non-whites, everyone listening to Temple knew that "taking care of the problem" would mean eliminating undesirables, such as blacks who were snared by the movement to give it a non-racist face. The point was to achieve a Christian government and then dispose of the enemy. To achieve this reach, patriots whose views were not widely known were enlisted for the cause of presenting a respectable front.

Louis Beam put this in perspective. On a leaflet that he distributed was printed an assessment that would prove all too true, now that the movement had martyrdom to add to its list of weapons:

> The federals have made a terrible error in the Weaver case that they will long regret. Their cruelty and callous disregard for the rules of civilized warfare will have the effect of solidifying opposition to them. Long after Weaver has been tried and has been freed by the courts as an innocent man wrongfully accused, there will be 10,000 White men in this country who harbor in their hearts a terrible hatred for the federals and all they stand for.[2]

In retribution for Ruby Ridge and the siege at Waco, TX, one such white man, Timothy McVeigh, went on to kill 168 people in the Oklahoma City Bombing of 1995.

---

[1] Ibid.
[2] Ibid.

CHAPTER 9. THE BRANCH DAVIDIAN SIEGE

As the product of a schism within The Davidian Seventh Day Adventist church, the Branch Davidians of Waco, Texas, were established by Benjamin Roden in 1955. Upon Roden's death, his wife Lois took over the church and later had an affair with Vernon Howell, a young man who joined the Branch Davidians in 1981. After Lois died in 1986, her son George attempted to lead but found himself contested by Vernon Howell, who claimed to be a prophet and later named himself David Koresh.[1] Proposing that true leadership would stem from power to raise the dead, George Roden challenged Koresh, who reported George to the authorities for exhuming a corpse. There was a gunfight between them that left Roden injured, after which he was jailed for contempt of court in another case. Koresh was then awarded a mistrial over his part in the shooting.[2]

Claiming that he could interpret Biblical Revelation and the significance of the Seven Seals, Koresh separated all married couples and took the wives as his own. As "God," Koresh asserted that they were handmaidens of the "Lord," with a duty to spread his seed and generate an army. Their true husbands, the so-called Mighty Men, became the guards of King Solomon's bed and Koresh's primary soldiers.[3]

---

[1] "The Standoff in Waco," Texas Observer, April 18, 2013, http://www.texasobserver.org/the-standoff-in-waco/
[2] "Federal agents raid the Branch Davidian compound in Waco, TX," This day in history, February 28, 1993, http://www.history.com/this-day-in-history/federal-agents-raid-the-branch-davidian-compound-in-waco-texas
[3] Ramsland, Katherine, "David Koresh: Millennial Violence," ‹crimelibrary›, http://www.crimelibrary.com/notorious_murders/not_guilty/koresh/11.html

In all, Koresh "married" a total of fifteen women and girls, some as young as twelve,[1] and according to later reports, he often regaled his flock with sexual stories and details inappropriate for children in order to prepare them for the honor of sharing his bed when they matured.

Although all Seventh Day Adventists believe that the second coming of Christ and the end of the world are imminent, by 1992 Koresh began to behave as if the Branch Davidians were already under siege. Weapons and food were stockpiled, and he began to question his followers on how far they were willing to fight the "Babylonian" government, up to and including taking their own lives. According to defectors, he taught the children to use a gun or cyanide as the means of suicide.[2]

ENTER THE BATF

There are two theories of why the BATF became involved. The first is that a UPS driver tipped them off to the delivery of supplies for grenades. The second (which is listed in the BATF investigation), is that a neighbor complained of hearing rapid machine gun fire, thereby inferring that the Branch Davidians were illegally altering weapons. This led the BATF to collect background on the case, although nothing surfaced to support the neighbor's complaint. According to the dealer who sold to the Branch Davidians, they kept proper records of their guns and would be willing to allow the BATF to inspect the weapons at their compound. That the BATF refused to speak with Koresh at this time meant the issue was more than guns. Aside from having knowledge that the local newspaper was about to run a story on Koresh entitled "The Sinful Messiah," those who defected from Koresh had alleged that he committed statutory rape, mandated child abuse, and even demanded suicide as proof of loyalty and obedience should the compound be invaded. Invoking the specter of Jonestown, he was, to the BATF, not a charismatic leader but a dangerous psychopath to be taken out root and branch.

To prove his true nature, they couldn't just grab him off the street. Instead, he had to be provoked, even if it meant acquiring an arrest warrant on the basis of conjecture, which is what took place.

> According to the affidavit presented by ATF investigator David Aguilera to U.S. Magistrate Dennis G. Green on February 25, 1993, the Branch Davidian gun business, the Mag Bag, had purchased many legal guns and gun parts from various legal vendors, such as 45 semi-automatic AR-15 lower receivers from Olympic Arms...None of the weapons and firearms were illegally obtained nor illegally owned

---

[1] Ibid.
[2] Ibid.

by the Mag Bag; however, Aguilera affirmed to the judge that in his training and experience, in the past other purchasers of such legal gun parts had modified them to make illegal firearms. The search warrant was justified not on the basis of there being proof that the Davidians had purchased anything illegal, but on the basis that they could be modifying legal arms to illegal arms, and that automatic weapon fire had been reported from the compound. The affidavit of Aguilera for the search warrant claimed that there were over 150 weapons in the compound. The paperwork on the AR-15 components cited in the affidavit showed that they were in fact legal semi-automatics; however, Aguilera told the judge: "I have been involved in many cases where defendants, following a relatively simple process, convert AR-15 semi-automatic rifles to fully automatic rifles of the nature of the M-16." Aguilera stated in the affidavit and later testified at trial that a neighbor had heard machine gun fire; however, Aguilera failed to tell the magistrate that the same neighbor had previously reported the noise to the local Waco sheriff, who investigated the neighbor's complaint.[1]

Similarly, the BATF claimed that Koresh was manufacturing methamphetamines, ignoring the evidence that a lab had indeed existed when the Branch Davidians purchased the property, but that Koresh had dismantled it and turned it over to the local Sheriff for destruction.[2]

In the meantime, BATF agents had tried to infiltrate the sect. Female agents, posing as college students, drew suspicion almost at once. A neighbor across the street who asked the Davidians to help fix up his house, strangely moved in with rifles instead of furniture. Then a man named Robert Rodriguez expressed interest in learning everything David could teach but declined to move into the compound.

"THE SINFUL MESSIAH"

As it happened, the local newspaper broke its story, and the first installment of "The Sinful Messiah" became available to the Branch Davidians the day before the arrest warrant was due to expire. The next day Agent Rodriguez informed the BATF that the Davidians were on to them. Having lost the element of surprise, they would put themselves at risk if they tried to serve the warrant.

From the BATF's point of view, it was a Sunday, when the Davidians were known to lock up their weapons and spend the day in prayer. Thus a coordinated attack could still work. If everything went according to plan,

---

[1] "The Waco Siege," Wikipedia,
[2] Ibid.

three teams would be deployed in thirteen seconds to "protect the children, neutralize the military force, and seize the arms."[1]

Instead, Koresh opened the door when they knocked and then slammed it shut. During the ensuing shootout, Koresh was shot in the wrist and side. In the dispute over who fired first, the Davidians claimed that bullets were fired by overhead helicopters, forcing the women to throw themselves over the children. Others claimed that the agents were shooting the dogs to get them out of the way.

In any case, the agents' preparedness for violence was evident. They wore Kevlar vests and body armor, and each agent had his blood type written on his neck or arm.[2]

TWO SIDES OF THE STORY

According to researcher Carol Moore, the Davidians were attacked with overwhelming force, both from the air and on the ground. They ultimately refused to leave the compound because they feared it would be destroyed, taking their evidence along with it—the bullet holes in the ceilings and walls—which proved that the BATF's mission was murder from the word go.

If this actually made sense, there would have been no need for the six weeks of painstaking negotiation leading up to the conflagration. Moreover, there were agents all over the rooftop within seconds of Koresh slamming the door in their face. The likelihood of helicopter fire is disproved by the actions of the BATF, during which agents were killed, and not by friendly fire:

> The first ATF casualty was an agent who had made it to the west side of the building before he was wounded. Agents quickly took cover and fired at the buildings while the helicopters began their diversion... The Branch Davidians fired on the helicopters...and the helicopters immediately stopped the mission... On the east side of the compound, agents hauled out two ladders and set them against the side of the building. Agents then climbed onto the roof...On the west slope of the roof, three agents reached Koresh's window and were crouching beside it when they came under fire. One agent was killed and another wounded. The third agent scampered over the peak of the roof and joined other agents attempting to enter the arms room. The window was smashed, a flashbang stun grenade thrown in, and three agents entered the arms room. When another tried to follow them, a hail of bullets penetrated the wall and wounded him, but he was able

---

[1] Ibid.

[2] "The Waco massacre, a fiery end to a whacko cult," April 18, 2013, news. com.au, http://www.news.com.au/world/the-waco-massacre-a-fiery-end-to-a-whacko-cult/story-fndir2ev-1226623449407

to reach a ladder and slide to safety. An agent fired with his shotgun at Branch Davidians who were shooting at him until he was hit in the head and killed. Inside the arms room, the agents killed a Branch Davidian gunman and discovered a cache of weapons but then came under heavy fire and two were wounded. As they escaped, the third agent laid down covering fire, killing a Branch Davidian. As he made his escape, he hit his head on a wooden support beam and fell off the roof, but survived. An agent outside provided them with covering fire but was shot by a Branch Davidian and killed instantly.[1]

From noises inside, said agents in later hearings, it was clear that the cult had some heavy artillery. Bullets even pierced the reporters' cars and then concussion grenades, known as "flash-bangs" exploded among the agents. Koresh and his crew appeared to have superior weapons. They also had the advantage of cover, while the agents were out in the open.[2]

At the end of the initial skirmish, the F.B.I. counted four dead and sixteen wounded.

According to Alan A. Stone, the Branch Davidians did not ambush the BATF. Rather they defended themselves and their compound, consistent with their view that the End Time was upon them.

THE MILLENNIALISM FACTOR

Portrayed by Alan A. Stone as "desperate religious fanatics expecting an apocalyptic ending in which they were destined to die defending their sacred ground and destined to achieve salvation,"[3] the Branch Davidians never took up the offensive. They respected the ceasefire that allowed the BATF to remove their dead and wounded, and talked for at least a thousand hours in ensuing negotiations.

To the analytic community, apocalyptic cults are either offensive or defensive. Defensive violence is used to defend an enclave specifically created to eliminate outside contact.

The Branch Davidians, who often worked in town or traveled to other regions on evangelizing missions, did not fit the isolationist profile. They did, however, fit the *political profile* associated with millennialsm:

...millennial thinking, however spiritually put, is political thinking. All millennialists hope that commitment to their beliefs will spread far and wide enough to bring about a transformation of the social, and therefore the political, universe. That is the very essence of

---

[1] Ramsland, Katherine.
[2] Ibid.
[3] "The Waco Siege," Wikipedia.

millennialism, as opposed to other forms of eschatology: the just live free in this world. It might be by and by, but the messianic promise is no pie in the sky. It's a transformation of humanity, an evolutionary leap to a different way of human interaction. To use the language of evolutionary epidemiology, millennialism is a meme programmed to spread as far and wide as possible. To use the language of political science, millennialism is a (the first?) revolutionary ideology.[1]

To suggest that millennialism is politics parading as religion is to miss the point entirely. Because it is religious conviction that inspires evangelism, the political world is one that religious groups must necessarily contend with.

Citing Saddam Hussein's 1990 invasion of Kuwait and the "New World Order" speech of former President George W. Bush as events which instigated cult formation, the F.B.I. Law Enforcement Bulletin of September 1999 goes on to say:

> ...in a speech before the Council of Christian Broadcasters, [Bush] talked about "a moral and just war to defeat the tyranny of Saddam, a madman who threatens the burgeoning New World Order...." Most individuals who heard these words believed that President Bush was talking about an international community united by a sense of justice and the rule of law. Others, however, have cited those statements as proof that the U.S. government is involved with international forces in a plot to replace democracy in America with a tyrannical, Communist-like dictatorship. Others suggest that foreign troops have arrived clandestinely in the United States to await orders to round up any Americans who oppose this presumed New World Order. Some individuals allege that gun control legislation represents a ploy to assemble lists of gun owners in order to arrest them and transport them to concentration camps, which supposedly are secretly under construction by [FEMA] the Federal Emergency Management Agency. Still others have gone so far as to assert that the tragedies at Ruby Ridge and Waco served as dry runs for future government actions by New World Order storm troopers.[2]

In effect:

> The examination of domestic extremist groups reveals three social-psychological components that appear to interact to produce an effect known as the Lethal Triad. In particular, extremist groups physically and psychologically isolate their members from mainstream society.

---

[1] Newport, Kenneth G.C. and Gribben, Crawford, eds., Expecting the End: Millennialism in Social and Historical Context (Baylor University Press: Waco, TX, 2006), p. 4.

[2] FBI Law Enforcement Bulletin, September 1999, Volume 68, Number 9, p. 3.

This isolation causes a reduction of critical thinking on the part of group members, who become more entrenched in the belief proposed by the group leadership. As a result, group members relinquish all responsibility for group decision making to their leader and blame the cause of all group grievances on some outside entity or force, a process known as projection. Finally, isolation and projection combine to produce pathological anger, the final component of the triad.[1]

While the "Lethal Triad" theory may apply to offensive militant movements, which, as I noted in Appendix A, may evolve from the dual growth of triangular representations, whereby perceptions of hurt and humiliation are both externalized and internalized in equal proportion as the most dangerous of all stable and unstable outcomes, it does not fit the Branch Davidian profile insofar as the group was neither hostile in public relations nor suffering repressed anger of pathological proportions. Being armed and ready, in this instance, does not equate to fury. Instead, it is a compromise between religious duty (to die as proof of final redemption— and the only way to earn it) and common pain avoidance (the hope that self-defense will overcome the forces of evil), allowing the group to survive Armageddon and take its place in the New Jerusalem promised by the Bible.

"GOOD" COP, "BAD" COP

After the initial violence, the BATF received backup from local police, Texas Rangers, members of the F.B.I.'s Hostage Rescue Team (HRT), the F.B.I.'s Special Agent in Charge from the San Antonio office, a bomb squad, and several U.S. Marshals. Almost from the start, the BATF disagreed with the Hostage Rescue Team. The latter preferred a show of force as the means to undermine Koresh's strength and the faith of his followers; a strategy that had backfired when the BATF attempted to serve their warrant. Since the use of force only played to Koresh's belief that the End Time was upon them, it provided a test of faith that strengthened the resolve of the Davidian group overall. To make matters worse, apostates of the group advised the BATF that a siege could trigger mass suicide.

In the meantime, Koresh used the ceasefire to contact the media, and particularly CNN, during which he described the danger to his flock and the many children involved. He also claimed to be mortally wounded, with little time to live.

Until the takeover by Jeffrey Jamar (the F.B.I.'s Special Agent-in-Charge), the BATF's Critical Incident Negotiation Team spoke to Koresh by phone and also enlisted the help of the Waco Police Department. As agents and police officers attempted to reason with the Davidians, Jamar apparently

[1] Ibid., p. 4.

decided to play "bad cop" to their "good cop," and commenced cutting the compound's electricity at irregular intervals, blasting recordings over the loudspeakers, and using high-powered lights to make sleep impossible.

This angered the BATF, as well as the team of psychologists brought in to assist with the siege. Jack Zimmerman, Steve Schneider's attorney later said:

> "The point was this—they were trying to have sleep disturbance and they were trying to take someone that they viewed as unstable to start with, and they were trying to drive him crazy. And then they got mad 'cos he does something that they think is irrational!"[1]

As described by Waco survivor David Thibodeau, who wrote of the siege in retrospect:

> It is hell. Day and night booming speakers blast us with wild sounds—blaring sirens, shrieking seagulls, howling coyotes, wailing bagpipes, crying babies, the screams of strangled rabbits, crowing roosters, buzzing dental drills, off-the-hook telephone signals. The cacophony of speeding trains and hovering helicopters alternates with amplified recordings of Christmas carols, Islamic prayer calls, Buddhist chants and repeated renderings of whiny Alice Cooper and Nancy Sinatra's pounding, clunky lyric, "These Boots Were Made for Walking." Through the night the glare of brilliant stadium lights turns our property into a giant fishbowl. The young children and babies in our care, most less than eight years old, are terrified.[2]

Speaking on behalf of the Davidians, Thibodeau underscores the psychological hurt sustained during the siege—that they viewed themselves as victims of arbitrary authority exercising religious intolerance:

> [The] torments are intended to sap our wills and compel us to surrender to an authority that refuses to accept that we are a valid religious community with deeply held beliefs. All our attempts to explain our commitment to what we believe has been dismissed as mere "Bible babble."[3]

As for why most of the Davidians refused to leave the compound, Thibodeau writes:

> The people who chose to leave...after the ATF attack, and the parents who stayed...but sent out some or all of their children, made agonizing decisions to trust the solemn word of the FBI that all would be treated with respect. The feds guaranteed that the children would be allowed to remain with their parents or be reunited with relatives

---

[1] "The Waco Siege, " Wikipedia,
[2] Thibodeau, David and Whiteson, Leon, A Place Called Waco: A Survivor's Story (New York: Public Affairs, 1999), p. v.
[3] Ibid.

waiting in Waco. But the feds promptly betrayed their word. They separated children from their parents, some of whom were arrested, and placed the kids in public care; they shackled the adults, even some of the elderly women, and threatened to indict them all for attempted murder. These broken promises and hostile actions on the part of the federal government certainly don't inspire the rest of us to leave the fragile security of our collective home.[1]

The release of children, however, persuaded the F.B.I. that Koresh might eventually give up. This was denied by a psychological consultant, who contended that Koresh would never surrender. As one writer put it, "God was not going to prison."[2]

THE PUBLICITY ANGLE

When the F.B.I. rerouted the phone lines so that all calls went straight to the F.B.I., Koresh became angry. Sheets were hung from the windows with lettering that read, "God help us. We need the press!" In response, the press held up their own sign. "God help us. We *are* the press."

Desperate to spread his message, Koresh offered to let everyone go if an hour-long tape he made would be shown on national television, to which the F.B.I. agreed. Hours after the tape was broadcasted by Christian radio stations, Koresh reneged on the agreement, saying that God had told him to wait. After this, negotiators made little to no headway. Koresh alternated between Bible readings and statements of resistance. Negotiators were exasperated, but they listened anyway, until Koresh admitted that the remaining children were his and would not be released.

On the advice of a psychiatrist, who diagnosed Koresh with "antisocial and narcissistic traits as well as paranoid and grandiose delusions," the F.B.I. agreed that its "best approach was to validate his ideas and get him to believe that his mission had not yet been accomplished."[3]

> Trying to resolve things quickly, the negotiators tried to put together a strategy that relied on those things that Koresh most wanted. They knew he had won in court against Boden, and that he appeared to be enjoying all the sudden fame, so they worked on that angle: The ATF had attacked, they could prove it from the crime scene, and Koresh could take them to court and win. He would then draw even more followers and the Branch Davidians would be known all over the world. They were already on the cover of the major news

---

[1] Ibid., p. vi.
[2] Ramsland, Katherine.
[3] Ibid.

magazines and the world was watching. Koresh could parlay this into something beneficial for himself and his followers.[1]

Presumably, this did not work because Koresh knew he would face murder and child abuse charges.

The F.B.I. then shifted to a strategy of taping the children who had been released to show they were being cared for and to urge their parents to join them. They also recorded phone conversations where Koresh cast doubt upon his own teachings, and then played them over the loudspeaker, hoping to shock his followers.

On March 12, Special Agent in Charge Jamar shut off the electricity for good. This too upset the negotiators as much as the Branch Davidians. Then "the HRT drained the compound's diesel storage tanks."[2]

More adults came out over the following days, such that another offer was made to Koresh:

> In prison he could communicate with his followers and make a worldwide broadcast on CNN. In order to have these privileges, Koresh and his people had to leave by 10:00 the following day, March 23.[3]

Koresh didn't bite.

THE PATH TO CONFLAGRATION

On March 25th an ultimatum passed to send out a minimum of twenty people, upon which the F.B.I. began to clear the yard of vehicles. Then the arrival of Passover provided another hiatus that lasted for seven days after.

By then, the F.B.I. could see that it would only face more delay tactics. Discussions concerning the use of tear gas were resumed. Attorney General Janet Reno was consulted. She asked whether the gas could harm the children, and she was told that it wouldn't.

The substance used by the F.B.I., chlorobenzylidene malononitrile (CS gas), was believed not to be flammable—but it was. There was also the added danger that it might come in contact with flames from kerosene lamps, which the Davidians had been using since Jamar cut off the power.

Koresh now professed a need to write of the Seven Seals. He asked for writing supplies and received them.

In the ensuing negotiations, taped and later released by the Justice Department, both sides in the standoff remained intransigent in their

---

[1] Ibid.
[2] Ibid.
[3] Ibid.

positions. As is clear from the following transcript, agents were losing their patience and Koresh's ability to stall them was no longer working:[1]

THE DIALOGUE

Tape One—April 16, 1993

> Koresh: ...I say that when I get through writing these, and they're given to my attorney, and my attorney hands them over—What's the two theologians names?

> Steve Schneider: Ah—Philip Arnold and Jim Tabor.

> Koresh: Philip Arnold and Jim Tabor who has shown that they have a sincere interest in these things—you see? Then I can spend all my time in jail, and people can go ahead and ask me all the stupid questions they want—cause they're not gonna ask me about the seals. They're gonna say, "Ah, do you molest young ladies?" "Ah, have you eaten babies?" "Do you sacrifice people?" "Ah, do you make automatic weapons?" "Ah, do you have [unintelligible]" That's what they're gonna be interested in—sensationalism.

> FBI: That's why you need to get it done before you leave there then.

> Koresh: That's why I'm gonna complete it, because you see, you know as well as I do that people in this world they want something dramatic and sensational. They don't want to have to sit—No one's gonna sit there—and let me sit there in front of a camera and read Psalms 40 to them—to prove the first seal. Dick, it's a real world, and that's why I'm sympathetic with your position. I realize you're frustrated, and I agree with you.

> FBI: I'm not frustrated. I went home and I'm back. I'm no longer frustrated. I never was frustrated.

> Koresh: Did you take a shower for me?

> FBI: Well, yeah. I took a couple of them for you.

> Koresh: Thank you. I appreciate it.

> FBI: Now listen. Let's get back to the point in hand. This ah—you know—the writing of the seals. OK. You've got to do that in there, and it's gonna take you x amount of time. But—just tell me this David— are you saying that when you finish that manuscript—

---

[1] "Transcript of Waco Negotiations," Serendipity, http://www.serendipity.li/waco/tapes.html

Koresh: Then I'm not bound any longer [unintelligible]—

FBI: No. But see, that doesn't answer the question.

Koresh: Then I'll be out—yes—definitely.

FBI: I know you'll be out, but that could—excuse me I've got a cold. That could mean a lot of things David. That could mean—

Koresh: I'll be in custody in the jailhouse. You can come down there and feed me bananas if you want.

FBI: I know—I know that some point in time that's true. But I'm getting from you—I'm asking you, "When that is finished, are you than telling me that you are coming out the next day, or two hours after you send that out or what?"

Koresh: Oh, I'll probably—when I—when I bring it out—see—my attorney is gonna get the—get to the copy.

FBI: Right.

Koresh: OK? And as soon as he hands it over to the scholars—the theologians—right?

FBI: Um, hm.

Koresh: That's when—he's gonna come back, and that's when I'm going to go out with him, because he said point blank that—you know—one of the guarantees of me arriving down there is that he is gonna go with me.

FBI: So you go on paper here and said that David Koresh told me that as soon as he finishes this manuscript—the seven seals—of which you've finished the first chapter dealing with the first seal—

Koresh: The first seal—right.

FBI: That you're gonna make that available—

Koresh: I'll be splitting out of this place. I'm so sick of MRE's—Dick— that ah—

FBI: Well, I just want to make sure that I have this right—that you're coming out. As soon as that's finished—

Koresh: That's what—it was said by the attorney's—

FBI: Well, I know—I know.

Koresh: That's what I'm saying—

FBI: OK.

Koresh: It's clarified. Lock, stock, and barrel it.

FBI: I mean—I've heard you say that you're coming out after, but that is not specific. You know—that's a game that we all can play.

Koresh: It's—look, I know. Dick—

FBI: But I'm asking you for your word. You say that you're coming out as soon as that's done, and you give up the manuscript to DeGuerin who is gonna make copies available for Arnold and the other—the other fella—

Koresh: Right.

FBI: The other Biblical scholar, and then you are coming out with that manuscript.

Koresh: I'm outta here. And he's he's gonna come, and the way the procession is to be—I'm to go out first with him, and then I think, "You're last, right Steve?"

Steve Schneider: Yeah.

Koresh: With his attorney, and the other people—the other people in between.

FBI: OK. Then—you know what? I'm keeping you from getting back to work. So I'm—you know what I'm gonna do? I'm gonna let you go so that you can get back to work, because David, frankly I'm eagerly awaiting this manuscript.

Koresh: Well, I'll tell you what. It's gonna blow your socks off.

FBI: Well—I'm—I'm perfectly willing to—to read it, and I'm looking forward to it as a member—

Koresh: You'll either hate me or love me then.

FBI: Well, I want to read it—and then—I'll—you know—make a decision then, and we'll see how it goes. And in the meantime, ah— you know—let's get that thing written.

Tape Two—April 16, 1993

FBI: Now are you telling me David—I want to get this clear in my own mind. Are you telling me here and now that as soon as you reduce the seven seals to a written form that you're coming out of there. I don't mean two days later—

Koresh: I have no reason—I have no reason to—

FBI: I know what you're saying, but answer my question if you would please—definitely. I mean—I want to get an answer to this, "Are you coming out as soon as your done—"

Koresh: I'm coming out.

FBI: Or are you coming out afterwards at some point in time.

Koresh: After I get the thing—see Dick, you don't seem to understand. We are going to fulfill our commitment to God. Now, if you would allow me to show you what has been pre-written by the prophets you would know what I am doing.

FBI: Well, I'm asking you—

Koresh: You see—

FBI: A simple question though. I—

Koresh: And I'm giving you the simple answer. Yes. Yes. Yes. I never intended to die in here.

April 18, 1993

FBI: This is Henry.

Koresh: Ah—Henry, this is Dave.

FBI: Hi Dave.

Koresh: Look. The ah—the generals out here—right? You have a hard time controlling them, right?

FBI: I don't control them. No.

Koresh: OK. Well look. We have done everything we can to be able to communicate in a nice, passionate way. We've ah—you know—I've told you what our work with God is. And ah—we've been kind. We've not been your everyday kind of cult. We've not been your everyday kind of terrorist which I'm sure you—you're familiar with having to deal with.

FBI: Um, hm.

Koresh: And a lot of the things that the FBI, or these generals are doing is just kinda way beyond the scope of reason. And they're not only destroying private property, they're also removing evidences. And this doesn't seem like that ah—these are—these are moves that should be made by a government who says to people that we're going to be able to take this up in a court of law. I mean—they're not ever— they're not going to be able to replace a lot of things here. Like that 68 SS El Camino that belonged to Paul Fatta?

FBI: Um, hm.

Koresh: They'll never be able to replace that. They don't have any more of those. And ah—the 68 Camaro and other things out here in the front.

FBI: Um, hm.

Koresh: They can't replace that. They just can't replace it.

FBI: Um, hm.

Koresh: And—ah—they keep—they keep doing these kind of things it's just proving to us that they're not—they're not showing good faith on their part, and I just—I just suggest they shouldn't do it.

FBI: I understand what you're saying, and I will impart that ah—

Koresh: In all courtesy's please—please impart that, because—because it's coming to the point to where ah—you know—God in heaven has somewhat to do also. And it's just really coming to the point of really, "What—What do you men really want?"

FBI: I think what—you know—just—this is—I'm just imparting to you what my perception is. And my perception is that—that—what they want is they want you and everybody to come out. You know—I—

Koresh: I don't think so. I think what they're showing is that they don't want that.

FBI: Well, I think that—that is exactly what they want.

Koresh: No. They're not gonna—they're not gonna—they're not gonna get that. They're not gonna get that by what they're doing right now. They're gonna get exactly the opposite—exactly the opposite. They're gonna get wrath on certain people. They're gonna get anger from certain guys. Now I can't control everybody here.

FBI: I think you can.

Koresh: No. I can't. You gotta understand John—

FBI: Henry.

Koresh: Henry—I'm sorry. In 1985, I presented a truth. And everybody that's here—I had to debate and I had to talk to, and I had to show from the scriptures. I had to prove my point for many hours, days, months, and sometimes years with certain people here.

FBI: Um, hm.

Koresh: They went to scholars. They went to theologians. I have a very unique group here.

FBI: Yes. You do.

Koresh: Not ignorant people—not stupid people. Now there are some people—that in the beginning—that went out like Kevin and Brad. Individuals that were—you know—people that were out there—bar rollers and stuff like that. Rough and tough guys. Now they're not—they're not the theologians of the world, but they're guys that need a lot of patience, and—you know—with a little bit of refinement and a little bit of proof to them—they can—they can be good people.

FBI: Um, hm.

Koresh: But ah—but I would really and in all honesty and in good faith tell these generals to ah—to—to back up. They don't need to tear up anymore of this property. You tell us out of one side of the mouth, we're going to be able to come back here and all this. And ah—you know—we're gonna take this up in court, and on the other hand you're showing us there's not gonna be nothing to come back to.

FBI: I think the problem with this thing David is that this thing has lasted way too long.

Koresh: Oh, it—it—it has. It should have never gotten started this way—

FBI: You're right.

Koresh: And that was not our fault.

FBI: Ok. But—

Koresh: Now you don't wish to speak to the issues of the beginning of this—

FBI: No. I don't. And—and what the issues were—you know at that time is something else. The problem is not what the issues were at that time—the problem is this has lasted way too long. You know—

Koresh: I'm gonna finish my book or I'm not gonna finish my book.

FBI: Well, I hope that you do.

Koresh: Well, let me tell you this. These men who every day we try to show them good faith. They've walked out in front of us, they've driven their tanks up to us, they've bust in the side of the building a little bit one time. You said that was a mistake—it was not in your control—that wasn't in the commander's wishes. You know—all of this has been shown that if these guys want to fight—Now I don't want to fight. I—I want—I'm a life too, and there's a lot of people in here that are lives. There's children in here.

FBI: That's right.

Koresh: And we're also Americans. And I think—I think that America has a patronage—a very clear patronage of individual citizens who—who—who—who have a breaking point.

FBI: Well, that's true.

Koresh: Now if the government is gotten this stronger—it can come on to something that we have worked for hard. We worked when we got on this property. A lot of hard hours. This place was a dump. We fixed it up. We built this little house here. It's not extravagant. You know—there's a lot of people here with a high commission and a lot of love and concern, not just for our own lives, but for everybody's life. And if this is the way our government is showing the world that its tactics are to get someone to—to—to—to—to do as they wish when realistically, our—our rights have been infringed upon right and left.

FBI: But there's a way to resolve that David.

Koresh: Yes. Yes.

FBI: And the way to resolve it is for you to come out and lead your people out.

Koresh: Your way—your way is that you're gonna keep—you're gonna keep destroying our property.

FBI: This—this probably would not have had to happen—

Koresh: It never did have to happen.

FBI: That's right. And—and then—you know—if you would have come out on—on the day that you indicated that you promised that you were gonna come out none of this would have taken place.

Koresh: Look. You denounce the fact that I have a God that communicates with me. That's—that's the first mistake that we—that we make.

FBI: Nobody—nobody—nobody is saying anything about your religious beliefs, your thoughts. your ideas—

Koresh: Listen. But you are—

FBI: Or anything like that.

Koresh: You're—you're saying—

FBI: The same things that you can do there you could do out—out here.

Koresh: That's what you say. I—I think that you are lying. As a matter of fact, I know that when the first month or so that I'm out, I'm gonna be bombarded all of the time with nothing but people wanting to know Koresh—asking this—asking that.

FBI: And if you were working on the seven seals—I mean—nobody would bother you. I mean—why would you—why would that have to happen?

Koresh: I have my responsibility also you know. Come on, look at the reality of things.

FBI: And the reality of things is that there are priorities.

Koresh: OK. But you put your priorities—

FBI: And you're priority and everybody's priority should be in the safety of the children—

Koresh: All right.

FBI: And the safety of the women, and the safety of everybody

Koresh: You're fixing—you are fixing to ruin—your commanders are fixing to ruin the safety of my...and my children. My life—the lives of my wives—the lives of my friends—my family. You're fixing to step across the ribbon.

FBI: I think that—that was something that you brought on. It has nothing to do with the commanders, David.

Koresh: All right. I brought on—if this—if this is the corner of the box that you place me into—

FBI: I think that you're placing yourself in that David. I don't think anybody is forcing it—

Koresh: No. No. You're the one who moving forward. You're the one who—who has violated—your generals have violated our constitutional rights. You have made us guilty before proving so.

FBI: I don't think so.

Koresh: You actively brought a band of—of—of people who didn't announce themselves. They came—I was at the front door. I was willing to talk to them. They shot at me first.

FBI: See, now you're talking about—you're talking about the ATF.

Koresh: About something that you don't want to prove as a matter of a fact. You're telling me—now you've—now you telling me that I am under arrest. I have to come out and I—

FBI: When somebody's under arrest that doesn't mean that it—that you've already been proven guilty. It just means that you've been charged.

Koresh: No. I'm being punished. We've already been punished. We've been placed in jail. We're being punished as guilty.

FBI: Well, that is something that you chose for everybody inside.

Koresh: That is not correct.

FBI: Sure it is because—

Koresh: That is something that you chose as a confinement.

FBI: Because if you had walked out on that day as you promised, by now who knows where we would have been. You know—you probably would be out on bail for God sakes.

Koresh: John—all I can say is—is that if you want to—to—to place this in the history books as one of the saddest days in the world—

FBI: Well, I think that the—the—the rules for your safety still apply. There's no reason—you know—to think that—that—that they shouldn't apply.

Koresh: OK. I understand your rules. I'm just simply asking you in all good faith, and all good manner to—you tell the general it's enough to tear up our property.

FBI: I will tell them exactly what you said. But you need to understand that—um—I'm talking up. It's not—you know—talking down. So—you know—what I suggest and what I will suggest is exactly what you said. I've suggested that and I've suggested other things. I have no—no problem in—ah—you know—

Koresh: You tell em we love em. We love em and—you know—

FBI: And you're willing to send out thirty people.

Koresh: Look.

FBI: Fifty?

Koresh: Whoever wants to go out can go out.

FBI: No. No. No. No. Don't tell me—don't tell me that. Tell me that you're sending somebody out.

Koresh: I'm not going to—you don't—see—you don't understand about these people yet.

FBI: And you don't understand about the people here yet either.

Koresh: OK. Well if that's the way we want to play then we come to a point where

FBI: I'm not wanting to play anything—

Koresh: But it—you are playing.

FBI: No. I'm not. I'm telling you.

Koresh: Everyone in the tanks—everyone in the tanks out there is playing.

FBI: No. Nobody is. People just want to see some progress.

Koresh: Look, some progress is being made. You don't realize what kind of progress is being made. There are people all over this world who are going to benefit from this book of the seven seals. You don't seem to understand.

FBI: And what you don't seem to understand is—is that the people here want to see that kind of progress, but other kind of progress. There's no reason why you couldn't be doing the same very thing that you are doing now within the place out here.

Koresh: That's not true. What you're saying is not based on truth.

FBI: Why not? Why not? What do you mean it's not

Koresh: Because it's just not.

FBI: Your attorney is gonna be your attorney whether you're in there or out here. Anything that you want your—all you—all you'd have to do is—is furnish it to him.

Koresh: An attorney—

FBI: Why would he not comply with your wishes?

Koresh: That's—the legal system is not the majority of the attorney. The legal system is a completely sophisticated—lots of—lots of Indian chief—ah—system. It's not just where you got one guy who is hired to speak in your behalf in a court case in front of a jury.

FBI: Yes. But—but what I'm saying—

Koresh: There's more to it than just—I was in jail in 1988.

FBI: And—and how did it come out?

Koresh: It came out wonderful, because—

FBI: Well, there you go. There you go.

Koresh: Well the thing of it is—is that you don't understand the amount of cost it takes to get that legal representation too.

FBI: Well—

Koresh: And this was something—this was something that the Sheriff's department got us in.

FBI: Well, that was—that was then. You have an attorney now. You know—the same work that you're doing there you can be doing out here.

Koresh: It's a different more high profile case type situation. I just—I just suggest that it—it would be a very bad thing for you to—to keep destroying all this evidence out here.

FBI: Well—you—know—I really don't have any control over that.

Koresh: I mean what are they doing? Are they—are you covering up the ATF? That's exactly what it appears you're doing.

FBI: David, what we're trying to do is we're trying—

Koresh: It's wrong! You're doing wrong before God—before man. You are doing wrong! You adding to your wrong.

FBI: David, you're the one that's doing wrong.

Koresh: No. No. No. No. No. No. No.

FBI: You seem to have—

Koresh: No.

FBI: No concern about—

Koresh: You know we can't stay in here forever.

FBI: Anybody within the place except yourself.

Koresh: You know that we can't stay in here forever.

FBI: You know—if you could send—OK. Well send fifty people out. Send fifty people out right now.

Koresh: Does fifty of you want to go out?

FBI: You don't have to ask. All you have to do is say, "Look, I want fifty volunteers," and they'll come out. If you send fifty people out.

Koresh: They're saying because of these things they want to stay the more.

FBI: And I guess that you have no control over anybody. You know—

Koresh: You've got to understand, what I have control

FBI: This is your responsibility. This is your responsibility because you're the leader. Their safety is in your hands.

On April 17, the day before the last negotiation, Attorney General Janet Reno approved the use of CS gas, to be inserted gradually over a period of 48 hours, in order to end the six-week standoff.[1]

Then an F.B.I. sniper reported seeing a sign on a window that read: "Flames await."[2]

FIRE CONSUMES THE HOLDOUTS

Three minutes before tanks punched holes in the compound to insert the CS gas, the F.B.I. called to speak to Steve Schneider, Koresh's top lieutenant. As recalled by David Thibodeau:

> Before six o'clock, just as dawn breaks, I'm awakened from a doze by the ringing of the telephone... "I want to speak to Steve," a rough voice says... "He's asleep," I reply curtly. "We have to speak to Steve right now," the voice insists. Shivering, I stumble along the corridor to the room where Steve is sleeping. While I'm shaking him awake...Jamie Castillo appears. He looks alarmed. "Something's going on" ...Looking out the window, we see a formation of the demolition tanks closing in on us... "Shit!" Steve exclaims. Just then the amplified speakers...start up again. A metallic voice shouts... "The siege is over. We're going to pour tear gas into the building. David and Steven, lead your people out of there!"...We stare at one another stunned. "This is not an assault," the loud voice continues. "The tear gas is harmless. But it will make your environment uninhabitable. Eventually, it will soak into your food and clothing." The tone of fake concern switches to an abrupt: "You are under arrest. Come out with your hands up!" "Get your gas masks," Steve orders. "Now!"[3]

> "The siege is over," brassy voices shout. "We will be entering the building. Come out with your hands up. Carry nothing. There will be no shooting." One phrase is repeated over and over. "This is not an assault, this is not an assault."[4]

> Not an assault? ...All at once I see a powdery cloud billowing into the building, and I hear the sinister hiss of tear gas. Windows shatter as small canisters, like miniature rockets shoot through the glass and explode, adding fumes to those spewing from the nozzles attached to the tank booms...I hurry to the ground-floor chapel at the east end of the building, my brain hammering with worry for the children.[5]

---

[1] Ramsland, Katherine.
[2] Ibid.
[3] Thibodeau, David and Whiteson, Leon, p. xi.
[4] Ibid.
[5] Ibid., p. xii.

About 9:30 A.M., Koresh came to the chapel to check on his followers. Holding his wounded side, he urged them to "Hold tight," saying, "We're trying to establish communication, maybe we can still work this out."[1]

Unfortunately, Steve had thrown the telephone out the window as soon as the tanks attacked.

Then Thibodeau recalls hearing a news flash:

> "Up to this point, no one has come out," the announcer rattles off breathlessly. The F.B.I. claims that eighty to one hundred gunshots have been directed at its agents." This stuns me...I can't swear that some of us aren't responding to the assault with firearms at the other end of the building, but I've heard no gunfire in the chapel or anywhere nearby. In my despair I begin to believe that we are truly doomed, that the F.B.I. may be setting the American public up for a massacre...[2]

As for the fire that broke out with the tanks' second assault, some contend that the Branch Davidians caused it, citing parts of a tape wherein the Branch Davidians referred to spreading fuel, as well as evidence of accelerants found on their clothing when police investigated the crime scene. Others insist that the tanks knocked over kerosene lamps and exploded a canister of propane gas. The outcome in any case is that only nine Branch Davidians emerged from the flames alive. Eighty were found dead, including twenty-three children under the age of seventeen. Due to evidence of gunshot wounds, many were thought to be mercy killings. Yet, according to the coroners and some FBI sources, "the pattern of most of the bodies was not consistent with a theory of mass suicide."[3] Koresh himself had been shot in the head.

Of course, the siege had never been a necessity. Koresh frequently went to town and could have been picked up alone, had that actually been the goal.

This leads me to conclude not that the agents desired his death but that they wanted to take down a dangerous and suicidal cult—which had to be proven as such—for the initial plan to be justified as well as where it led.

---

[1] Ibid., p. xiv.
[2] Ibid., p. xv
[3] "Waco: the Inside Story," Frontline PBS, http://www.pbs.org/wgbh/pages/frontline/waco/topten2.html

CHAPTER 10. THE BRANCH DAVIDIAN FALLOUT

As a researcher, I believe I have thus far provided an unflinching account of government extremism when and where it occurred while remaining watchful for the worst of spin doctors at work. Naturally, I grieve for the losses of law enforcement as for those of the Weaver family and the Branch Davidian group. That each case influenced the other was shown as the government's means to prove by association during the Weaver Trial that all militant separatist groups are intractable, dangerously hostile, and (in the Waco case) suicidal as victims of their own beliefs. However, the notion of the self-fulfilling prophecy—that rejecting the laws of the government and/or society as a whole by creating alternate polities will entail a fight to the death—is a sword that cuts both ways. Law enforcement in both cases seemed to conduct a test of extremism—to prove the validity of their threat profiles—even conscious of the fact that they might suffer casualties, which they did. Then, the government became more extremist, calling on overwhelming backup to resolve the situations they had provoked. In a day and age when law enforcement must face the increasing willingness of criminals to engage in cop killing and worse, group solidarity is based on more than grief. They are fighting against disrespect for their office and the government itself.

Much as I posited earlier that a constant state of nervosa creates psychological tensions that are resolved through internalization, externalization, or both, the same must apply to the nation. It cannot for long be viewed as the enemy without creating similar tension. Thus, the responses of law enforcement must be viewed along a continuum of which we have not yet seen the end.

In this, the government has learned at least that it need not test its self-declared enemies in such a way that private extremism provokes the government in turn.

Those who do wish to peacefully coexist will prove it by their actions. Those who don't will lean on the help of spin doctors, or worse, propagandists: those who ruthlessly twist the knife in society's open wounds.

This chapter is therefore devoted to revealing hateful agendas, much as it disturbs me to do so. But first, I will deal with commendations to the F.B.I. as well as citizens' umbrage.

LETTERS FROM HOME

Beginning with a few of the letters collected by the F.B.I., some are addressed to William Sessions, the Director of the F.B.I., while others are addressed to the President, or Attorney General Janet Reno:

Exhibit 1

April 20, 1993

Judge William Sessions, Director
Federal Bureau of Investigation
J. Edgar Hoover Building
Washington, DC 2005

Dear Judge Session:

In my opinion, the F.B. I. showed remarkable restraint and a high degree of competence and professionalism in handling the most difficult David Koresh matter. The "Monday morning quarterbacks" who are critical have conveniently forgotten that David Koresh could have surrendered peacefully at any point in the 51-day siege, and could have saved everyone in the compound by electing to face the consequences of his own actions. He simply elected to die rather than face prison, and shamefully took women, children, and his other followers with him. What an ogre!
I know the tremendous pressure Bob Ricks and his colleagues were under in Waco, and would appreciate you forwarding my comments to them. They performed superbly and with a high degree of restraint.
You have my total support. Please let me know if there is anything I can do to help.
F.B.I. Document No.: 63-HQ-1650365=432

Exhibit 2

April 30, 1993

Mr. William Sessions, Director
Federal Bureau of Investigation

Washington, D.C. 20537

Dear Mr. Sessions:

I have observed the Congressional Hearings concerning the procedures followed in the Waco, Texas situation. I would like to offer a few words of support to you and the people in the Bureau.

First, we have all heard plenty of criticisms of the manner in which this situation was handled. I have yet to hear anyone present an alternative plan, in which the outcome would have been any different.

Second, it seems to me that the news media must bear some responsibility for interfering in an already very complex and dangerous situation. I might add that I have already written a letter to ABC News regarding their lack of ethical conduct in this situation.

I realize that what information that people like me receive is obtained from the media. We have no way of knowing if this information is valid.

You and the dedicated people who serve with the F.B.I. and other law enforcement agencies have been unmercifully criticized. I would like for you to know that I along with many other average citizens support you and your Bureau. The average citizen of this country may be silent in this matter, but I really feel that there is much support in the country for what you and your dedicated people do each day to help protect us from criminal activity.

Please realize that we support you and pray for your safety.

Thanks for all that you do to protect our great country.

F.B.I. Document No.: 63-HQ-1050305-443

Exhibit 3

April 28, 1993

Mr. William Sessions, Director
Federal Bureau of Investigation
J. Edgar Hoover Building
Washington, DC

Dear Mr. Sessions:

Your actions in handling the crisis in Waco seem to me to have been appropriate. Everyone regrets the fire and the death of the people in the compound, but the outcome was not the fault of the government. The government agents on the scene did all they could in a virtually impossible situation.

It makes me mad when I see the media and the Congress jump in after the fact criticizing and passing judgment. They had no solutions to offer. They didn't have to take responsibility. They didn't have cameras passing moral judgments. The stupid questions and comments some of those congressmen made at the hearing were appalling.

I also find it offensive that they try to make a national issue out of this one incident. The government has other things to worry about besides the Branch Davidians. Yet the media expect everyone from the President on down to drop everything and listen to them carp and complain about it.

Let's get on with governing the country. The administration should set the national agenda, not the reporters and the crackpots like Koresh.

The country continues to be proud of the F.B.I. Best wishes.

F.B.I. Document No.: 63-HQ-1050305

Exhibit 4

April 19, 1993

Attorney General Janet Reno
Department of "Justice"
10th St. and Constitution Ave. N.W.
Washington, D.C. 20530

Dear Ms. Reno:

How can the FBI say it is "shocked"? Only days ago, their spokesman whined about David Koresh's threats of suicide. How can you call the Branch Davidians' end as "tragic and horrible"? You were the one who decided to "escalate" the pressure.

How can the ATF claim the end should have been "negotiated"? They were the ones who, instead of even trying to negotiate, set the events moving with their abortive assault on February 28th. I had heard that, under Steven Higgins, the ATF has made a lot of "show-boat" assaults on people. I thought, when the FBI took over, things would be more professional.

How can you claim your actions were a part of law enforcement? They were not. They were military actions. Law enforcers are taught to save people. Warriors are trained to assault the enemy. You declared war on those people.

By branding the Davidians as cultists, fanatics, and child abusers, you tried to dehumanize them in our eyes. But no propaganda can erase seeing their home going up in flames, knowing men, women, and—especially—children were gone forever.

The end should have been no surprise. After destroying their life, their property, and their future, you left them nothing. They left us a little more: the image of a family of human beings eradicated by your intolerance.

I am ashamed of our officials.

F.B.I. Document No.: 63-HW-1050305-43

Exhibit 5

May 1, 1993

William Sessions
Director of the F.B.I.
9th Street and Pennsylvania Ave N.W.
Washington, D.C. 20535

Dear Mr. Sessions:

After witnessing the response of our federal agents and elected officials to the situation of the Branch Davidian compound in Waco Texas, I feel it is necessary for me to voice my strongest disapproval in this formal letter. At every stage of the incident, including the aftermath, our federal and elected officials displayed the highest levels of incompetence. In this letter, I will systematically review how our nation's public servants mismanaged each stage of the operation.

The first stage of the government operation began with the initial raid of the Davidian compound by federal agents, charging that David Koresh and some of his followers possessed illegal weapons. It's a sad commentary that a raid which was motivated by nine months of planning and included undercover agents would end in such tragedy. Four agents and two Davidians were killed in an exercise that was intended to save lives and protect innocent people, in and out of the compound, from illegal firearms.

The massive blunder evident at this stage raises many questions that reflect the ineptness of our federal law enforcement agents who are supposed to be intelligent and well trained. Why did the agents have to storm the compound with force, putting innocent women and children inside the compound in jeopardy? The whole crisis could have been averted, at this stage, if federal agents had avoided an initial siege by force and waited to arrest Koresh (the absolute ruler of the accused) when he left the compound, doing such things as going out for a morning jog or a trip to the supermarket. After nine months of planning, one would like to think that our public servants would be smart enough to take this form of action that would avoid putting innocent women and children in harms way.

Shortly before the initial raid took place, it became evident that the people within the compound may have been aware of the impending federal assault. This was due to the fact that officials from the press were already waiting outside, even before federal agents had arrived. After witnessing this, why didn't the agent in charge abort the operation and proceed with another plan, such as secretly staking out the compound and arresting Koresh when he leaves? In short, if we had competent federal law enforcement officials who were more apt at using their brains first rather than arrogantly displaying force, lives would have been saved and the entire crisis avoided.

The multiplicity of mistakes made by federal agents during the first stage of the entire incident were grave and irreversible. The explanation given by them was that they were simply outgunned, but I say that they were simply arrogant and incompetent. Whoever planned, organized, or led the initial raid should be dismissed from their post.

I would categorize the second stage of the Waco affair as including the F.B.I.'s attempts of using negotiations and psychological tactics to bring the standoff to a successful conclusion. On T.V. news, I saw William Sessions (Director of the F.B.I.) describe the F.B.I.'s "closing the perimeter of the compound" tactic which on the surface seemed interesting but in reality it brought the whole incident to a horrible conclusion. The F.B.I.'s psychological tactics were elementary at best. They included playing bizarre, loud sounds or music in a pathetic attempt to drive David Koresh and his followers out of the compound. In all probability, the net effect of these tactics were that it drove a madman even madder.

The F.B.I. has departments that spend millions of dollars of our tax money in researching behavioral sciences or the psychological behavior of human beings. Taking this into account, it's pitiful that one of the best psychological strategies that they could think of was playing loud sounds outside the compound. It is also obvious that the F.B.I. dramatically failed in negotiating with David Koresh and his followers. After 51 days of negotiating and playing bizarre, loud sounds, it was the F.B.I. that lost patience and stamina, not the Davidians. It was the F.B.I. who compromised its position by making a rash seize of the compound, which resulted in the deaths of 80+ people, the very same people the F.B.I.'s operation was designed to protect.

Let's look at the third stage of the incident, which I would categorize as being the tragic conclusion of the standoff. I have one major question in regard to this stage and that is why did the F.B.I. decide to move when it did? Their answer was that their agents were getting tired and they had no relief for them. I find this answer completely false as well as unacceptable.

I believe, although I cannot prove, that the real reason the F.B.I. moved when it did was because of political pressure based on press releases concerning the cost of the operation. One such press release stated that during the 51 day standoff at Waco, federal agents spent close to a million dollars on food costs alone. This does not even include the millions of dollars spent on other expenses to finance the operation, such as servicing M-1 battle tanks. In short, the public was outraged at the unwarranted costs (one million dollar food bill) of the operation and this is what probably motivated the premature attack by the F.B.I.

It's also absurd that a trapped, outnumbered, untrained, unpaid, and probably malnourished cult could outlast an extensively trained, organized, paid, and well-fed group of federal agents. David Koresh's group was not willing to give up. Why was the F.B.I. so fatigued and in dire need of being replaced? Also, how come there was no available unit to replace the federal agents who had been there throughout the incident? With the hundreds of billions of tax dollars our government spends on federal, state, and local law enforcement officials nationwide, one would think that at least one team would be available for relief.

The tear gas assault on the Davidian compound by the F.B.I. was obviously marred with flaws. Plan "A" of the F.B.I.'s final siege involved using armored vehicles to punch holes in the Davidian compound, while injecting tear gas inside to flush out the occupants. When it became obvious that Plan "A" was not working, where was Plan "B"? Why did the F.B.I. stake all of its apples in one basket by not having a contingency plan?

Another major question concerning the final assault is what was the Fire Department not included in any part of the F.B.I.'s plan? I find this dilemma shocking, considering that only a week earlier Koresh announced that any attempts to seize his compound would be followed by an apocalypse of fire.

In the final analysis of the first three stages of the Waco incident, one must conclude that every stage was consumed with flaws and failure on the part of our federal officials. This is highly unacceptable because billions of dollars of our tax money is spent training and paying the salaries of these inept federal law enforcement agents. It is pitiful that with all this money spent on their behalf, their job performance is no better than amateurs off the street.

The final stage of the Waco affair would include the aftermath of the tragic destruction of the compound. This stage is categorized by federal law enforcement leaders and politicians, trying to shift the entire blame on David Koresh for the Waco incident's horrible conclusion, in a feeble attempt to cover up their own massive blunders. I don't think any American citizens believe that David Koresh is not at least partly responsible for the many deaths that resulted from the Waco situation. However, our government must also come forward and assume responsibility.

The response to the Waco catastrophe by our government leaders reflects indecisiveness, incompetence, and even cowardice. President Clinton's reaction was very similar to his notorious statement "I smoked marijuana but I didn't inhale it." He claimed that he approved Attorney General Janet Reno's decision to go ahead with the F.B.I. tear gas assault, but the final decision was hers. President Clinton expects the American people to believe that there is no difference between approving a decision and making a decision, especially when he is President of the United States.

William Sessions, Director of the F.B.I., and Attorney General Janet Reno both claimed that if they thought that David Koresh would order a mass suicide they would not have ordered the final federal assault. Both of them should be dismissed from their posts for making such an absurd statement. How could anyone not even consider that David Koresh and his followers might commit a mass suicide? There were many factors which indicated that David Koresh might order a mass suicide. These factors include: the fact that the Davidian compound had "Apocalypse" as one of its nicknames; Koresh had promised one week before the final raid that the compound would be engulfed in fire; and finally, using the Jonestown example as a reference point in history for the F.B.I., one can see what cult leaders are willing to do. Also, if the first use of force by federal agents failed, why did the F.B.I. think that a second show of force would be successful? In short, it was probably clear to most American citizens that Koresh might order a mass suicide, it should have been taken into account by the F.B.I. The F.B.I. should have had an alternative plan to deal with the possibility of a mass suicide taking place when they assaulted the Branch Davidian compound.

In the final analysis, with government intervention, over 80 people are dead. Without government intervention, it is safe to assume that these people would be alive today. Our government failed to protect the women and children inside the Davidian compound and must take at least partial responsibility for its failures. The government failed at every stage of the Waco incident. If the mistakes of this magnitude took place in a private sector organization, the planners would be held accountable and fired. Our government must resume some form of responsibility for the Waco catastrophe and be held liable by the American people. The organizers, planners, and leaders of the Waco operation should all be dismissed from their posts, if the government inquiry that is now taking place is to mean anything.

F.B.I. Document No.: 63-HQ-1050305

Exhibit 6

May 10, 1993

William S. Sessions
Director, Federal Bureau of Investigation
9th Street and Pennsylvania N.W.
Washington, D.C. 20535

Subject: Gassing and cremation of the Branch Davidian Cult in Waco, Texas

Dear Mr. Sessions:

Your decision to use tanks to break down the walls of the Branch Davidian Cult Headquarters and subsequent gassing of the building, resulted in the deaths of everyone inside.
This plan was obviously very poorly conceived and very poorly executed, all in the name of expediency. Before the tanks crashed into the building all the people were alive.
After 51 days there was no need to take this abrupt kind of action. Patience and time would have been far more effective.

F.B.I. Document No.: 63-HQ-1050305-541

Exhibit 7

May 22, 1993

The Honorable President of the USA
Mr. William Jefferson Clinton
The White House, 1600 Pennsylvania Ave.
Washington, D.C. 20500

Re: The BATF, FBI, the Randall Weaver Family, Naples, Idaho
And the Branch Davidians, Waco, Texas

Dear Mr. President
:

It is appalling that you have appeared to be more concerned about Serbian–Bosnian atrocities than about those perpetrated on certain of our own people by our own government, i.e., the BATF and the FBI.

How could you possibly justify what happened to the Branch Davidian children by recalling that they were, after all, being abused? *Whatever* kind of abuse those innocent children may have suffered at the hands of their misled parents, or others in the compound: It was of no consequence whatever in comparison to their ultimate abuse, suffering, and deaths; essentially at the hands of our own government; which is supposed to protect the innocent! And I assert that as an adult survivor of child sexual, emotional, verbal, and physical abuse; as well as an officer of the Court in my capacity as a Court Appointed Special Advocate for children, or Guardian Ad Litem.

One needn't have a degree in psychology *or* an active imagination to comprehend the abject terror of those children (and adults) must have suffered when the tanks began demolishing the walls of their home and dousing them with tear gas. And whomever or whatever was responsible for the ensuing firestorm: There is simply no excuse or justification for the initial onslaught and the 50-day siege which led up to it!

The same is true of the Randall Weaver case in Idaho. The killings of Vicki Weaver and her son were atrocities, plain and simple. As with David Koresh: The firearms violations charges involved were against Randall Weaver—NOT his wife—NOT his son—and *certainly* not against the son's *dog*; the killing of which by lawmen provoked the youngster into firing on them; which resulted in the boy's death from a gunshot in the back as lawmen returned fire.

That Weaver elected to defend his home when it was attacked by unknown assailants: and that he declined to surrender once their identities were established; does NOT justify the BATF's and the FBI's willingness to kill the essentially innocent in their determination to exercise absolute dominion and control over the situation. Vicki Weaver was shot dead (in the forehead) as she stood with her baby in her arms, in the doorway of her home, by a sniper with a 20-power scope at 120 yards. It was *NO* accident!

That such atrocities could, and actually did happen in this country, of *all* countries (Thomas Jefferson must be spinning in his grave); clearly indicates that almost any family or religious community could wind up at risk of, or actually being terrorized or destroyed by our own government, depending on their degree of departure or "difference" from what is generally considered the accepted "norm" or mainstream of American life.

Aside from all of the above, the bottom line is that the civil rights of both the innocent and the accused were violated by the BATF and the FBI.

According to Thomas Jefferson, ours was to be a government of laws, not men;

with every citizen presumed innocent until proven guilty through due process in a court of law.

It follows then that any accused person(s); regardless of the nature of the allegations or charges against them; ARE STILL ENTITLED TO THEIR FULL RIGHTS OF PROTECTION UNDER THE LAW; and no less so than any and all innocent or non-accused persons in their immediate proximity!

F.B.I. Document No.: 63-HQ-1050305-553

Exhibit 8

June 11, 1993

Federal Bureau of Investigation
Director William S. Sessions
Washington, DC 20600

Director:

I am appalled by your use of public opinion and the context of telephone calls to determine that the actions of the United States Government (and the FBI) in the Koresh case were correct, proper, and moral (your letter, Time magazine June 14, 1993, page 7).

You did not receive a comment from me as I am not in the habit of expressing my anger, disbelief, and disgust to the perpetrators of crimes. I have however, expressed earlier my opinion to President Clinton and to my Congressional delegation.

In brief, the United States Government (Justice Department, CAN, FBI, and BATF) acted in a shameful way by ignoring the Constitutional protection afforded citizens, by hiding the indictment, by acting as jury in determining guilt, by attacking and killing them, and then by destroying all the evidence. Not a proud day.

In replacing the power of the jury with your judgment, you have demonstrated your disdain for the single body that protects us from a tyrant. You have done a monstrous disservice to the citizens of the United States.

F.B.I. Document No.: 63-HQ-1050305-578

***

In the files that I surveyed, there were as many letters expressing support for the government as letters conveying the opposite. I will now turn to posts obtained on the Internet.

UMBRAGE ON THE INTERNET

In "Waco, Texas: Where Part of America's Heart and Soul Died," author Robert McCurry does not pull any punches, nor does he need to since his work relies on facts. Getting straight to the heart of the matter he writes:

> [I]s it rational and humane to send 150 ATF and other law enforcement officers with guns drawn to storm a home on a quiet Sunday morning to "rescue" children from alleged child abuse? What the ATF did on that February 27 Sunday morning was child abuse of the worst kind. If this is the government's way of saying, "Good morning, we're here to help you and serve the best interests of the children" then I hope and pray they will never "protect" my children and grandchildren.[1]

As to his specific complaint, McCurry goes on to say:

> Interestingly, the tear gas that the government poured into the Branch Davidian home has been banned from use in warfare anywhere in the world after January 1994...Think about this. The tear gas that has been banned in warfare by 120 countries was poured into the Branch Davidian home in Waco, Texas, by the American government.[2]

The use of CS gas was among the most controversial measures taken during the siege but has since been addressed in an article from FRONTLINE, which lays out the facts:

> According to medical examiners who performed the autopsies, CS gas did not directly kill any of the more than 80 Branch Davidians, including 22 children, who died in the fire on April 19. Nor did anyone perish from inhalation of CS gas—or its byproduct from a fire, cyanide...Other experts have [said] that CS gas may have totally incapacitated the children and others so that when the fire occurred, it would have rendered them incapable of escape. It should be noted that Mount Caramel had not been gassed preceding the last hour of the fire. Experts also noted that CS gas only has a persistence factor of about ten minutes. Holes that the FBI's armored vehicles punched in the walls of the compound to insert the gas also allowed the high winds on that day to disperse it.[3]

This does not excuse the use of CS gas. However, it does explain why asphyxiation by fire and the collapse of the structure (rather than exposure to CS gas) were among the causes of death.

---

[1] McCurry, Robert, "Waco, Texas: Where a Part of America's Heart and Soul Died," http://www.islandone.org/Politics/Waco.McCurry.html
[2] Ibid.
[3] "Waco: the Inside Story," Frontline PBS, http://www.pbs.org/wgbh/pages/frontline/waco/topten2.html

Nevertheless, Gary Null perpetuates the belief that CS gas was to blame for most, if not all, of the deaths:

> According to investigators, C.S. gas was pumped into the compound from 6:00 AM to 12:00 noon on the day of the fire. C.S. is a toxic tear gas designed for open-air use to disperse riots. In confined spaces, it has been known to combine with other compounds to form the deadly hydrogen cyanide gas. At noon, government tanks hit the compound with a big injection of an atomized mixture of orthochlorobenzylidene malononitrile and ethanol. The mixture was heated so that it would release hydrogen cyanide and carbon monoxide into a vapor. Autopsies indicate that large numbers of people were already dead from hydrogen cyanide gas before the fire. People died from cyanide poisoning within four to five minutes.[1]

Then, taking it one step further, Null goes on to say:

> In a documentary videotape produced by KPOC-TV...last year, Novel states, "I believe [the government's] intent was to trap them, and to incapacitate them, and to poison them with cyanide gas, and they probably came through there in the last three or four minutes, right when the fire began to ignite and the hydrogen cyanide was in there—we have indications of that from the F.B.I. agents taking their respirators off right after the fire started, and you can see them exiting the building—so based upon...the fact that the Davidians had no .45-caliber pistols, one can reasonably deduct that they were shot while they were wriggling on the ground, including the babies.[2]

This is where the line is crossed into sensationalism. Presumably, Novel based his statement that the Davidians had no .45-caliber pistols on the work of the BATF, which specifically looked for guns that could be transformed to assault rifles. This does not mean that the Davidians possessed no other weapons. It simply means they were not the focus during the investigation. Moreover, no one from the government side was in the building just prior to or during the fire. The only time the agents gained entry was during the initial botched assault intended to neutralize military force, protect the women and children, and secure and seize the weapons. The nine people who did leave the compound just before and during the fire were all Branch Davidians who wore gas masks and layers of protective clothing, which were stripped off as they left.

---

[1] Null, Gary, "Holocaust at Waco," Virtual School, http://www.virtualschool.edu/ mon/SocialConstruction/HolocaustAtWaco.html
[2] Ibid.

Addressing another issue with a quote from Catherine Wessinger, a religious historian at Loyola University in New Orleans and authority on apocalyptic groups:

> "[T]he agency's actions are indefensible. If the FBI believed they were dealing with members of a cult who were not in their right minds, then why would the FBI put so much pressure on them and then ultimately carry out an assault which just confirmed David Koresh's prophecies?"[1]

From my own perspective, I have already addressed this as a test of the threat profile—which, if valid, could have allowed the government to root out *all* the Davidians based on their behavior once provoked to act.

According to others, the failure to take Koresh's faith seriously was apparent in the lack of theological experts enlisted by the F.B.I. to negotiate during the siege. In answer, F.B.I. agent Byron Sage replied:

> In the early stages, there was an extremely heavy emphasis on David needing to get his biblical message out—that's what we would refer to as a hook. It was a critical objective of his so we could exploit it. But trust me—you don't want to debate theology with somebody who believes they are Christ. You're never going to win.[2]

This is supported by the following dialogue extracted from F.B.I. records,[3] wherein Max (the negotiator) attempts to reason with Wayne, one of Koresh's lieutenants—as a layman and not a specialist, so as not to approach Koresh and his people from a position of educational superiority that would only demean their intelligence:

Max: Well, I think recently we've been showing a lot of patience and so in that respect we're godly I suppose.

Wayne: Well, James Chapter 1 says...

Max: And I think patience is what's going to help end this situation because God is certainly going to have use—utilize patience in some degree to, to keep people from getting hurt and if we use that patience then we're working with him on this thing.

Wayne: Yes.

Max: And not being a great scholar, scholar and not being a great theologian, and I mentioned this the other night from a person who lives in the day-to-day real factual world, I just think that there needs

---

[1] Ibid.
[2] "The Standoff in Waco," Texas Observer, April 18, 2013, http://www.texasobserver.org/the-standoff-in-waco/
[3] U.S. Department of the Treasury Bureau of Alcohol, Tobacco, and Firearms, Tape 1x, March 9, 1993, 3:10 AM—4:00 AM,

to be some interpretation of what this sign might be. That you know I have heard the phrase somewhere that God works in mysterious ways and I don't know—and I've also heard somewhere along the way that everybody perceives things religious and sacred through different eyes and different hearts and minds. And if we are tuned to accepting some kind of sign, what we can, if someone in there should decide to lead out to safety or if someone, the right person would come and meet you would that not be a sign of some type? For instance—if your Joe and Helen from Newark, New Jersey were here and standing at the end of the driveway and motioning you to, to come out, would that not be a sign of some kind? Would you not put faith in that?

Wayne: Well, Max, I don't have a comment for you.

Max: Well, I really wanted one.

Wayne: I feel that if God asked me to wait, and you asked me once well, how would I be sure that God had given the message to David Koresh? Well, how could a person know as much about God's mysteries as he does, open up vast areas of knowledge about the Scriptures as he has and not be able to communicate with God?

Max: Does, does, does that process shut off your communication with him? Again, I'm, I'm sorting, acting as a, you know, observer in this thing. But does that automatically shut off your interpretation?

Wayne: My interpretation really doesn't matter.

Max: Oh really?

Wayne: Listen, listen. Isaiah 50—

Max: I got a hard time with that one.

Wayne: Isaiah 50 verse 10 says. "When God's servants are in darkness..."

Max: Well, I just—it's so conflicting to me. It's, it's one day it's one thing and it's the next day it's the next thing. I just—

Wayne: But—

Max: —this seems to be whatever, whatever serves David's the purpose the best is what it always is. And, you know, from what little I know of it, it—I thought it was supposed to be more of an equal situation, that everybody had their own, own line in if they wanted it.

Wayne: That's a promise. That's a promise in the Scriptures. However, at this time Isaiah 50 verse 10 is my position and—

Max: Can you tell, tell me without a verse?

Wayne: It says, well, who is there that obeys God's servant and walks in darkness and has no light.

Max: That means that everybody's got to listen to David.

Wayne: Let him put his trust in the Lord.

Max: Well, I really wish there was as much confusion in there about what's going on as there was in my mind and the people out here. We can't—from the articles we read and the people we interview and from people who used to be in there and came out—

Wayne: Well—

Max: —really, honestly, we can't, can't see how this situation is, is, is continuing the way it is and under the circumstances that it has and with people under the influence that they're under and that the cause is that orthodox and that proper and that religious.

Wayne: Well, it is a mystery how so many dumb people that are brainwashed and unable to think for themselves are able to reach a consensus on what the Scriptures teach. That's, in the words of Bob, unusual. But we're learning how to see eye-to-eye on the Scriptures. And it's our standard, it's our reference. It's a biblical standard, and it's what we intend to keep and we're—we feel that as, as Americans we have a constitutional right to our religious freedom and we're going to keep the Bible.

Max: Well, certainly you, you do have those rights and the constitution does give them, but it also gives the rest of us some and, you know, it doesn't give, you know, the right to bear certain types of arms and, and other things. You know, there are some laws of man that enter into it, but you know that's, that's another issue for another court. The one thing that has to be resolved, it has to be resolved here now or, or in this time period, this time frame, is getting people out of there in a safe manner—God's going to have His way anyway, whether you're in there or whether you're out here. There's nobody, nothing that any of us can do to change it if he's going to have His way. So, if you had come into a position—

Wayne: (Indiscernible)

Max: —you know, that everyone could be safe first in man's world and then, you know, say God's going to have His way anyway.

Wayne: Well, the Lord is good and a stronghold in the day of trouble and knows those who put their trust in Him, in Nahum, Chapter 1. And we have a song in Isaiah in Chapter 25 and we have waited for God, he will save us and we have waited for the Lord. We will rejoice in his salvation. So, the word is to wait and that it came from God. And so we're going to exercise our patience and our faith in this message from God.

Max: Do you, do you think in all of that then that everybody who has gone about any type of religious—anybody that has gone about accomplishing any religious goals in the past have gone about it the wrong way, that they all should have done as you all have done and prepared as you all have prepared and challenged the laws that you all have challenged in order to be right?

Wayne: Well, I'm not commenting on that last clause, but

Max: Well—

Wayne: No, no, I'm not—

Max: —gee, that's what this is all about, is, you know, if this is—you know, is everybody else wrong because they haven't armed themselves and prepared as you have prepared and—

Wayne: I'm not commenting about arms. But in answer to the first part of your, your first question, I would say that the dispensation that God has given to people in other times has been different. God has saved people in different ways at different times. Noah's time, people were told to get in the ark; Abraham's time, people were told to get out of Sodom; in Moses' time people were told to sacrifice the lamb, put it on the door post and then the next morning they were told to leave Egypt. Now, each time people were told a different way to be saved. In our time, we are told that there is a certain person that has credentials from God, and to check it out by hearing what he has to say about the seven seals and seeing whether it's made plain in the prophesies, and Isaiah 55 says that person is our commander, all right? Now, the second part of your question is about arms. We've talked about that before you and I.

Max: Um-hum. Everybody I think that's been on either of these telephones has talked about that and nobody out here has been really able to understand it yet.

Wayne: Well—

Max: And we probably won't reach an understanding in this conversation about it, but go ahead.

Wayne: Well, didn't Christ have a conversation with Pilate? That was the government in his day, 2,000 years ago, and they talked about things like truth. What is truth? Well, didn't Christ say the truth will set you free? Well, we believe the seven seals will set us free. Now, getting back on the subject. Talked with Pilate, talked about the kingdom and why it wasn't going to be set up 2,000 years ago. And, you know, we've talked to you about that before.

Max: Um-hum.

Wayne: Because his servants weren't willing to fight for him the kingdom would not be set up. Earlier that week, Christ had told his Disciples to sell whatever they owned and do what with the money? To even borrow. To do what? Buy swords.

Max: You know, your phrasing, your, your every comment, every sound that you make when you get into this is exactly parroting David. You stop and you pause and you ask the questions the same time he does, you quote some of the same verses he does, you stop and want us to fill in the blank. It's—I can't take it seriously that it's you believing it because you're—it's just an exact tape recording of what David says. So, you know, I can't really think that you're in there in spite of your education, in spite of your experience, thinking for yourself.

Wayne: Well, well then reason with me for a bit. How could I go to the city of Waco, practice law, exercise judgment and then come home and be totally brainwashed and then the next day go back to the city of Waco, practice law, exercise reason and judgment no one detecting that I was a moron? Figure that out.

Max: No, no, I would never—

Wayne: No, I resent—

Max: —call anyone a moron.

Wayne: I resent all these comments in the media about the people here not knowing how to think. We have science teachers, we have lawyers, we have medical people, we have computer engineers.

Max: Well, sanity is not always a matter of IQ, you know.

Wayne: Oh, so I was mentally defective in practicing law?

Max: No. You mentioned brainwashing.

Wayne: Well, what are we talking about?

Max: You know, that's, that's an affectation of the sanity to—

Wayne: Doesn't the brain have something to do with the mental health of a person?

Max: At times. But a person on many occasions—you're a lawyer so you know, you know that you can be—you can have a severe personality malformation—

Wayne:	An interactive social worker—
Max:	—that will cause, that will cause crime.
Wayne:	—interactive psychiatrist—
Max:	But at the same time you will not be ruled insane in a court of law. So, we both know that we're talking about here...

As the dialogue demonstrates, the negotiator is a plain-spoken person, which forces Koresh's lieutenant to have to break down the elaborate construct of quotes and scriptures absorbed from David Koresh consistent with the F.B.I.'s efforts to engage the Davidians in reason rather that accepting what they said by rote. At the same time, the F.B.I. did work closely, albeit behind the scenes, with specialists in every related profession from psychology to behavioral science. Nor did they lack volunteers, some of which were people who claimed to be the "real" Jesus Christ or somehow related to him. Others believed that their own command of scripture would be sufficient to resolve the Davidians' "confusion."

SPIN DOCTORS

Those who sought more compelling reasons for the siege at Waco, Texas, often recounted the tale of his disaffected followers and how they hired a private detective to dig up dirt on Koresh in order to prove their allegations as presented to legal authorities. Others thought that the Cult Awareness Network had undue influence in pushing the F.B.I. toward persecution and violence.

As noted by one writer:

> The Cult Awareness Network (CAN) actively urges the press, Congress and law enforcement to act against any non-mainstream religious, psychological or even political movement which it describes as a "cult."...According to CAN critic Dr. Gordon Melton of the Institute for the Study of Religion in Santa Barbara, California, CAN has used a number of means to try to destroy small religious groups: they unsuccessfully tried to expand "conservatorship" to allow families to remove members from "cults"; they unsuccessfully tried to have laws passed against "cults"; they unsuccessfully sued the American Psychological Association for rejecting their views on "brainwashing." However, they have found one successful method of disrupting groups: false anonymous charges of child abuse. Anonymous reports are legal under current law. [1]

---

[1] Moore, Carol, "The Massacre at Waco," http://www.jeffhead.com/liberty/waco_mas.htm

For its part, CAN claimed to have offered invaluable assistance to members of law enforcement during the Branch Davidian siege:

> CAN representatives made numerous television and radio appearances during the siege. Ross bragged on the "Up to the Minute" public television program that he "consulted with ATF agents on the Waco sect and told them about the guns in the compound." On April 19th he told the "Today Show," "I was a consultant offering ideas, input that was filtered by their team and used when they felt it was appropriate"[1]

The following documents, extracted from F.B.I. files, materially demonstrate how CAN claimed to be effectual and even indispensable during the Waco case, according to "The Family," a Christian organization that has been targeted by CAN and wished to prevent it from influencing law enforcement regarding the siege at Waco. The final document is a response from the F.B.I. to a Congressman, for whom "The Family" represented constituents. It notably denies the allegation that CAN was a driving influence.

Exhibit 9

The Family
A Fellowship of Independent Christian Missionary Communities
14118 Whittier Blvd., Suite 116, Whittier, CA 90605

Congressman Hamilton Fish Jr.
2354 Rayburn Hob
Washington, DC 20515

WACO
WHO'S RESPONSIBLE?—
CULT AWARENESS NETWORK? (CAN)

—*"The FBI should use any means necessary...including lethal force."* (CAN Director Patricia Ryan—*Houston Post*, April 9)

OUR PROPOSAL
THAT A THOROUGH INVESTIGATION INTO CAN'S ACTIVITIES BE CONDUCTED
THAT ACCREDITED, UNBIASED ACADEMICS BE CONSULTED ON RELIGIOUS GROUPS
THAT AN EDUCATION CAMPAIGN BE LAUNCHED TO COUNTER MIS-INFORMATION

---

[1] Ibid.

Dear Congressman Fish,

Thank you for taking your time to read this. We appreciate your willingness to take public office to represent the people of this land and to tackle the serious issues and responsibilities involved in forging the direction of our country. Our prayers are with you.

We are a Christian missionary movement known as *The Family*. We are writing you to express our concern that the actions and stance taken by our government in the Waco situation portend to set a serious precedent for future unconstitutional hostilities and bigotry which will threaten the freedom of religion in our country.

One of the major issues we feel needs to be addressed is how our well-intentioned law enforcement agencies seem to have been deliberately misled by an anti-religious organization known as the Cult Awareness Network (CAN). This organization of so-called "cult experts" injected prejudice, distrust, and fear into what should have been an objective, unemotional investigation of the Branch Davidians. In fact, CAN leaders, including convicted felon and deprogrammer Rick Ross, have openly boasted of influencing FBI and ATF authorities, both before the initial raid as well as during the standoff. Instead of common sense and reason prevailing, the misinformation spread by CAN led to the tragic mishandling of the entire Waco incident, resulting in the sad loss of life on the part of the authorities, and a tragic ending for this small religious group.

These self-styled "cult experts" of CAN have falsely established their credibility to the point they have now become the advisors of our nation's law enforcement agencies. This in spite of the fact that the vast majority of our nation's academic and professional community clearly do not endorse the views or activities of this biased, anti-religious organization. Had our country's accredited and internationally recognized authorities on religion and human behavior been consulted, their sensible and educated counsel could have helped officials make sound judgments based on fact and empirical evidence, thereby averting this tragedy.

Our apprehension is that this anti-religious propaganda will endanger many innocent people whose beliefs and practices happen to run outside those of this country's mainstream religions. We feel that the media, politicians, law enforcement agencies and the general public are being heavily prejudiced and swayed by these anti-religious elements. The whole world has now seen the devastating power of this 'provocation by misinformation' tactic in Waco, much akin to those coercive techniques used by totalitarian states this nation has condemned.

We, The Family, have also been targets of CAN's "dirty tricks department" via media smear campaigns and deprogramming attacks. CAN and its affiliates have frequently stirred up local officials, often via the media, to take action against our Christian communities in several countries, causing untold trauma and heartache for our children and parents. Of course none of their slanderous accusations have ever been proven true—To the contrary, our community involvement, as well as our home education and childcare programs have been hailed as exemplary by educators, sociologists, psychologists and government officials the world over.

Therefore, having stated the above, we would like to make 3 proposals:

1) That a thorough investigation be conducted into CAN's activities, including its influence on decisions made in Waco

2) That accredited and unbiased academics who have scientifically studied New Religious Movements (NRMs) for years, be put in a position to consult with local and federal officials should situations such as this arise again.

3) That an education campaign be launched, by those same professionals, to disseminate factual and unbiased information regarding NRMs.

We appeal to you, Congressman Fish, as an elected official of our democratic society, to help preserve our legacy of freedom. It seems this generation has forgotten that our government was largely founded to protect the rights of minority religious movements, most of its founders having been members of just such religious groups in its inception. Please help stem the rising tide of ignorance, hate and fear now being fostered by these enemies of our country.

F.B.I. Document No.: 63-HQ-1050305-595

Exhibit 9 Attachment

U.S. Justice Department Indicts Deprogrammer a Second Time
Press Release from Dr. Isaac N. Brooks, Jr.
President of Deprogramming Survivors Network
March 8, 1993

WASHINGTON DC—A man who stood trial in December 1992 for conspiring to kidnap and deprogram an heir to the duPont fortune has been indicted for kidnapping the second time in five months. The indictment is for kidnapping and imprisoning a Washington, D.C. woman.

The Federal grand jury charges were brought in the Alexandria Division of the U.S. District Court for the Eastern District of Virginia against Galen Kelly, a self-styled kidnapper and deprogrammer.

Kelly, according to court papers, helped kidnap Debra Dobkowski off the streets of Washington, D.C. and transported her in a van from Washington, D.C. to Leesburg, Virginia. It was discovered upon arrival that they had mistaken Dobkowski for her roommate, the real objective of the kidnapping.

At the end of the duPont conspiracy trial, presiding Judge T.S. Ellis III admonished Kelly saying: "Mr. Kelly, I don't know where matters stand with you, but this trial ought to be a clear message to you that under no circumstances is it ever justified to snatch, lift, or pull anybody off the street against their will."

Edgar Newbold Smith, co-defendant and millionaire in the duPont trial, testified that Pricilla Coates, head of the Los Angeles chapter of the Cult Awareness Network, (CAN) referred him to deprogrammer Galen Kelly. Critics have charged for years that CAN is an anti-religious group and clearing house for kidnapping and deprogrammings. Kelly is a long-time paid consultant to CAN.

The victim told the FBI that she was grabbed near her car when leaving work in Washington, D.C. about midnight May 5, 1992, and pinned against the hood of the car. "The taller one had hold of my legs..." said Dobkowski. "I thought I was going to be raped....The other guy (Galen Kelly) grabbed my upper body, twisting my arm and banging me against the car. I was thrashing and screaming as loud as I could."

The victim said Kelly threatened her: "He said they could do things to make me cooperate...that they had a whole slew of techniques, from drugs to other various methods that would force me to cooperate."

Only after Kelly threw her into a van and drove her across state lines did he learn that he had kidnapped the wrong woman. He then drove her back to Washington, D.C., and dumped her in the streets in the early hours of the next morning.

Dr. Isaac N. Brooks, Jr., president of the Deprogramming Survivors Network (DSN) said, "The tragedy of the Debra Dobkowski, the duPont man, and other similar incidents can be laid at the feet of the Cult Awareness Network and the deprogrammers, like Kelly, for whom CAN constantly drums up business. These deprogrammers are only interested in profiting from the violence they create."

DSN is an organization of religious leaders and victims of deprogramming who work to eradicate deprogramming and stress meaningful dialogue in place of violence.

The Cult Awareness Network has been fomenting hatred against religious groups, churches, and political organizations for years. They have kidnapped Evangelical Christians, Catholics, Scientologists, Episcopalians and others. It is time their violations of the law and the Constitution of the United States come to an end.

Exhibit 10

Honorable Esteban E. Torres
House of Representatives
Washington, DC 20515-0534

Dear Congressman Torres:

This is in further reply to your May 26th correspondence to the Department of Justice which was referred to the FBI on June 11 on behalf of [redacted] who represents a group called The Family. This group is requesting that the Cult Awareness Network (CAN) be investigated, particularly regarding its alleged role as an advisor in the standoff with the Branch Davidians in Waco, Texas.

As an investigative arm of the United States Department of Justice, the FBI investigates violations of Federal law which fall within our jurisdiction. We do not, however, infringe on the rights of groups to participate in activities protected by the First Amendment. If there is evidence that any group or member of a group has violated a law within the FBI's investigative authority, we would, of course, initiate an investigation. If you have such information regarding CAN, you should bring it to the attention of our local offices.

The FBI became involved in the Waco situation because Federal officers were killed, a violation of Federal law that falls within our investigative jurisdiction. A principal FBI negotiator during the standoff with the Branch Davidians has advised that to his knowledge, the Cult Awareness Network did not contact the FBI about the Branch Davidians, nor was it a driving force behind law enforcement's strategy in handling this siege.

I hope this information will assist you in responding to your constituent.

F.B.I. Document No.: 63-HQ-1050305-596

TWISTING A KNIFE IN THE WOUND

Of the two Internet posts to be reviewed in this section, the first states that the documentary film "Waco: The Rules of Engagement" (WTROE) was a hoax designed to:

- Hide the most damaging truths and direct attention to false issues;
- Neutralize the outrage that would be felt if the true facts were known; and
- Inoculate the public against the real evidence that the Davidians murdered.

Below is a summarization of the author's ten points, which she employs to prove that WTROE was a hoax.[1]

1) WTROE makes its gravest charge against the FBI—that adult Davidians were machine-gunned as they ran from the burning Mt. Carmel Center on April 19, 1993—on a single piece of contested evidence. That evidence is Forward-Looking Infra Red (FLIR) film taken by government forces on April 19, 1993.

2) WTROE does not question the veracity of this evidence, even though the source is the FBI, the very agency WTROE is accusing of murder.

3) WTROE argues that the Davidian mothers and children were not deliberately murdered and that their deaths were the unintended result of the CS attack and fire.

4) WTROE ignores a wealth of convincing evidence from a number of sources which confirms the charge that the Davidian mothers and children were deliberately murdered.

5) WTROE fabricates a "they died of cyanide poisoning" story to explain the deaths of the children.

6) WTROE makes blatantly false statements about the Davidian Autopsy Reports and "official" causes of death.

---

[1] Valentine, Carol A., "Waco Documentary is a Hoax! A Review of Waco: the Documentary," 1997, http://www.serendipity.li/waco/valent01.html

7) WTROE dilutes outrage over Waco by showcasing the most repulsive accusation against the Davidians.

8) WTROE dilutes outrage over Waco by suggesting the atrocity was, in part, a product of the Davidians' belief system.

9) WTROE reasserts the obviously false accounts of April 19 events, as told by some Davidian "survivors"—that the majority of Davidians were alive during the CS attack and fire and died as a result of those events.

10) WTROE protects the US military by casting Waco as a "law enforcement" event.

The author concludes her list of points, saying that the murders of children, committed with malice aforethought, is the real, politically explosive issue being covered up by the film. But to support her allegations, she must tear down the Branch Davidians themselves. Those who died were defenseless and good. Those who survived were duplicitous and even spineless "curs."

Citing the same film that, in her own words, is widely contested, she asserts that the FLIR video "strongly suggests" that an F.B.I. agent lobbed an incendiary grenade to start the second fire. The same film, supposedly, shows Delta Force commandos shooting the survivors as they exit the burning building and (even more unsustainably) sneaking into the building to place plastic explosives on the roof of the concrete room where the women and children sheltered.

Really? Delta Force?

If you do not recognize that the gist of this author's story fits the long-established conspiracy theory of "jackbooted thugs" to be used on innocent civilians at the orders of a neo-Nazi government that will spare no effort (nor limit to the author's imagination) in terms of its depravity, then perhaps an unrelated example will acquaint you with the storyboard.

On an Internet site that sells survivalist instruction videos, a disembodied (and unidentified) voice reports that the U.S. military has supplied plastic coffins for an entire mid-Western township in readiness for genocide. Meanwhile, FEMA has plans to seize your property and stuff you into a trailer.

Those who conceive of and propagate conspiracy theories begin with the basic premise that:

1) Their victims are always good, ergo

2) They cannot possibly be violent, ergo

3) There is immediate evidence of a cover-up in progress, ergo

4) The observer's initial suspicions may only be scratching the surface in terms of what *could have* occurred, ergo

6) The survivors (and victims) who tell a different story must be lying, ergo

7) The survivors are either "spineless curs" rather than victims or they must have been brainwashed, ergo

8) Something *truly* heinous and diabolical must have occurred, ergo...

Is there a precedent for such a belief?

Since the answer to the last question is obviously "yes," the fertile ground of conspiracy theory proves that it is quite willing to grow another monstrosity. And there you have it: women and children were not just killed with malice aforethought. Instead, their bodies were mutilated, dismembered, rearranged, and disappeared, albeit in a way to which the FLIR was blind.

To that end, all experts employed by the government must also be "known incompetents," especially in identifying the true causes of death. This unfortunately requires us to enter the world of "war porn," complete with shocking and gruesome details.

To wit:

> Some [bodies] were charred beyond recognition or slightly charred... Some bodies were severely decomposed, some only moderately; some dismembered and badly mutilated, while others were whole...Some corpses were so decomposed that the connective tissue between the bones had disintegrated, causing the bodies to fall apart...[although] this degree of decomposition is usually effected over a long period of time. Other corpses were so decomposed that the internal organs were unrecognizable, had turned to mush, or were liquefied...In one case, the body parts of eleven...people were reformed into an agglutinated mass, as if compacted in a press...It is obvious that these people died in different environments, and their remains gathered after death and pressed together.[1]

It also manifests like this with open-ended questions disguising innuendo:

> The Autopsy reports present even further problems... For example, whose child was Mt. Carmel Doe 51A? ...Is it likely that one of the Davidian mothers had a two-year-old, and no one noticed? Hardly... What about Doe 65...Doe 31DE...and Doe 59? ...If these were Davidians, why have they not been identified? And if those people were not Davidians, who were they, and how did their bodies come to rest in the concrete room? And why are the Davidian survivors...not talking about the bodies that are entirely MISSING? Where on earth could those bodies be? And why have there been no comments or questions

---

[1] Valentine, Carol A., "Waco Documentary is a Hoax! A Review of Waco: the Documentary," 1997, http://www.serendipity.li/waco/valent01.html

from Davidian survivors...about the mutilation, beheading, and selective incineration of bodies in the concrete room? ...In Western culture, defilement of human remains is one of the most heinous acts one can perform. This is particularly true if you are a Christian and believe the body is the vessel of the soul, to be resurrected on the Last Day and rejoined with the soul to live in Everlasting Glory with God. But not one of the survivors talks about this defilement. Instead, we hear about how the FBI agents pulled their pants down and mooned the Davidians while they were driving the tanks around....[1]

Then the survivors themselves are attacked:

Without the survivors' stories, our attention would be focused on the evidence, and the evidence SCREAMS that the mothers and children were murdered with malice aforethought. The evidence SHOUTS that their bodies were laundered—mutilated, decapitated, blown apart, and selectively burned—to disguise the time, cause, circumstances, and even the identities of the dead...Without the survivors' stories, no one would believe the government's tale. The unbelievable stories of the Waco "fire survivors" are essential elements in the cover-up of the Waco Holocaust.[2]

Finally, there must be a larger purpose for something so patently evil:

Linda Thompson's opinion is that "Waco was merely one of the first tests of using federal law enforcement with military, and using military tactics. The government proved it could use the major media to tell the government's version of the story to the public. It was a victory for mass propaganda...They murdered 96 people in front of our eyes on national TV, and the public bought it.[3]

In the words of Gary Null:

[W]aco has one final, totally chilling message to the people of America: "It is useless to resist...Don't confront your government, or you'll be dealt with." Anyone who accepts without question the official version of the government's war against the Branch Davidians has, in reality, already surrendered.[4]

THE SONG, THE TUNE, AND THE WORDS

In the text for this book's back cover, I originally wrote:

---

[1] Valentine, Carol A., "Waco Survivor's Story: True or False?" http://www.public-action.com/SkyWriter/WacoMuseum/burial/page/b_a.html
[2] Ibid.
[3] Null, Gary.
[4] Ibid.

Because white supremacists are not yet strong enough to seize the American government and/or destroy Corporate Governance, its leaders advocate proxy wars—pitting average, ordinary citizens who claim to be white separatists against the monolith of the state—in hopes of promoting a backlash against government extremism.

The message?

If the government crushes a "no one," then the same can happen to anyone.

This is the drumbeat of the standoff—one that would march us into the world of white supremacists, creating a new dark age of enemies and conspiracy theories.

As indicated above, conspiracy theorists have a twisted and blind logic regarding their propaganda, but this does not mean that they are "deaf" in any sense. Attracted by the drum beat of the standoff, they provide the song, the tune, and the words that they need for a revolution—one that is based on falsehoods to hide the world as they would remake it—a place where Jews, non-whites, non-Christians, and liberal policy-makers will either be repressed, cleansed from Christian territories, or violently eliminated.

To fight it, and simultaneously counter Corporate Governance, we must tune out the song, the words, and the drumbeat to focus on actionable facts and evidence—eschewing hostility to favor humanity—thereby choosing to stand for tolerance and tangible equality against the probable pitfall of falling as a nation.

APPENDIX A. VISUALIZING THE STANDOFF

When poised overlong between the need to fight or flee, a person suffering from nervosa will either make a decision between them (to internalize or externalize their hurt and humiliation—the most dangerous reaction being a dual outcome). We can therefore use triangles to represent the potential for internalization (leading toward implosion), externalization (leading toward explosion), or both.

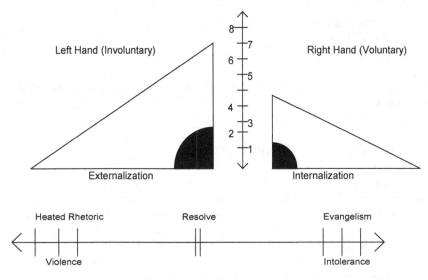

When the triangles point upward, the lack of inverted structures represents mental stability, which is further reinforced by arcs of potential action projecting outward rather than inward. The gap between the triangles indicates resolve, which increases exponentially once the triangles connect. Individuals and groups portrayed by non-inverted triangles are in their strongest positions at the lines forming their bases. According to the right hand (voluntary) triangle, they will internalize their grievances, giving rise to stronger and/or reinforced belief systems, while limiting exposure to, and interaction with, the offensive world outside them. In contrast, the left hand (involuntary) triangle portrays externalization as a matter of survival. Thus subjects fitting this profile will engage in evangelism and other forms of recruitment in an effort to subvert and ultimately superimpose their own views on societal opposition.

The proportional evolution of both triangles is important. If the right hand (voluntary) triangle grows larger than that of the (involuntary) left hand, individuals or groups fitting this profile will tend to be most withdrawn from the outside world, exclusive in terms of their membership, hyper-suspicious, and secretive. Therefore, their externalization may be more inclined toward violence, even if it only pertains to their rhetoric. The numbers 1–8 along the vertical axis indicate the transition from a non-combative to a combative state and the states in between:

> Non-combative
> Altruistic
> Helpful
> Passive
> Aggressive
> Antagonistic
> Suicidal
> Combative

When both triangles are equally proportionate violence becomes a necessity, both as a tactic and matter of leadership.

VISUALIZING RETRIBUTION

Because we must also deal with violence in and outside the standoff—an attack on oneself, society, or officers of the law—the triangles below represent a psychological crisis, which, in the crossover from the stable state represented by non-inverted triangles to the unstable state represented by inverted triangles, may induce delusions (particularly of grandeur and elevated narcissism) or perceptual distortions, such as extreme paranoia or the interpretation of visions and world events as sinister "signs" and biblical portents.

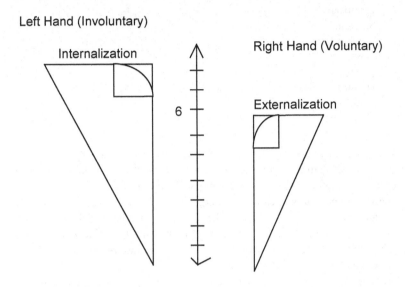

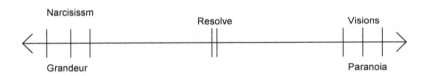

Here, the triangles are inverted and the arcs representing potential are correspondingly concave. This means that instability is at its maximum potential and the person may be mentally unbalanced. Such a person is capable of violence, but such violence is self-referential. Again, the gap between the triangles indicates resolve, which increases exponentially once the triangles connect. If the triangles remain in the proportion shown above or the left hand (involuntary) triangle grows ever larger than that of the (voluntary) right hand, the subject may be viewed as suicidal. If, however, the right hand (voluntary) triangle is pushed to a greater proportion than the left hand (involuntary) triangle, then the subject may kill without resorting to self-harm because externalization is prioritized over internalization, consistent with the subject's perception that he or she is in command of the situation. If both triangles are realigned in equal proportion, command of the situation requires murder-suicide to resolve pressure from both directions.

Again, the numbers along the vertical axis indicate the transition from a non-combative to a combative state and the states in between:

Combative
Suicidal
Antagonistic
Aggressive
Passive
Helpful
Altruistic
Non-combative

These are the dynamics of individual motivations, which may apply to a loner or group of loners. In the latter case assessments must still be made with respect to each individual because one loner among the group may be responsible for killing the other loners once murders are committed before taking his or her own life. Otherwise, some or all members may plan to die in a shootout once responders arrive at the scene. The remaining possibility is that one or more members may surrender to responders in a last, desperate bid to be saved from their own inclinations, whether or not remorse is present.

Although it may be argued that the last analysis applies to the Columbine Massacre, this does not mean that action by one loner or a limited group of loners necessarily involves mental instability, including or excluding suicidal intentions.

IDENTITIES AND CROSSOVERS

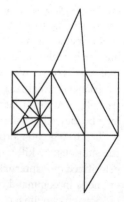

In the diagrams shown above, three different scenarios emerge as a result of either combining identities, illustrating their crossover and attendant potentialities, or a partial loss of identity when dependents are submerged within a dominant identity. When defined from left to right, the first figure depicts an unstable identity capable of influencing a stable identity. Although both have similar resolve (as shown by the space between each set of triangles), the dominant size of the inverted, right-hand triangles indicates more power.

Moving to the central diagram, where one triangle is missing its inverse opposite, indicates a crossover, where the uppermost stable identity lends partial stability to the lower unstable identity. The space between the sets of triangles depicts similar resolve, and because all three triangles are equally proportionate, the effect of the crossover is one of co-dependency.

In the much larger diagram depicted on the right, there is a sole stable identity represented by two conjoined triangles that subsume many smaller triangles on the (involuntary) left side. There is a partial loss of identity with respect to the smaller triangles, representing complete, one-sided dependency. Simultaneously, the one stable identity is conjoined on the right to many unstable identities, representing a crossover. In this scenario, the sole stable identity is clearly the dominant power, both because it subsumes other identities *and either needs or causes* the uncertainties of the conjoined unstable identities. Overall, the lack of space between any triangles confirms universal resolve.

INTERPRETING THE PATTERNS

Recalling Chapter Eight, it will be argued that the central diagram represents the relationship between Randall and Vicki Weaver as one of co-dependence, rather than the left-hand diagram, which portrays Vicki Weaver as the dominant, unstable influence, consistent with the unproven allegation (offered by Bo Gritz) that law enforcement responders perceived her as such.

The larger left-hand diagram pertains to the Branch Davidians, controlled and led by David Koresh.

Where to Draw the Line(s)

Looking at the right-most diagram representing David Koresh and the relationships of his followers, we can see that he does indeed subsume the identities of women and children by half on the left side of his profile (where the children are represented by the smallest triangles embedded in Koresh's left-hand (involuntary) side through which he externalized his power.

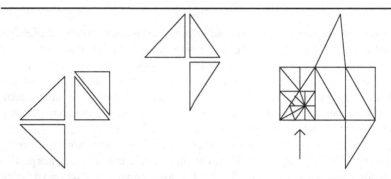

Below, the triangles of co-dependence representing the women are conjoined outside Koresh's left-hand (involuntary) side in a manner that reflects their internalization of Koresh's power:

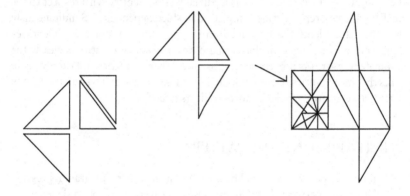

In contrast, Koresh's Mighty Men, or chief lieutenants, are kept unbalanced by Koresh's teachings and their military preparedness. Believing unreservedly and completely that obedience to "God" meant adhering to Koresh, their plight was poignantly underscored when Steve Schneider told negotiators, "You don't understand. I'm a God-fearing man." Therefore, the lieutenants' paired triangles are conjoined to Koresh's right-hand (voluntary) triangle, not as co-dependents but men he kept off balance. Koresh's first act to achieve this was to take away their wives, denying them the support of anyone but himself.

Viewed from this perspective, the F.B.I.'s mistaken belief—that extracting the women and children, and thereby shrinking the size of Koresh's world, was the means to undermine him—produced the opposite instead. Both Koresh and his supporters believed he was being set up for a violent end, which is what occurred.

Appendix B. Terror From the Right

July 28, 1995

Antigovernment extremist Charles Ray Polk is arrested after trying to purchase a machine gun from an undercover police officer, and is later indicted by federal grand jury for plotting to blow up the Internal Revenue Service building in Austin, Texas. At the time of his arrest, Polk is trying to purchase plastic explosives to add to the already huge arsenal he's amassed. Polk is sentenced to almost 21 years in federal prison.

October 9, 1995

Saboteurs derail an Amtrak passenger train near Hyder, Ariz., killing one person and injuring about 70 others. Several antigovernment messages, signed by the "Sons of Gestapo," are left behind. The perpetrators remain at large.

November 9, 1995

Oklahoma Constitutional Militia leader Willie Ray Lampley, his wife Cecilia and another man, John Dare Baird, are arrested as they prepare explosives to bomb numerous targets, including the Southern Poverty Law Center, gay bars and abortion clinics. The three, along with another suspect arrested later, are sentenced to terms of up to 11 years in 1996. Cecilia Lampley is released in 2000, while Baird and Willie Lampley—who wrote letters from prison urging others to violence—are freed in 2004 and 2006, respectively.

December 18, 1995

An Internal Revenue Service (IRS) employee discovers a plastic drum packed with ammonium nitrate and fuel oil in a parking lot behind the IRS building in Reno, Nev. The device failed to explode a day earlier when a three-foot fuse went out prematurely. Ten days later, tax protester Joseph Martin Bailie is arrested. Bailie is eventually sentenced to 36 years in federal prison, with a release date of 2027. An accomplice, Ellis Edward Hurst, is released in 2004.

January 18, 1996

Peter Kevin Langan, the pseudonymous "Commander Pedro" who leads the underground Aryan Republican Army, is arrested after a shootout with the FBI in Ohio. Along with six other suspects arrested around the same time, Langan is charged in connection with a string of 22 bank robberies in seven Midwestern states between 1994 and 1996. After pleading guilty and agreeing to testify, co-conspirator Richard Guthrie commits suicide in his cell. Two others, Kevin McCarthy and Scott Stedeford, enter plea bargains and do testify against their co-conspirators. Eventually, Mark Thomas, a leading neo-Nazi in Pennsylvania, pleads guilty for his role in helping organize the robberies and agrees to testify against Langan and other gang members. Shawn Kenny, another suspect, becomes a federal informant. Langan is sentenced to a life term in one case, plus 55 years in another. McCarthy is released from prison in 2007, while Stedeford's release date is set in 2022. Thomas receives eight years and is released in early 2004.

April 11, 1996

Antigovernment activist and self-described "survivalist" Ray Hamblin is charged with illegal possession of explosives after authorities find 460 pounds of the high explosive Tovex, 746 pounds of ANFO blasting agent and 15 homemade hand grenades on his property in Hood River, Ore. Hamblin is sentenced to almost four years in federal prison, and is released in March 2000.

April 12, 1996

Apparently inspired by his reading of a neo-Nazi tract, Larry Wayne Shoemake kills one black man and wounds seven other people, including a reporter, during a racist shooting spree in a black neighborhood in Jackson, Miss. As police close in on the abandoned restaurant he is shooting from, Shoemake, who is white, sets the restaurant on fire and kills himself. A search of his home finds references to "Separation or Annihilation," an essay on race relations by neo-Nazi National Alliance leader William Pierce, along with an arsenal of weapons that includes 17 long guns, 20,000 rounds of ammunition, and countless military manuals.

April 26, 1996

Two leaders of the Militia-at-Large of the Republic of Georgia, Robert Edward Starr III and William James McCranie Jr., are charged with manufacturing shrapnel-packed pipe bombs for distribution to militia members. Later in the year, they are sentenced to terms of up to eight years. Another Militia-at-Large member, Troy Allen Kayser (alias Troy Spain), is arrested two weeks later and accused of training a team to assassinate politicians. Starr is released from prison in 2003, while McCranie gets out in 2001. Kayser, convicted of conspiracy, is released in early 2002.

July 1, 1996

Twelve members of an Arizona militia group called the Viper Team are arrested on federal conspiracy, weapons and explosive charges after allegedly surveilling and videotaping government buildings as potential targets. All 12 plead guilty or are convicted of various charges, drawing sentences of up to nine years in prison. The plot participants are all released in subsequent years. Gary Curds Baer, who drew the heaviest sentence after being found with 400 pounds of ammonium nitrate, a bomb component, is freed in May 2004.

July 27, 1996

A nail-packed bomb goes off at the Atlanta Olympics, which are seen by many extremists as part of a Satanic "New World Order," killing one person and injuring more than 100 others. Investigators will later conclude the attack is linked to 1997-1998 bombings of an Atlanta-area abortion clinic, an Atlanta gay bar and a Birmingham, Ala., abortion facility. Suspect Eric Robert Rudolph—a reclusive North Carolina man tied to the anti-Semitic Christian Identity theology—flees into the woods of his native state after he is identified in early 1998 as a suspect in the Birmingham attack, and is only captured five years later. Eventually, he pleads guilty to all of the attacks attributed to him in exchange for life without parole.

July 29, 1996

Washington State Militia leader John Pitner and seven others are arrested on weapons and explosives charges in connection with a plot to build pipe bombs to resist a feared invasion by the United Nations. Pitner and four others are convicted on weapons charges, while conspiracy charges against all eight end in a mistrial. Pitner is later retried on that charge, convicted and sentenced to four years in prison. He is released in 2001.

October 8, 1996

Three "Phineas Priests"—racist and anti-Semitic Christian Identity terrorists who feel they've been called by God to undertake violent attacks— are charged in connection with two bank robberies and bombings at the two banks, a Spokane newspaper and a Planned Parenthood office. Charles Barbee, Robert Berry and Jay Merrell are eventually convicted and sentenced to life terms. Brian Ratigan, a fourth member of the group arrested separately, draws a 55-year term; he is scheduled for release in 2045.

October 11, 1996

Seven members of the Mountaineer Militia are arrested in a plot to blow up the FBI's national fingerprint records center, where 1,000 people work, in West Virginia. In 1998, leader Floyd "Ray" Looker is sentenced to 18 years in prison, with a release date of 2012. Two other defendants are sentenced on explosives charges and a third draws a year in prison for providing blueprints of the FBI facility to Looker, who then sold them to a government informant who was posing as a terrorist.

January 16, 1997

Two anti-personnel bombs—the second clearly designed to kill arriving law enforcement and rescue workers—explode outside an abortion clinic in Sandy Springs, Ga., a suburb of Atlanta. Seven people are injured. Letters signed by the "Army of God" claim responsibility for this attack and another, a month later, at an Atlanta gay bar. Authorities later learn that these attacks, the 1998 bombing of a Birmingham, Ala., abortion clinic and the 1996 Atlanta Olympics bombing, were all carried out by Eric Robert Rudolph, who is captured in 2003 after five years on the run. Rudolph avoids the death penalty by pleading guilty in exchange for a life sentence, but simultaneously releases a defiant statement defending his attacks.

January 22, 1997

Authorities raid the Martinton, Ill., home of former Marine Ricky Salyers, an alleged Ku Klux Klan member, discovering 35,000 rounds of heavy ammunition, armor piercing shells, smoke and tear gas grenades, live shells for grenade launchers, artillery shells and other military gear. Salyers was discharged earlier from the Marines, where he taught demolitions and sniping, after tossing a live grenade (with the pin still in) at state police officers serving him with a search warrant in 1995. Following the 1997 raid, Salyers, an alleged member of the underground Black Dawn group of extremists in the military, is sentenced to serve three years for weapons violations. He is released from prison in 2000.

March 26, 1997

Militia activist Brendon Blasz is arrested in Kalamazoo, Mich., and charged with making pipe bombs and other illegal explosives. Prosecutors say Blasz plotted to bomb the federal building in Battle Creek, the IRS building in Portage, a Kalamazoo television station and federal armories. But they recommend leniency on his explosives conviction after Blasz, a member of the Michigan Militia Corps Wolverines, renounces his antigovernment beliefs and cooperates with them. He is sentenced to more than three years in federal prison and released in late 1999.

April 22, 1997

Three Ku Klux Klan members are arrested in a plot to blow up a natural gas refinery outside Fort Worth, Texas, after local Klan leader Robert Spence gets cold feet and goes to the FBI. The three, along with a fourth arrested later, expected to kill a huge number of people with the blast—authorities later say as many as 30,000 might have died—which was to serve, incredibly, as a diversion for a simultaneous armored car robbery. Among the victims would have been children at a nearby school. All four plead guilty to conspiracy charges and are sentenced to terms of up to 20 years. Spence enters the Witness Protection Program. Carl Jay Waskom Jr. is released in 2004, while Shawn and Catherine Adams, a couple, are freed in 2006. Edward Taylor Jr. is released in early 2007.

April 23, 1997

Florida police arrest Todd Vanbiber, a member of the neo-Nazi National Alliance's Tampa unit and the shadowy League of the Silent Soldier, after he accidentally sets off pipe bombs he was building, blasting shrapnel into his own face. He is accused of plotting to use the bombs on the approach to Disney World to divert attention from a planned string of bank robberies. Vanbiber pleads guilty to weapons and explosives charges and is sentenced to more than six years in federal prison. He is released in 2002. Within two years, Vanbiber is posting messages on neo-Nazi Internet sites boasting that he has built over 300 bombs successfully and only made one error, and describing mass murderer Timothy McVeigh as a hero.

April 27, 1997

After a cache of explosives stored in a tree blows up near Yuba City, Calif., police arrest Montana Freemen supporter William Robert Goehler. Investigators looking into the blast arrest two Goehler associates, one of them a militia leader, after finding 500 pounds of explosives—enough to level three city blocks—in a motor home parked outside their residence. Six others are arrested on related charges. Goehler, with previous convictions for rape, burglary and assault, is sentenced to 25 years to life in prison. He is later accused of stabbing his attorney with a shank and charged with attacking prison psychologists.

May 3, 1997

Antigovernment extremists set fire to the IRS office in Colorado Springs, Colo., causing $2.5 million in damage and injuring a firefighter. Federal agents later arrest five men in connection with the arson, which is conceived as a protest against the tax system. Ringleader James Cleaver, former national director of the antigovernment Sons of Liberty group, is accused of threatening a witness and eventually sentenced to 33 years in prison, with a release date of 2030. Accomplice Jack Dowell receives 30 years and is scheduled to be freed in 2027. Both are ordered to pay $2.2 million in restitution. Dowell's cousin is acquitted of all charges, while two other suspects, Ronald Sherman and Thomas Shafer, plead guilty to perjury charges in connection with the case.

July 4, 1997

Militiaman Bradley Playford Glover and another heavily armed antigovernment activist are arrested before dawn near Fort Hood, in central Texas, just hours before they planned to invade the Army base and slaughter foreign troops they mistakenly believed were housed there. In the next few days, five other people are arrested in several states for their alleged roles in the plot to invade a series of military bases where the group believes United Nations forces are massing for an assault on Americans. All seven are part of a splinter group from the Third Continental Congress, a kind of militia government-in-waiting. In the end, Glover is sentenced to two years on Kansas weapons charges, to be followed by a five-year federal term in connection with the Fort Hood plot. The others draw lesser terms. Glover is released in 2003, the last of the seven to get out.

December 12, 1997

A federal grand jury in Arkansas indicts three men on racketeering charges for plotting to overthrow the government and create a whites-only

Aryan People's Republic, which they intend to grow through polygamy. Chevie Kehoe, Daniel Lee and Faron Lovelace are accused of crimes in six states, including murder, kidnapping, robbery and conspiracy. Kehoe and Lee will also face state charges of murdering an Arkansas family, including an 8-year-old girl, in 1996. Kehoe ultimately receives a life sentence on that charge, while Lee is sentenced to death. Lovelace is sentenced to death for the murder of a suspected informant, but because of court rulings is later resentenced to life without parole. Kehoe's brother, Cheyne, is convicted of attempted murder during a 1997 Ohio shootout with police and sentenced to 24 years in prison, despite his helping authorities track down his fugitive brother in Utah after the shootout. Cheyne went to the authorities after Chevie began talking about murdering their parents and showing sexual interest in Cheyne's wife.

January 29, 1998

An off-duty police officer is killed and a nurse terribly maimed when a nail-packed, remote-control bomb explodes outside a Birmingham, Ala., abortion facility, the New Woman All Women clinic. Letters to media outlets and officials claim responsibility in the name of the "Army of God," the same entity that took credit for the bombings of a clinic and a gay bar in the Atlanta area. The attack also will be linked to the fatal 1996 bombing of the Atlanta Olympics. Eric Robert Rudolph, a loner from North Carolina, is first identified as a suspect when witnesses spot his pickup truck fleeing the Birmingham bombing. But he is not caught until 2003. He ultimately pleads guilty to all four attacks in exchange for a life sentence.

February 23, 1998

Three men with links to a Ku Klux Klan group are arrested near East St. Louis, Ill., on weapons charges. The three, along with three other men arrested later, formed a group called The New Order, patterned on a 1980s terror group called The Order (a.k.a. the Silent Brotherhood) that carried out assassinations and armored car heists. New Order members plotted to assassinate a federal judge and civil rights lawyer Morris Dees, blow up the Southern Poverty Law Center that Dees co-founded and other buildings, poison water supplies and rob banks. Wallace Weicherding, one of the men, came to a 1997 Dees speech with a concealed gun but turned back rather than pass through a metal detector. In the end, all six plead guilty or are convicted of weapons charges, drawing terms of up to seven years in federal prison. New Order leader Dennis McGiffen is released in 2004, the last of the six to regain his freedom.

March 18, 1998

Three members of the North American Militia of Southwestern Michigan are arrested on firearms and other charges. Prosecutors say the men conspired to bomb federal buildings, a Kalamazoo television station and an interstate highway interchange, kill federal agents, assassinate politicians and attack aircraft at a National Guard base—attacks that were all to be funded by marijuana sales. The group's leader, Ken Carter, is a self-described member of the neo-Nazi Aryan Nations. Carter pleads guilty, testifies against his former comrades, and is sentenced to five years in prison. The others, Randy Graham and Bradford Metcalf, go to trial and are ultimately handed sentences of 40 and 55 years, respectively. Carter is released from prison in 2002.

May 29, 1998

A day after stealing a water truck, three men shoot and kill a Cortez, Colo., police officer and wound two other officers as they try to stop the suspects during a road chase. After the gun battle, the three—Alan Monty Pilon, Robert Mason and Jason McVean—disappear into the canyons of the high desert. Mason is found a week later, dead of an apparently self-inflicted gunshot. The skeletal remains of Pilon are found in 1999 and show that he, too, died of a gunshot to the head, another apparent suicide. McVean is not found, but most authorities assume he died in the desert. Many officials believe the three men intended to use the water truck in some kind of terrorist attack, but the nature of their suspected plans is never learned.

July 1, 1998

Three men are charged with conspiracy to use weapons of mass destruction after threatening President Clinton and other federal officials with biological weapons. Officials say the men planned to use a cactus thorn coated with a toxin like anthrax and fired by a modified butane lighter to carry out the murders. One man is acquitted of the charges, but Jack Abbot Grebe Jr., and Johnnie Wise—a 72-year-old man who attended meetings of the separatist Republic of Texas group —are sentenced to more than 24 years in prison. The men are set for release in 2019.

July 30, 1998

South Carolina militia member Paul T. Chastain is charged with weapons, explosives and drug violations after allegedly trying to trade drugs for a machine gun and enough C-4 plastic explosive to demolish a five-room house. The next year, Chastain pleads guilty to an array of charges, including threatening to kill Attorney General Janet Reno and FBI Director Louis

Freeh. He is sentenced to 15 years in federal prison, with release scheduled in 2011.

October 23, 1998

Dr. Barnett Slepian is assassinated by a sniper as he talks with his wife and children in the kitchen of their Amherst, N.Y., home. Identified as a suspect shortly after the murder, James Charles Kopp flees to Mexico, driven and disguised by friend Jennifer Rock, and goes on to hide out in Ireland and France. Two fellow anti-abortion extremists, Loretta Marra and Dennis Malvasi, make plans to help Kopp secretly return. Kopp, also suspected in the earlier sniper woundings of four physicians in Canada and upstate New York, is arrested in France as he picks up money wired by Marra and Malvasi. He eventually admits the shooting to a newspaper reporter—claiming that he only intended to wound Slepian—and is sentenced to life in prison plus 10 years. In 2003, Marra and Malvasi are sentenced to time served after pleading guilty to federal charges related to harboring a fugitive.

June 10, 1999

Officials arrest Alabama plumber Chris Scott Gilliam, a member of the neo-Nazi National Alliance, after he attempts to purchase 10 hand grenades from an undercover federal agent. Gilliam, who months earlier paraded in an extremist T-shirt in front of the Southern Poverty Law Center's offices in Montgomery, tells agents he planned to send mail bombs to targets in Washington, D.C. Agents searching his home find bomb-making manuals, white supremacist literature and an assault rifle. Gilliam pleads guilty to federal firearms charges and is sentenced to 10 years in prison. He is released in early 2008.

July 1, 1999

A gay couple, Gary Matson and Winfield Mowder, are shot to death in bed at their home near Redding, Calif. Days later, after tracking purchases made on Mowder's stolen credit card, police arrest brothers Benjamin Matthew Williams and James Tyler Williams. At least one of the pair, Matthew Williams (both use their middle names), is an adherent of the anti-Semitic Christian Identity theology. Police soon learn that the brothers two weeks earlier carried out arson attacks against three synagogues and an abortion clinic in Sacramento. Both brothers, whose mother at one point refers in a conversation to her sons' victims as "two homos," eventually admit their guilt—in Matthew's case, in a newspaper interview. Matthew, who at one point badly injures a guard in a surprise attack, commits suicide in 2002.

Tyler, who pleads guilty to an array of charges in the case, and is given two sentences amounting to 50 years to be served consecutively.

July 2, 1999

Infuriated that neo-Nazi leader Matt Hale has just been denied his law license by Illinois officials, follower Benjamin Nathaniel Smith begins a three-day murder spree across Illinois and Indiana, shooting to death a popular black former college basketball coach and a Korean doctoral student and wounding nine other minorities. Smith kills himself as police close in during a car chase. Hale, the "Pontifex Maximus," or leader, of the World Church of the Creator, at first claims to barely know Smith. But it quickly emerges that Hale has recently given Smith his group's top award and, in fact, spent some 16 hours on the phone with him in the two weeks before Smith's rampage. Conveniently, Hale receives a registered letter from Smith just days after his suicide, informing Hale that Smith is quitting the group because he now sees violence as the only answer.

August 10, 1999

Buford Furrow, a former member of the neo-Nazi Aryan Nations who has been living with the widow of slain terrorist leader Bob Mathews, strides into a Jewish community center near Los Angeles and fires more than 70 bullets, wounding three boys, a teenage girl and a woman. He then drives into the San Fernando Valley and murders Filipino-American mailman Joseph Ileto. The next day, Furrow turns himself in, saying he intended to send "a wake-up call to America to kill Jews." Furrow, who has a history of mental illness, eventually pleads guilty and is sentenced to two life terms without parole, plus 110 years in prison.

November 5, 1999

FBI agents arrest James Kenneth Gluck in Tampa, Fla., after he wrote a 10-page letter to judges in Jefferson County, Colo., threatening to "wage biological warfare" on a county justice center. While searching his home, police find the materials needed to make ricin, one of the deadliest poisons known. Gluck later threatens a judge, claiming that he could kill 10,000 people with the chemical. After serving time in federal prison, Gluck is released in early 2001.

December 5, 1999

Two California men, both members of the San Joaquin Militia, are charged with conspiracy in connection with a plot to blow up two 12-million-gallon propane tanks, a television tower and an electrical substation in hopes of provoking an insurrection. In 2001, the former militia leader, Donald Rudolph, pleads guilty to plotting to kill a federal judge and blow up the propane tanks, and testifies against his former comrades. Kevin Ray Patterson and Charles Dennis Kiles are ultimately convicted of several charges in connection with the conspiracy. They are expected to be released from federal prison in 2021 and 2018, respectively.

December 8, 1999
Donald Beauregard, head of a militia coalition known as the Southeastern States Alliance, is charged with conspiracy, providing materials for a terrorist act and gun violations in a plot to bomb energy facilities and cause power outages in Florida and Georgia. After pleading guilty to several charges, Beauregard, who once claimed to have discovered a secret map detailing a planned UN takeover mistakenly printed on a box of Trix cereal, is sentenced to five years in federal prison. He is released in 2004, a year after accomplice James Troy Diver is freed following a similar conviction.

March 9, 2000
Federal agents arrest Mark Wayne McCool, the one-time leader of the Texas Militia and Combined Action Program, as he allegedly makes plans to attack the Houston federal building. McCool, who was arrested after buying powerful C-4 plastic explosives and an automatic weapon from an undercover FBI agent, earlier plotted to attack the federal building with a member of his own group and a member of the antigovernment Republic of Texas, but those two men eventually abandoned the plot. McCool, however, remained convinced the UN had stored a cache of military materiel in the building. In the end, he pleads guilty to federal charges that bring him just six months in jail.

April 28, 2000
Immigration attorney Richard Baumhammers, himself the son of Latvian immigrants, goes on a rampage in the Pittsburgh area against non-whites, killing five people and critically wounding a sixth. Baumhammers had recently started a tiny white supremacist group, the Free Market Party, that demanded an end to non-white immigration into the United States. In the end, the unemployed attorney, who is living with parents at the time of his murder spree, is sentenced to death.

March 1, 2001
As part of an ongoing probe into a white supremacist group, federal and local law enforcement agents raid the Corbett, Ore., home of Fritz

Springmeier, seizing equipment to grow marijuana and weapons and racist literature. They also find a binder notebook entitled "Army of God, Yahweh's Warriors" that contains what officials call a list of targets, including a local federal building and the FBI's Oregon offices. Springmeier, an associate of the anti-Semitic Christian Patriots Association, is eventually charged with setting off a diversionary bomb at an adult video store in Damascus, Ore., in 1997 as part of a bank robbery carried out by accomplice Forrest Bateman Jr. Another 2001 raid finds small amounts of bomb materials and marijuana in Bateman's home. Eventually, Bateman pleads guilty to bank robbery and Springmeier is convicted of the same charges. Both are sentenced to nine years, and have release dates in 2011.

April 19, 2001

White supremacists Leo Felton and girlfriend Erica Chase are arrested following a foot chase that began when a police officer spotted them trying to pass counterfeit bills at a Boston donut shop. Investigators quickly learn Felton heads up a tiny group called Aryan Unit One, and that the couple, who had already obtained a timing device, planned to blow up black and Jewish landmarks and possibly assassinate black and Jewish leaders. They also learn another amazing fact: Felton, a self-described Aryan, is secretly biracial. Felton and Chase are eventually convicted of conspiracy, weapons violations and obstruction, and Felton is also convicted of bank robbery and other charges. Felton, who previously served 11 years for assaulting a black taxi driver, is sentenced to serve more than 21 years in federal prison, while his one-time sweetheart draws a lesser sentence and is released in 2007.

October 14, 2001

A North Carolina sheriff's deputy pulls over Steve Anderson, a former "colonel" in the Kentucky Militia, on a routine traffic stop as he heads home to Kentucky from a white supremacist gathering in North Carolina. Anderson, who is an adherent of racist Christian Identity theology and has issued violent threats against officials for months via an illegal pirate radio station, pulls out a semi-automatic weapon and peppers the deputy's car with bullets before driving his truck into the woods and disappearing for 13 months. Officials later find six pipe bombs in Anderson's abandoned truck and 27 bombs and destructive devices in his home. In the end, Anderson apologizes for his actions and pleads guilty. He is sentenced on a variety of firearms charges to 15 years in federal prison.

December 5, 2001

Anti-abortion extremist Clayton Lee Wagner, who nine months earlier escaped from an Illinois jail while awaiting sentencing on weapons and carjacking charges, is arrested in Cincinnati, Ohio. Wagner's odyssey began in September 1999, when he was stopped driving a stolen camper in Illinois and told police he was headed to Seattle to murder an abortion provider. He escaped in February 2001 and, while on the lam, mailed more than 550 hoax anthrax letters to abortion clinics and posted an Internet threat warning abortion clinic workers that "if you work for the murderous abortionist, I'm going to kill you." Wagner is eventually sentenced to 30 years on the Illinois charges. In Ohio, he is sentenced to almost 20 years more, to be served consecutively, on various weapons and car theft charges related to his time on the run. In late 2003, he also is found guilty of 51 federal terrorism charges. He is scheduled to be released in 2046.

December 11, 2001

Jewish Defense League chairman Irving David Rubin and a follower, Earl Leslie Krugel, are arrested in California and charged with conspiring to bomb the offices of U.S. Rep. Darrel Issa (R-Calif.) and the King Fahd Mosque in Culver City. Authorities say a confidential informant taped meetings with the two in which the bombings were discussed and Krugel said the JDL needed "to do something to one of their filthy mosques." Rubin later commits suicide in prison, officials say, just before he is to go on trial in 2002. Krugel pleads guilty to conspiracy in both plots, and testifies that Rubin conspired with him. Krugel dies in prison in 2005.

January 4, 2002

Neo-Nazi National Alliance member Michael Edward Smith is arrested after a car chase in Nashville, Tenn., that began when he was spotted sitting in a car with a semi-automatic rifle pointed at Sherith Israel Pre-School, run by a local synagogue. In Smith's car, home and storage unit, officials find an arsenal that includes a .50-caliber rifle, 10 hand grenades, 13 pipe bombs, binary explosives, semi-automatic pistols, ammunition and an array of military manuals. They also find teenage porn on Smith's computer and evidence that he carried out computer searches for Jewish schools and synagogues. In one of his E-mails, Smith wrote that Jews "perhaps" should be "stuffed head first into an oven." Smith is sentenced to more than 10 years in prison, with an expected release date in 2011.

February 8, 2002

The leader of a militia-like group known as Project 7 and his girlfriend are arrested after an informant tells police the group is plotting to kill judges and law enforcement officers in order to kick off a revolution. David Burgert, who has a record for burglary and is already wanted for assaulting police officers, is found in the house of girlfriend Tracy Brockway along with an arsenal that includes pipe bombs and 25,000 rounds of ammunition. Also found are "intel sheets" with personal information about law enforcement officers, their spouses and children. Although officials are convinced the Project 7 plot was real, Burgert ultimately is convicted only of weapons charges and draws a seven-year sentence; he is to be released in 2010. Six others are also convicted of or plead guilty to weapons charges. Brockway gets a suspended sentence for harboring a fugitive, but is sent to prison for violating its terms. She is released in early 2008.

July 19, 2002

Acting on a tip, federal and local law enforcement agents arrest North Carolina Klan leader Charles Robert Barefoot Jr. for his role in an alleged plot to blow up the Johnson County Sheriff's Office, the sheriff himself and the county jail. Officers find more than two dozen weapons in Barefoot's home. They also find bombs and bomb components in the home of Barefoot's son, Daniel Barefoot, who is charged that same day with the arson of a school bus and an empty barn. The elder Barefoot—who broke away from the National Knights of the KKK several months earlier to form his own harder-line group, the Nation's Knights of the KKK—is charged with weapons violations and later sentenced to more than two years. In 2003, Barefoot's wife and three men, including Barefoot Sr., are charged with the murder of a former Klan member. In 2007, a judge rules Barefoot Sr. mentally incompetent to stand trial for murder and commits him indefinitely to a mental hospital. Sharon Barefoot was released from prison in July 2009.

August 22, 2002

Tampa area podiatrist Robert J. Goldstein is arrested after police, called by Goldstein's wife after he allegedly threatened to kill her, find more than 15 explosive devices in their home, along with materials to make at least 30 more. Also found are homemade C-4 plastic explosives, grenades and mines, a .50-caliber rifle, semi-automatic weapons, and a list of 50 Islamic worship centers in the area. The most significant discovery is a three-page plan detailing plans to "kill all 'rags'" at the Islamic Society of Pinellas County. Eventually, two other local men are also charged in connection with the plot, and Goldstein's wife is arrested for possessing illegal destructive devices.

Goldstein pleads guilty to plotting to blow up the Islamic Society and is sentenced to more than 12 years in federal prison, with a release date in 2013. His wife was released in 2006.

October 3, 2002

Officials close in on long-time antigovernment extremist Larry Raugust at a rest stop in Idaho, arrest him and charge him with 16 counts of making and possessing destructive devices, including pipe bombs and pressure-detonated booby traps. He is accused of giving one explosive device to an undercover agent, and is also named as an unindicted co-conspirator in a plot with colleagues in the Idaho Mountain Boys militia to murder a federal judge and a police officer, and to break a friend out of jail. A deadbeat dad, Raugust is also accused of helping plant land mines on property belonging to a friend whose land was seized by authorities over unpaid taxes. He eventually pleads guilty to 15 counts of making bombs and is sentenced to federal prison. Raugust was released in early 2008.

January 8, 2003

Federal agents arrest Matt Hale, the national leader of the neo-Nazi World Church of the Creator (WCOTC), as he reports to a Chicago courthouse in an ongoing copyright case over the name of his group. Hale is charged with soliciting the murder of the federal judge in the case, Joan Humphrey Lefkow, who he has publicly vilified as someone bent on the destruction of his group. (Although Lefkow originally ruled in WCOTC's favor, an appeals court found that the complaint brought by an identically named church in Oregon was legally justified, and Lefkow reversed herself accordingly.) In guarded language captured on tape recordings, Hale is heard agreeing that his security chief, an FBI informant, should kill Lefkow. Hale is found guilty and sentenced to serve 40 years in federal prison; he is not expected to be released until 2037.

January 18, 2003

James D. Brailey, a convicted felon who once was selected as "governor" of the state of Washington by the antigovernment Washington Jural Society, is arrested after a raid on his home turns up a machine gun, an assault rifle and several handguns. One informant tells the FBI that Brailey was plotting to assassinate Gov. Gary Locke, both because Locke was the state's real governor and because he was Chinese-American. A second informant says that Brailey actually went on a "dry run" to Olympia, carrying several guns into the state Capitol building to test security. Eventually, Brailey pleads guilty to weapons charges and is sentenced to serve 15 months in prison. He is released in 2004.

February 13, 2003

Federal agents in Pennsylvania arrest David Wayne Hull, imperial wizard of the White Knights of the Ku Klux Klan and an adherent of the anti-Semitic Christian Identity theology, alleging that Hull arranged to buy hand grenades to blow up abortion clinics. The FBI says Hull also illegally instructed followers on how to build pipe bombs. Hull, who published a newsletter in which he urged readers to write Oklahoma bomber Tim McVeigh "to tell this great man goodbye," is found guilty of weapons violations and sentenced to 12 years in federal prison. He is to be released in 2012.

April 3, 2003

Federal agents arrest antigovernment extremist David Roland Hinkson in Idaho and charge him with trying to hire an assassin on two occasions in 2002 and 2003 to murder a federal judge, a prosecutor and an IRS agent involved in a tax case against him. Hinkson, a businessman who earned millions of dollars from his Water Oz dietary supplement company but refused to pay almost $1 million in federal taxes, is convicted in 2004 of 26 counts related to the tax case. In early 2005, a federal jury finds him guilty in the assassination plot as well. He is not expected to be released until 2040.

April 10, 2003

The FBI raids the Noonday, Texas, home of William Krar and storage facilities that Krar rented in the area, discovering an arsenal that includes more than 500,000 rounds of ammunition, 65 pipe bombs and remote-control briefcase bombs, and almost two pounds of deadly sodium cyanide. Also found are components to convert the cyanide into a bomb capable of killing thousands, along with white supremacist and antigovernment material. Investigators soon learn Krar was stopped earlier in 2003 by police in Tennessee, who found several weapons and coded documents in his car that seemed to detail a plot. But Krar refuses to cooperate, and details of that alleged plan are never learned. He pleads guilty to possession of a chemical weapon and is sentenced to more than 11 years in prison, where he dies.

June 4, 2003

Federal agents in California announce that former accountant John Noster, in prison since November 2002 for car theft, is under investigation for plotting a major terrorist attack. Noster was first arrested as part of a car theft ring investigation, but officials who found incendiary devices in his stolen camper continued to probe his activities. Eventually, they find in various storage facilities three pipe bombs, six barrels of jet fuel, five assault weapons, cannon fuse, a large amount of ammunition and $188,000 in cash. Law enforcement officials, who describe Noster as an "antigovernment extremist," allege at a press conference that he "was definitely planning" on an attack but do not elaborate. In addition to prison time in that case, Noster draws another five years in 2009, after pleading guilty to two weapons charges.

October 10, 2003

Police arrest Norman Somerville after finding a huge weapons cache on his property in northern Michigan that includes six machine guns, a powerful anti-aircraft gun, thousands of rounds of ammunition, hundreds of pounds of gunpowder, and an underground bunker. They also find two vehicles Somerville calls his "war wagons," and on which prosecutors later say he planned to mount machine guns as part of a plan to stage an auto accident and then massacre arriving police. Officials describe Somerville as an antigovernment extremist enraged over the death of Scott Woodring, a Michigan Militia member killed by police a week after Woodring shot and killed a state trooper during a standoff. Somerville eventually pleads guilty to weapons charges and is sentenced to six years in prison. He is scheduled to be released in late 2009.

April 1, 2004

Neo-Nazi Skinhead Sean Gillespie videotapes himself as he firebombs Temple B'nai Israel, an Oklahoma City synagogue, as part of a film he is preparing to inspire other racists to violent revolution. In it, Gillespie boasts that instead of merely pronouncing the white-supremacist "14 Words" slogan ("We must secure the existence of our people and a future for White children"), he will carry out 14 violent attacks. A former member of the neo-Nazi Aryan Nations, Gillespie is found guilty of the attack and later sentenced to 39 years in federal prison, with an expected release date of 2038.

May 24, 2004

During the attempted robbery of a Tulsa bank by Wade and Christopher Lay, a father-and-son pair of political extremists, security guard Kenneth Anderson is shot to death. Both robbers are wounded, and are arrested a short time after fleeing the bank. At trial, Wade Lay testifies that he and his son acted "for the good of the American people" and in an effort to "preserve liberty." Other evidence shows the pair hoped to get money to pay for weapons that they intended to use to kill Texas officials who they believed were responsible for the deadly 1993 standoff between the authorities and religious cultists in Waco. In the end, Wade Lay is sentenced to death for first-degree murder, while his son gets 25 years for armed robbery.

October 13, 2004

Ivan Duane Braden, a former National Guardsman discharged from an Iraq-bound unit after superiors noted signs of instability, is arrested after checking into a mental health facility and telling counselors about plans to blow up a synagogue and a National Guard armory in Tennessee. The FBI reports that Braden told agents that he planned to go to a synagogue wearing a trench coat stuffed with explosives and get himself "as close to children and the rabbi as possible," a plan Braden also outlined in notes found in his home. In addition, he intended to take and kill hostages at the Lenoir City Armory, before blowing the armory up. Eventually, Braden, who also possessed neo-Nazi literature and reportedly hated blacks and Jews from an early age, pleads guilty to conspiring to blow up the armory. He is sentenced to prison, where his release is expected in 2017.

October 25, 2004

FBI agents in Tennessee arrest farmhand Demetrius "Van" Crocker after he tried to purchase ingredients for deadly sarin nerve gas and C-4 plastic explosives from an undercover agent. The FBI reports that Crocker, who local officials say was involved in a white supremacist group in the 1980s, tells the agent that he admires Hitler and hates Jews and the government. He also says "it would be a good thing if somebody could detonate some sort of weapon of mass destruction on Washington, D.C." Crocker is convicted of trying to get explosives to destroy a building and imprisoned until an expected release in 2030.

May 20, 2005

Officials in New Jersey arrest two men they say asked a police informant to build them a bomb. Craig Orler, who has a history of burglary arrests, and Gabriel Carafa, said to be a leader of the neo-Nazi World Church of the Creator and a member of a racist Skinhead group called The Hated, are charged with illegally selling 11 guns to police informants. Carafa gave one informant 60 pounds of urea to use in building him a bomb, but never said what the bomb was for. Police say they moved in before the alleged bombing plot developed further because they were concerned about the pair's activities. They taped Orler saying in a phone call that he was seeking people in Europe to help him go underground. Orler is sentenced to more than 10 years in prison, while Carafa draws seven.

June 10, 2005

Daniel J. Schertz, a former member of the North Georgia White Knights of the Ku Klux Klan, is indicted in Chattanooga, Tenn., on federal weapons charges for allegedly making seven pipe bombs and selling them to an undercover informant with the idea that they would be used to murder Mexican and Haitian immigrant workers. The informant says Schertz demonstrated how to attach the pipe bombs to cars, then sold him bombs that Schertz expected to be used against a group of Haitians and, separately, Mexican workers on a bus headed to work in Florida. Schertz eventually pleads guilty to six charges—including teaching how to make an explosive device; making, possessing and transferring destructive devices; and possessing a pistol with armor-piercing bullets—and is sentenced to 14 years in prison. He is to be released in 2017.

March 19, 2006

U.S. Treasury agents in Utah arrest David J. D'Addabbo for allegedly threatening Internal Revenue Service employees with "death by firing squad" if they continued to try to collect taxes from him and his wife. D'Addabbo, who was reportedly carrying a Glock pistol, 40 rounds of ammunition and a switchblade knife when he was seized leaving a church service, allegedly wrote to the U.S. Tax Court that anyone attempting to collect taxes would be tried by a "jury of common people. You then could be found guilty of treason and immediately taken to a firing squad." In August D'Addabbo pleads guilty to one charge of threatening a government agent in exchange for the dismissal of three other charges of threatening IRS agents. He is sentenced to time served and released the same year as his arrest.

April 26, 2007

Five members of the Alabama Free Militia are arrested in north Alabama in a raid by federal and state law enforcement officers that uncovers a cache of 130 homemade hand grenades, an improvised grenade launcher, a Sten Mark submachine gun, a silencer, 2,500 rounds of ammunition and almost 100 marijuana plants. Raymond Kirk Dillard, the founder and "commander" of the group, pleads guilty to criminal conspiracy, illegally making and possessing destructive devices and being a felon in possession of a firearm. Other members of the group—Bonnell "Buster" Hughes, James Ray McElroy, Adam Lynn Cunningham and Randall Garrett—also plead guilty to related charges. Although Dillard, who complained about the collapse of the

American economy, terrorist attacks and Mexicans taking over the country, reportedly told his troops to open fire on federal agents if ever confronted, no shots are fired during the April raid, and the "commander" even points out booby-trap tripwires on his property to investigators. Dillard and Garrett draw the harshest sentences, with releases scheduled for 2012 and 2018, respectively.

June 8, 2008

Six people, most of them tied to the militia movement, are arrested in rural north-central Pennsylvania after officials find stockpiles of assault rifles, improvised explosives and homemade weapons, at least some of them apparently intended for terrorist attacks on U.S. officials. Agents find 16 homemade bombs during a search of the residence of Pennsylvania Citizens Militia recruiter Bradley T. Kahle, who allegedly tells authorities that he intended to shoot black people from a rooftop in Pittsburgh and also predicts civil war if Barack Obama or Hillary Clinton are elected president. A raid on the property of Morgan Jones results in the seizure of 73 weapons, including a homemade flame thrower, a machine that supposedly shot bolts of electricity, and an improvised cannon. Also arrested and charged with weapons violations are Marvin E. Hall, his girlfriend Melissa Huet and Perry Landis. Landis, who is to be sentenced in late 2009, allegedly tells undercover agents he wanted to kill Gov. Ed Rendell. Hall is sentenced to more than two years.

August 24, 2008

White supremacists Shawn Robert Adolf, Tharin Robert Gartrell and Nathan D. Johnson are arrested in Denver during the Democratic National Convention on weapons charges and for possession of amphetamines. Although police say they talked about assassinating presidential candidate Barack Obama, they are not charged in connection with that threat because officials see their talk as drug-fueled boasting. Police report the three had high-powered, scoped rifles, wigs, camouflage clothing and a bulletproof vest, along with the crystal methamphetamine. Gartrell is released from prison in June 2009, while Johnson is to be freed in 2010. Adolf, who was already wanted on other charges, draws a longer sentence.

October 24, 2008

Two white supremacists, Daniel Cowart and Paul Schlesselman, are arrested in Tennessee for allegedly plotting to assassinate Barack Obama and murder more than 100 black people. Officials say Schlesselman and Cowart, a probationary member of the racist skinhead group Supreme

White Alliance, planned to kill 88 people, then behead another 14. (Both numbers are significant in white supremacist circles. H is the eighth letter of the alphabet, so double 8s stand for HH, or "Heil Hitler." The number 14 represents the "14 Words," a popular racist saying.) The pair are indicted on charges that include threatening a presidential candidate, possessing a sawed-off shotgun, taking firearms across state lines to commit crimes, planning to rob a licensed gun dealer, damaging religious property, and using a firearm during the commission of a crime.

December 9, 2008

Police responding to a shooting at a home in Belfast, Maine, find James G. Cummings dead, allegedly killed by his wife after years of domestic abuse. They also find a cache of radioactive materials, which Cummings was apparently using to try to build a radioactive "dirty bomb," along with literature on how to build such a deadly explosive. Police also discover a membership application filled out by Cummings for the neo-Nazi National Socialist Movement. Friends say that Cummings had a collection of Nazi memorabilia. The authorities say Cummings was reportedly "very upset" by the election of Barack Obama.

December 16, 2008

Kody Ray Brittingham, a lance corporal in the U.S. Marine Corps, is arrested with four others on attempted robbery charges. A search of his barracks room at Camp Lejeune, N.C., allegedly turns up white supremacist materials and a journal written by Brittingham containing plans to kill Barack Obama. Brittingham is indicted for threatening the president-elect of the United States, a crime that carries a maximum penalty of five years in federal prison and a fine of up to $250,000.

January 21, 2009

On the day after Barack Obama is inaugurated as the nation's first black president, Keith Luke of Brockton, Mass., is arrested after allegedly shooting three black immigrants from Cape Verde, killing two of them, as part of a racially motivated killing spree. The two murders are apparently only part of Luke's plan to kill black, Latino and Jewish people. After being captured by police, he reportedly says he planned to go to an Orthodox synagogue near his home that night and "kill as many Jews as possible." Police say Luke, a white man who apparently had no contact with white supremacists but spent the previous six months reading racist websites, told them he was "fighting for a dying race." Luke also says he formed his racist views in large part after watching videos on Podblanc, a racist video-sharing website run by longtime white supremacist Craig Cobb. When he later appears in court for a hearing, Luke, charged with murder, kidnapping and aggravated rape, has etched a swastika into his own forehead, apparently using a jail razor.

April 4, 2009

Three Pittsburgh police officers—Paul Sciullo III, Stephen Mayhle and Eric Kelly—are fatally shot and a fourth, Timothy McManaway, is wounded after responding to a domestic dispute at the home of Richard Andrew Poplawski, who had posted his racist and anti-Semitic views on white supremacist websites. In one post, Poplawski talks about wanting a white supremacist tattoo. He also reportedly tells a friend that America is controlled by a cabal of Jews, that U.S. troops may soon be used against American citizens, and that he fears a ban on guns is coming. Poplawski later allegedly tells investigators that he fired extra bullets into the bodies of two of the officers "just to make sure they were dead" and says he "thought I got that one, too" when told that the fourth officer survived. More law enforcement officers are killed during the incident than in any other single act of violence by a domestic political extremist since the 1995 Oklahoma City bombing.

April 25, 2009

Joshua Cartwright, a Florida National Guardsman, allegedly shoots to death two Okaloosa County, Fla., sheriff's deputies—Burt Lopez and Warren "Skip" York—at a gun range as the officers attempt to arrest Cartwright on domestic violence charges. After fleeing the scene, Cartwright is fatally shot during a gun battle with pursuing officers. Cartwright's wife later tells investigators that her husband was "severely disturbed" that Barack Obama has been elected president. He also reportedly believed the U.S. government was conspiring against him. The sheriff tells reporters that Cartwright had been interested in joining a militia group.

May 31, 2009

Scott Roeder, an anti-abortion extremist who was involved with the antigovernment "freemen" movement in the 1990s, allegedly shoots to death Kansas late-term abortion provider George Tiller as the doctor is serving as an usher in his Wichita church. Adherents of "freemen" ideology claim they are "sovereign citizens" not subject to federal and other laws, and often form their own "common law" courts and issue their own license plates. It was one of those homemade plates that led Topeka police to stop Roeder in April 1996, when a search of his trunk revealed a pound of gunpowder, a 9-volt battery wired to a switch, blasting caps and ammunition. A prosecutor in that case called Roeder a "substantial threat to public safety," citing Roeder's refusal to acknowledge the court's authority. But his conviction in the 1996 case is ultimately overturned. In the more recent case, Roeder is charged with murder and could face up to life in prison if convicted.

June 10, 2009

Eighty-eight-year-old James von Brunn, a longtime neo-Nazi, walks up to the U.S. Holocaust Memorial Museum and allegedly shoots to death security guard Stephen Johns before he is himself shot and critically wounded by other officers. Von Brunn, who earlier served six years in connection with his 1981 attempt to kidnap the members of the Federal Reserve Board at the point of a sawed-off shotgun, has been active in the white supremacist movement for more than four decades. As early as the early 1970s, he worked at the Holocaust-denying Noontide Press, and in subsequent decades, he comes to know many of the key leaders of the radical right. A search of von Brunn's car after the museum attack turns up a list of other apparent targets, including the White House, the Capitol, the National Cathedral and The Washington Post. A note allegedly left by von Brunn in his car reads: "You want my weapons; this is how you'll get them ... the Holocaust is a lie ... Obama was created by Jews. Obama does what his Jew owners tell him to do. Jews captured America's money. Jews control the mass media." He is charged with murder.

June 12, 2009

Shawna Forde—the executive director of Minutemen American Defense (MAD), an anti-immigrant vigilante group that conducts "citizen patrols" on the Arizona-Mexico border—is charged with two counts of first-degree murder for her alleged role in the slayings of a Latino man and his 9-year-old daughter in Arivaca, Ariz. Forde allegedly orchestrated the May 30 home invasion because she believed the man was a narcotics trafficker and wanted to steal drugs and cash to fund her group. Authorities say the murders, including the killing of the child, were part of the plan. Also arrested and charged with murder are the alleged triggerman, MAD Operations Director Jason Eugene "Gunny" Bush, and Albert Robert Gaxiola, 42, a local member of MAD. Authorities say that Bush had ties to the neo-Nazi Aryan Nations in Idaho, and that Forde has spoken of recruiting its members.

June 25, 2009

Longtime white supremacist Dennis Mahon and his brother Daniel are indicted in Arizona in connection with a mail bomb sent in 2004 to a diversity office in Scottsdale that injured three people. Mahon, formerly tied to the neo-Nazi White Aryan Resistance (WAR) group, allegedly left a phone message at the office saying that "the White Aryan Resistance is growing in Scottsdale. There's a few white people who are standing up." In a related raid, agents search the Indiana home of Tom Metzger, founder of WAR, but he is not arrested. On the same day, white supremacist Robert Joos is arrested in rural Missouri, apparently because phone records show that Dennis Mahon's first call after the mail bombing was to Joos' cell phone. Joos is charged with being a felon in possession of firearms and is sentenced in May 2010 to 6½ years in prison. Dennis Mahon is found guilty of three bombing charges in February 2012 and faces a maximum 60 years in prison and a $250,000 fine. Daniel Mahon is acquitted of the one charge against him.

Oct. 28, 2009

Luqman Ameen Abdullah, identified by authorities as a member of a black Muslim group hoping to create an Islamic state within U.S. borders, is shot dead at a warehouse in Dearborn, Mich., after he fires at FBI agents trying to arrest him on conspiracy and weapons charges. The FBI says Abdulla encouraged violence against the United States, adding that 10 other group members are being sought.

Feb. 18, 2010

Joseph Andrew Stack, who had earlier attended meetings of radical anti-tax groups in California, sets fire to his own house and then flies his single-engine plane into an Austin, Texas, building housing IRS offices. Stack and an IRS manager are killed, and 13 others are injured. Stack leaves a long online rant about the IRS and the tax code, politicians and corporations.

March 25, 2010

A man later identified as Brody James Whitaker opens fire on two Florida state troopers during a routine traffic stop on I-75 in Sumter County. Whitaker flees, crashing his vehicle and continuing on foot. He is arrested two weeks later in Connecticut, where he challenges the authority of a judge and declares himself a "sovereign," not American, citizen. Sovereigns typically believe that police have no right to regulate road travel. Whitaker is later extradited to Florida to face charges of assaulting and fleeing from a police officer.

March 27–28, 2010

Nine members of the Hutaree Militia are arrested in raids in Michigan, Ohio and Indiana and charged with seditious conspiracy and attempted use of weapons of mass destruction. The group, whose website said it was preparing for the imminent arrival of the anti-Christ, allegedly planned to murder a Michigan police officer, then use bombs and homemade missiles to kill other officers attending the funeral, all in a bid to set off a war with the government. . Joshua Clough pleads guilty to a weapons charge in December 2011. A federal judge dismisses charges against seven members of the group during a trial in March 2012, saying their hatred of law enforcement did not amount to a conspiracy. Militia leader David Stone and his son Joshua Stone plead guilty to gun charges two days after the trial. Another member, Jacob Ward, awaits a separate trial.

April 15, 2010
Matthew Fairfield, who is president of a local chapter of an antigovernment "Patriot" organization called the Oath Keepers, is indicted on 28 explosives charges, 25 counts of receiving stolen property and one count of possessing criminal tools. Authorities searching his home discover a napalm bomb built by Fairfield, along with a computer carrying child pornography. Fairfield later pleads guilty to explosives charges, but still faces trial on other counts.

April 30, 2010
Darren Huff, an Oath Keeper from Georgia, is arrested and charged with planning the armed takeover of a Madisonville, Tenn., courthouse and "arrest" of 24 local, state and federal officials. Authorities say Huff was angry about the April 1 arrest there of Walter Francis Fitzpatrick III, a leader of the far-right American Grand Jury movement that seeks to have grand juries indict President Obama for treason. Several others in the antigovernment "Patriot" movement accuse Huff of white supremacist and anti-Semitic attitudes in Internet postings. He is sentenced in May 2012 to four years in federal prison.

May 10, 2010
Sandlin Matthew Smith detonates a pipe bomb at a rear entrance to a mosque in Jacksonville, Fla., while worshippers are inside. Armed only with a fuzzy videotape, authorities only identify Smith, based on talking to witnesses to whom he admits the attack, a year later. They track Smith, a bus driver from Julington Creek, Fla., to a campsite near Fairview, Okla., where he resists arrest with a gun and is killed. A search of Smith's two homes turns up explosive materials.

May 20, 2010
A father and son team of "sovereign citizens" who believe police have no right to regulate road travel murder West Memphis, Ark., police officers

Robert Brandon Paudert, 39, and Thomas William "Bill" Evans, 38, during a routine traffic stop on an I-40 exit ramp. The incident begins when Jerry Kane, 45, starts to argue with the officers over his bogus vehicle paperwork and then pushes Evans into a roadside ditch. Kane's 16-year-old son then kills both officers with an AK-47 before the pair flees. Authorities catch up with them about 45 minutes later. In the ensuing shootout, two more officers are badly wounded and both Kanes are killed. The pair had been traveling the country offering seminars in bogus sovereign techniques for avoiding foreclosure and related matters.

June 8, 2010

A bomb packed into a soda can is planted outside Osage Baptist Church in Carroll City, Ark., where a polling station for a Democratic Senate primary runoff between Sen. Blanche Lincoln and Lt. Gov. Bill Halter is located. The device does not explode, although authorities say it was capable of causing death or serious bodily injury. Officials later receive a tip from contractors who hired to clean out the foreclosed home of self-described "Patriot" Mark Krause, where they find bomb-making materials, manuals, and materials related to antigovernment militias. Krause, who earlier posted antigovernment messages to MySpace, eventually is arrested in Seattle.

July 18, 2010

An unemployed parolee with two bank robbery convictions, apparently enraged at liberals and what he sees as the "left-wing agenda" of Congress, allegedly opens fire on California Highway Patrol troopers who pull him over in Oakland. No one is killed, but two troopers are slightly injured and Byron Williams is shot in the arms and legs. Williams allegedly later tells authorities that he was on his way to attack offices of the American Civil Liberties Union and the Tides Foundation, a liberal organization that, although little known to most Americans, has been repeatedly pilloried on air by Fox News host Glenn Beck.

July 21, 2010

Attorney Todd Getgen is shot to death at a gun range in Cumberland County, Penn., and his weapon, a silenced AR-15 rifle, is stolen. Authorities arrest prison guard Raymond Peake nine days later, saying Peake was trying to accumulate weapons for an unnamed organization that intended to overthrow the government. Fellow prison guard Thomas Tuso is also arrested for allegedly helping Peake hide Getgen's custom-built weapon.

August 30, 2010

White supremacist Wayde Lynn Kurt is arrested in Spokane, Wash., on federal gun and forgery charges. Authorities later release audio recordings to support their allegation that he was planning a terrorist attack he called his "final solution," which included killing President Obama. Wayde, a convicted felon who is associated with neo-Nazis and Odinists, is sentenced in May 2012 to 13 years in prison on firearms and false identification convictions after federal prosecutors sought and received a "terrorism enhancement" to his sentence.

Sept. 2, 2010

A pipe bomb is thrown through the window of a closed Planned Parenthood clinic in Madera, Calif., along with a note that reads, "Murder our children? We have a 'choice' too." The note is signed ANB, apparently short for the American Nationalist Brotherhood. Six months later, law enforcement officials arrest school bus driver Donny Eugene Mower, who allegedly also threatened a local Islamic Center and has the word "Peckerwood," a reference to a white supremacist gang, tattooed on his chest. Mower reportedly confesses to the attack.

Sept. 7, 2010

The FBI arrests 26-year-old Justin Carl Moose, a self-described "freedom fighter" and "Christian counterpart to Osama bin Laden," for allegedly planning to blow up a North Carolina abortion clinic. After earlier receiving tips that Moose was posting threats of violence against abortion providers and information about explosives on his Facebook page, the FBI set up a sting operation to capture him. Moose later pleads guilty to distributing information on manufacturing and use of an explosive and is sentenced to 30 months in prison.

Sept. 19, 2010

An antigovernment extremist with ties to the separatist Republic of Texas organization allegedly opens fire on an oil company worker and two sheriff's deputies who show up at White's property in West Odessa, Texas, to access an oil well to which the company has rights. Victor White, 55, allegedly wounds all three men before they retreat, and a 22-hour standoff follows. White eventually surrenders and is charged with three counts of attempted capital murder of a peace officer, one count of attempted capital murder, and aggravated assault.

Jan. 14, 2011

Federal agents in Arizona arrest Jeffery Harbin, a member of the neo-Nazi National Socialist Movement, for allegedly building homemade grenades and pipe bombs that he apparently intended to supply to anti-immigration groups patrolling the Mexican border. A prosecutor says that Harbin constructed the devices, using model rocket engines and aluminum power, "in such a way as to maximize human carnage." Harbin is indicted on two counts of possessing a destructive device and a third of transporting destructive devices. Jeffery Harbin is the son of Jerry Harbin, a Phoenix-area activist with past ties to the neo-Nazi National Alliance and the racist Council of Conservative Citizens.

Jan. 17, 2011

Bomb technicians defuse a sophisticated improvised explosive device (IED) found in a backpack along the Spokane, Wash., route of a Martin Luther King Jr. Day parade with 1,500 marchers. Using forensic clues found in the dismantled bomb, officials about two months later identify and arrest Kevin William Harpham, a long-time neo-Nazi. Harpham had posted more than 1,000 messages to the neo-Nazi Vanguard News Network since 2004, when he was a member of the neo-Nazi National Alliance. Harpham also had contributed to the white supremacist Aryan Alternative newspaper. He is indicted on one count of attempted use of a weapon of mass destruction and one count of possessing an IED. Later, federal hate crime charges are added.

March 10, 2011

Six members of the antigovernment Alaska Peacemakers Militia, including its leader Francis Schaeffer Cox, are arrested and charged with plotting to kill or kidnap state troopers and a Fairbanks judge. The group already has a large cache of weapons, including a .50-caliber machine gun and grenades and a grenade launcher. Cox earlier identified himself as a "sovereign citizen."

May 14, 2011

Three masked men break into the Madrasah Islamiah, an Islamic center in Houston, and douse prayer rugs with gasoline in an apparent attempt to burn the center down. Images of the men are captured on surveillance cameras, but they are not identified. The fire is put out before doing major damage.

May 25, 2011

A man with a long history of menacing abortion clinics is arrested on weapons charges after he accidentally shoots a pistol through the door of a

Madison, Wis., motel room. Ralph Lang, 63, tells police he planned to kill a doctor and workers at a nearby Planned Parenthood clinic.

August 24, 2011

Cody Seth Crawford, 24, is arrested on federal charges accusing him of the Nov. 28, 2010, arson of the Salman Alfarisi Islamic Center in Corvallis, Ore. The firebombing occurred two days after a former Oregon State University student was arrested in a plot to detonate a car bomb during Portland's annual tree-lighting. Crawford had ranted about Muslims and described himself as a Christian warrior during previous run-ins with police.

October 5, 2011

White supremacist ex-convict David "Joey" Pedersen, 31, and his girlfriend, Holly Ann Grigsby, 24, are arrested in California after a murderous rampage in three states. Grigsby tells police that she and Pedersen "were on their way to Sacramento to kill more Jews." The first killed were Pedersen's father and stepmother in Everett, Wash. Another man was killed in Lafayette, Ore., because the pair thought he was Jewish. An African-American man was found shot to death in Eureka, Calif. Pederson earlier served time for threatening to kill the federal judge who handled the Ruby Ridge case of white separatist Randy Weaver. Pederson pleads guilty in March 2012. He will receive a mandatory life sentence without possibility of parole. Grigsby pleads not guilty and awaits trial.

November 1, 2011

Four members of an unnamed North Georgia militia are arrested in an alleged plot to bomb federal buildings, attack cities including Atlanta with deadly ricin, and murder law enforcement officials. The men—Frederick Thomas, 73, Samuel J. Crump, 68, Dan Roberts, 67, and Ray H. Adams, 65—allegedly discussed dispersing ricin powder in a series of cities, "taking out" a list of officials to "make the country right again," and scouting buildings in Atlanta to bomb. Authorities say the plot was inspired by an online novel, Absolved, written by longtime Alabama militiaman Mike Vanderboegh. Thomas, the accused ringleader, and Roberts plead guilty in April 2012 to charges of conspiring to possess explosives and firearms.

April 17, 2012

Joseph Benjamin Thomas and Samuel James Johnson of Mendota Heights, Minn., are indicted on federal weapons and drug charges following a federal investigation into their alleged plans to form a white supremacist group called the "Aryan Liberation Movement" and commit violence against minorities, leftists and government officials. Prosecutors allege that Thomas planned to attack the Mexican consulate in St. Paul on May 1 with a truck loaded with barrels of oil and gas that he would set on fire, believing that the attack would stir debate on immigration amnesty prior to the 2012 elections. An affidavit unsealed in federal court reveals that Johnson, a former leader of the neo-Nazi National Socialist Movement in Minnesota with past convictions for armed crimes, was trying to recruit others to his cause and scouted for a training compound in Illinois and Minnesota. Johnson pleads not guilty and awaits trial.

BIBLIOGRAPHY

Ahmed, Habib, *Product Development in Islamic Banks* (Edinburgh University Press: Edinburgh, 2011)

Arendt, Hannah, *The Origins of Totalitarianism* (Harcourt, Inc., New York, NY, 1976)

Arendt, Hannah, ed., *Kant* (Harcourt Brace Jovanovich: San Diego, CA, 1962)

Barkey, Karen, ed., *After Empire: Multiethnic Societies and Nation-Building: The Soviet Union and the Russian, Ottoman, and Hapsburg Empires* (Westview Press: Boulder, CO, 1997)

Batra, Ravi, *Greenspan's Fraud: How Two Decades of His Policy Have Undermined the Global Economy* (Palgrave Macmillan: New York, 2005)

Bell, Daniel, *The Coming of Post-Industrial Society: A Venture in Social Forecasting* (Basic Books: New York, 1973)

Bierman, Harold Jr., *The Causes of the 1929 Stock Market Crash: A Speculative Orgy or a New Era?* (Greenwood Press: Westport, CT, 1998)

Brown, Dee, *Bury My Heart at Wounded Knee* (St. Martin's Press: New York, NY, 1970)

Blum, William, *Killing Hope: U.S. Military and C.I.A. Interventions Since World War II* (Common Courage Press: Monroe, ME 2004)

Cammisa, Anne Marie, *Governments as Interest Groups: Intergovernmental Lobbying and the Federal System* (Praeger Publishers: Westport, CT 1995)

Corrigan, John, ed., *Religious Intolerance in America: A Documentary History* (University of North Carolina Press: Chapel Hill, NC, 2010)

Dizard, Jan E., ed., *Guns in America: a Reader* (New York University Press: New York, NY, 1999)

Engdahl, F. William, *Seeds of Destruction: The Hidden Agenda of Genetic Manipulation* (Global Research: Montreal, Quebec, 2007)

Enlow, Robert C., ed., *Liberty and Learning: Milton Friedman's Voucher Idea at Fifty* (Cato Institute: Washington, DC, 2006)

Fitzgerald, Randall, *The Hundred-Year Lie* (Penguin Group: New York, 2007)

Friedman, Thomas L., *From Beirut to Jerusalem* (Random House, Inc.: New York, 1995)

Göcek, Fatma Müge, *Rise of the Bourgeoisie, Demise of Empire: Ottoman Westernization and Social Change* (Oxford University Press: New York, 1996)

Goffman, Daniel, *The Ottoman Empire and Early Modern Europe* (Cambridge University Press: Cambridge, England, 2002)

Greider, William, *Secrets of the Temple: How the Federal Reserve Runs the Country* (Simon & Schuster: New York, 1989)

Gribben, Crawford and Newport, Kenneth G.C., eds., *Expecting the End: Millennialism in Social and Historical Context* (Baylor University Press: Waco, TX, 2006)

Hanjoğlu, Sükrü M., *A Brief History of the Late Ottoman Empire* (Princeton University Press: Princeton, NJ, 2010)

Haskin, Jeanne M., *Ageless* (Artema Press: Chattanooga, TN, 2013)

_____, *Bosnia and Beyond: the "Quiet" Revolution That Wouldn't Go Quietly* (Algora: New York, 2006)

_____, *From Conflict to Crisis: The Danger of U.S. Actions* (Algora: New York, 2012)

_____, *The Tragic State of the Congo: From Decolonization to Dictatorship* (Algora: New York, 2005)

_____, *Unbreakable* (Artema Press: Chattanooga, TN, 2013)

Hayek, F.A., *The Road to Serfdom* (University of Chicago Press: Chicago, 2007)

Holbrooke, Richard, *To End a War* (Random House: New York, 1998)

Huntington, Samuel P., *The Clash of Civilizations and the Remaking of World Order* (Simon & Schuster: New York, NY 1996)

Jahoda, Gloria, *The Trail of Tears* (Random House: New York, 1975)

Kennedy, David M., *Freedom From Fear: The American People in Depression and War, 1929-1945* (Oxford University Press: New York, 1999)

Kennedy, Paul, ed., *Communities Across Borders: New Immigrants and Transnational Cultures* (Routledge: London, 2002)

_____, *Globalization and National Identities: Crisis or Opportunity?* (Palgrave: New York, 2001)

Khorshid, Aly, *Islamic Insurance: A Modern Approach to Islamic Banking* (RoutledgeCurzon, New York, 2004)

Klein, Naomi, *The Shock Doctrine: The Rise of Disaster Capitalism* (Henry Holt and Company: New York, 2007)

Lasch, Christopher, *The Culture of Narcissism: American Life in an Age of Diminishing Expectations* (Warner Books: New York, NY, 1979)

Lewis, James R., ed., *Odd Gods: New Religions and the Cult Controversy* (Prometheus Books: Amherst, NY, 2001)

Lindauer, Susan, *Extreme Prejudice* (Lindauer: Lexington, KY, 2010)

Mandel, Michael J., *The Coming Internet Depression: Why the High-Tech Boom Will Go Bust, Why the Crash Will Be Worse Than You Think, and How to Prosper Afterwards* (Basic Books: New York, 2000)

Marrs, Jim, *Rule by Secrecy* (Harper Collins Publishers: New York, NY, 2000)

Mazzetti, Mark, *The Way of the Knife: The CIA, a Secret Army, and a War at the Ends of the Earth* (Penguin Press: New York, 2013)

McNamara, Robert S., *In Retrospect: the Tragedy and Lessons of Vietnam* (Vintage Books: New York, 1995)

Mitchell, Broadus, *Depression Decade: From New Era Through New Deal, 1929-1941* (Rinehart: New York, 1947)

Morgan, Ted, *FDR: A Biography* (Simon & Schuster: New York, 1985)

Newport, Kenneth G.C., *The Branch Davidians of Waco: The History and Beliefs of an Apocalyptic Sect* (Oxford University Press: New York, 2006)

Perkins, John, *Confessions of an Economic Hit Man* (Berrett-Koehler Publishers, Inc.: San Francisco, CA, 2004)

Rand, Ayn, *Atlas Shrugged* (Signet: New York, NY, 1996)

_____, *We the Living* (Signet: New York, NY, 1996)

Rank, Mark Robert, *One Nation, Underprivileged* (Oxford University Press: New York, 2005)

Reagan, Michael D., *The Accidental System: Health Care in America* (Westview Press: Boulder, CO, 1999)

Reston, James Jr., *Dogs of God: Columbus, the Inquisition, and the Defeat of the Moors* (Random House: New York, 2005)

Ritzer, George, *The McDonaldization of Society* (Pine Forge Press: Thousand Oaks, CA, 2000)

Roberson, B.A., *Shaping the Current Islamic Reformation* (Frank Cass: London, 2003)

Rodogno, Davide, *Against Massacre: Humanitarian Interventions in the Ottoman Empire 1815-1914* (Princeton University Press: Princeton, NJ 2012)

Russell, Bertrand, *History of Western Philosophy* (Routledge: London, 2004)

Saeed, Abdullah, *Islamic Banking and Interest: A Study of the Prohibition of Riba and its Contemporary Interpretation* (Brill: Boston, 1999)

Salzmann, Ariel, *Tocqueville in the Ottoman Empire: Rival Paths to the Modern State* (Brill: Boston, 2004)

Schlatter, Evelyn A., *Aryan Cowboys: White Supremacists and the Search for a New Frontier 1970-2000* (University of Texas Press: Austin, TX, 2006)

Shull, Steven A., *American Civil Rights Policy From Truman to Clinton: The Role of Presidential Leadership* (M.E. Sharpe: Armonk, NY, 2000)

Silverman, Bertram, ed., *Labor and Democracy in the Transition to a Market System: a U.S.-Post-Soviet Dialogue* (M.E. Sharpe: Armonk, NY, 1992)

Sklar, Holly, ed., *Trilateralism: The Trilateral Commission and Elite Planning for World Management* (South End Press: Boston, MA 1980).

Soley, Lawrence C., *Leasing the Ivory Tower: The Corporate Takeover of Academia* (South End: Boston, 1995)

Sornette, Didier, *Why Stock Markets Crash: Critical Events in Complex Financial Systems* (Princeton University Press: Princeton, NJ, 2004)

Soros, George, *The Crash of 2008 and What it Means: The New Paradigm for Financial Markets* (Public Affairs: New York, 2009)

Stannard, David E., *The American Holocaust: Columbus and the Conquest of the New World* (Oxford University Press: New York, 1992)

Stern, Kenneth S., *A Force Upon a Plain: The American Militia Movement and the Politics of Hate* (Simon & Schuster: New York, 1997)

Thibodeau, David and Whiteson, Leon, *A Place Called Waco: A Survivor's Story* (Public Affairs: New York, 1999)

Thucydides, *The History of the Peloponnesian War* (E.P. Dutton: New York, 1950)

Toffler, Alvin, *The Third Wave* (Bantam Books, New York, NY, 1981)

Vizzard, William J., *In the Crossfire: A Political History of the Bureau of Alcohol, Tobacco, and Firearms* (Lynne Rienner Publishers: Boulder, CO, 1997)

Wagner-Pacifici, Robin, *Theorizing the Standoff: Contingency in Action* (Cambridge University Press: Cambridge, England, 2000)

Walzer, Michael, *Just and Unjust Wars: A Moral Argument With Historical Illustrations* (Basic Books: New York, 2000)

Warde, Ibrahim, *Islamic Finance in the Global Economy*, Second Edition (Edinburgh University Press: Edinburgh, 2010)

West, Richard, *Tito and the Rise and Fall of Yugoslavia* (Carroll & Graf Publishers, Inc.: New York, NY, 1994)

Witte, John F., *The Market Approach to Education: Analysis of America's First Voucher Program* (Princeton University Press: Princeton, NJ, 2000)

Zeskind, Leonard, *Blood and Politics: The History of the White Nationalist Movement from the Margins to the Mainstream* (Farrar, Straus and Giroux: Kindle Edition, 2009)

INDEX

Printed in the United States
By Bookmasters